THE CHILDREN'S BIBLE STORY BOOK

200 Stories by Peter Palmer
417 Illustrations by Manning DeV. Lee

THE CHILDREN'S BIBLE STORY BOOK

200 Stories by Peter Palmer
417 Illustrations in Color by Manning DeV. Lee

Sovereign Grace Publishers
P.O. Box 4998
Lafayette, Indiana 47904
United State of America

The Children's Bible Story Book
Copyright © 1962, 1998
By Jay P. Green, Sr.
All Rights Reserved

This book or parts thereof may not be reproduced in any form without written permission of the Copyright Holder

I.S.B.N. 1-878442-89-9

Printed in the United States of America

Table of Contents

Old Testament Stories

The Beginning Of The World	Gen. 1:1-25	6
The First Man And Woman	Gen. 1:26-2:25	8
The First Sin	Gen. 3:1-6	10
The Punishment	Gen. 3:7-24	12
The First Murder	Gen. 4:1-15	14
Noah Builds The Ark	Gen. 4:25-7:16	16
The Flood	Gen. 6-8	18
The Tower Of Babel	Gen. 11:1-9	20
God Calls Abram	Gen. 11:27-12:7	22
Sarai In Pharaoh's House	Gen. 12:10-20	24
Abram And Lot Separate	Gen. 13	26
Ishmael Is Born	Gen. 15 and 16	28
Isaac Is Promised	Gen. 17 and 18	30
Fire And Brimstone From Heaven	Gen. 19	32
Hagar And Ishmael Are Sent Away	Gen. 21:1-21	34
Abraham's Faith Is Tested	Gen. 22:1-19	36
A Wife For Isaac	Gen. 24:1-51	38
Esan Sells His Birthright	Gen. 25:20-34	40
Isaac Is Tricked	Gen. 26:34-27:40	42
Jacob's Dream	Gen. 27:41-28:22	44
The Tricker Is Tricked	Gen. 29:1-28	46
Jacob Flees From Laban	Gen. 29:30-31:55	48
Jacob Meets Esau Again	Gen. 32 and 33	50
Jacob's Favorite Son	Gen. 35; 37:1-11	52
Sold As A Slave	Gen. 37:12-36	54
Thown Into Prison	Gen. 39:1-20	56
The Butler And The Baker	Gen. 39:20-40:23	58
Pharaoh's Dreams	Gen. 41:1-36	60
Joseph Becomes Governor	Gen. 41:37-57	62
Joseph's Brothers Come To Egypt	Gen. 42:1-25	64
The Brothers Come A Second Time	Gen. 42, 43	66
Joseph's Silver Cup	Gen. 43:25-44:13	68
Joseph Makes Himself Known	Gen. 44, 45	70
Jacob Goes To Egypt	Gen. 45:16-50:26	72
A Boat In The Buirushes	Exod. 1-2:9	74
Moses Flees To Midian	Exod. 2:10-22	76
The Burning Bush	Exod. 3-4:17	78
No Straw For Bricks	Exod. 4:27-6:8	80
Waters Turned To Blood	Exod. 6, 7	82
Frogs, Lice, And Flies	Exod. 8	84
Dead Animals, Boils, And Hail	Exod. 9	86

Old Testament Stories Continued

Locusts And Darkness	Exod. 10:1-23	88
Moses' Last Warning To Pharaoh	Exod. 10-12	90
The Passover	Exod. 12:29-13:22	92
A Path Through The Sea	Exod. 13:17-14:29	94
Bread From Heaven	Exod. 14:30-16:36	96
The Israelites' First Battle	Exod. 17	98
God Gives The Ten Commandments	Exod. 19, 20	100
The Golden Calf	Exod. 32-34; Dent. 9, 10	102
The Tabernacle	Exod. 35-40	104
The Day of Atonement	Lev. 23:27-44	106
Miriam Is Punished	Num. 12	108
Korah, Dathan, and Abiram	Num. 16	110
Spies Into Canaan	Deut. 1:19-46; Num. 13,14	112
The Death of Moses	Num. 20, 27; Deut.3-31-32-34	114
Jericho Is Taken	Joshua 6	116
Achan's Sin	Joshua 7	118
With Torch And Trumpet	Judges 6:33-7:25	120
Samson And Delilah	Judges 16	122
Ruth	Ruth 1-4	124
Samuel, The Prophet Of God	I Sam. 2:12-4:1	126
Saul Becomes King	I Sam. 10:17-12:25	128
Jonathan's Bravery	I Sam. 18:15-14:23	130
Saul Disobeys God	I Sam. 15	132
Saul's Hatred Of David	I Sam. 18, 19	134
David And Goliath	I Sam. 17	136
David Spares Saul's Life	I Sam. 24	138
David Is Betrayed	II Sam. 15	140
The Advice of Hushai	II Sam. 16:15-19; 17:1-14	142
Adonijah Tries To Become King	I Kings 1	144
The Temple	I Kings 5-7; II Chron. 2-4	146
The Queen Of Sheba's Visit	I Kings 10:4	148
The Kingdom Is Split	I Kings 12	150
The Test On Mt. Carmel	I Kings 18:20-39	152
Solomon's Wisdom	Proverbs 10:11	154
Elijah Goes To Heaven	II Kings 2:1-15	156
Hezekiah's Faith Is Rewarded	Kings 18-19; Isaiah 36, 37	158
Naboth's Vineyard	I Kings 21	160
Ahab's Family Is Destroyed	II Kings 9-10	162
A Boy Made Alive	II Kings 4:8-37	164
God's Care Over All His Creation	Psalm 104	166
Naaman The Leper	II Kings 5:1-14	168
The Lord's Battle	IIChron. 20:1-30	170
A Good Beginning, But A Sad Ending	IIChron. 14	172
A Little Boy Becomes King	IIChron. 22:1-23:21; II Kings 11	174
Good King Josiah	II Chron. 34; II Kings 22	176
The Decree Of Cyrus	Ezra 1:1-3:5	178
The Walls Of Jerusalem	Nehemiah 1-6	180
Haman's Decree	Esther 3-4	182

Old Testament Stories Continued

The Jews Are Saved	Esther 5, 7	184
The Shepherd's Care	Psalm 23	186
David Prays For Mercy	Psalm 51	188
The Suffering Servant	Phil. 2:9-11, Isaiah 52:13-53:12	190
A Scroll Is Burned	Jeremiah 36	192
Dry Bones	Ezek. 37:1-14	194
The Fiery Furnace	Daniel 3	196
The Den Of Lions	Daniel 6	198
Jonah Flees	Jonah 1-2	200
Jonah's Lesson	Jonah 3-4	202
The Second Temple Is Finished	Haggai; Ezra 5-6	204

New Testament Stories

John The Baptist Is Born	Luke 1:5-25, 57-80	206
The Voice in the Wilderness	John 1:19-34; Matt. 3; Mark 1	208
Gabriel's Message to Mary	Luke 1:26-56	210
Jesus is Born	Luke 2:1-20; Matt. 1:18-25	212
Wise Men From The East	Matt. 2:1-12	214
The Flight Into Egypt	Matt. 2:13-23	216
In His Father's House	Luke 2:40-52	218
The Temptations of Jesus	Matt. 4:1-11; Luke 4	220
The Kingdom of Heaven	Matt. 5:1-6 — 6:18	222
Treasures In Heaven	Matt. 6:19-34	224
Jesus Chooses His Disciples	John 1:35-51	226
Doers of the Word	Matt. 7:13-29	228
The Great Catch of Fish	Luke 5:1-11	230
The Wedding Feast at Cana	John 2:1-11	232
A Visit by Night	John 3:1-21	234
The Roman Centurion	Luke 7:1-10; Matt. 8	236
Pigs Into the Sea	Mark 5:1-20; Matt. 8; Luke 8	238
Jairus' Daughter is Raised	Mark 5:21-43; Matt. 8; Luke 8	240
Through the Roof	Mark 2:1-12; Matt. 9; Luke 5	242
Jesus and the Sabbath	Mark 12:1-14; Mark 2,3; Luke 6	244
Anointed by a Sinful Woman	Luke 7:36-50	246
Four Kinds of Soil	Mark 4:1-20; Matt. 13; Luke 8	248
The Samaritan Woman	John 4:1-42	250
The Parable of the Tares	Matt. 13:24-30; 36:43	252
A Birthday Party	Mark 6:14-29; Matt. 14; Luke 9	254
Jesus Walks on the Water	Matt. 14:22-23; Mark 6; John 6	256
Five Loaves and Two Fishes	Mark 6:30-46; Matt. 14; Luke 9	258
The Lame Man at Bethesda	John 5:1-18	260
A Heathen Woman's Faith	Matt. 15:21-28; Mark 7	262
The Deaf Hear and the Blind See	Mark 7:31-37; 8-22-26	264
A Blind Man is Healed	John 9:1-38	266
Jesus is Transfigured	Matt. 17:1-9; Mark 9, Luke 9	268

New Testament Stories Continued

The Good Samaritan	Luke 10:25-37	270
Ask and It Shall Be Given	Luke 11:1-13	272
The Umerciful Servant	Matt. 18:21-35	274
The Good Shepherd	John 10:1-18	276
The Prodigal Son	Luke 15:11-32	278
The Rich Man and Lazarus	Luke 16:19-31	280
Lazarus Raised from the Dead	John 11:1-44	282
The Lord of the Vineyard	Matt. 20:1-16	284
The Wicked Farmers	Mark 12:1-12; Matt. 21; Luke 20	286
Hosanna to the Son of David	Luke 11; Matt. 21; Mark 11	288
The Wise and Foolish Virgins	Matt. 24, 25	290
The Wedding Feast	Matt. 22:1-14	292
Zaccheus	Luke 19:1-10	294
Two Prayers and Two Gifts	Luke 18:9-14; 21:1-4	296
A Den of Thieves	Mark 11:15-18; Matt. 21; Luke 19	298
The Last Supper	Matt. 26:17-29; Mark 14; Luke 22;9 John 13	300
Jesus' Last Words to His Disciples	John 13-17	302
Gethsemane	Mark 14:32-42; Matt. 26; Luke 22	304
The Kiss of Judas	Mark 14:43-50; Mat. 26; Luke 22: 5 John 18	306
Peter Denies His Lord	Mark 14:53-72; Matt. 26; Luke 22	308
Jesus Before Pilate	John 18-19; Matt. 27; Mark 15	310
Sentenced to Death	John 18-19; Matt. 27; Mark 15	312
Jesus is Crucified	John 19	214
The Burial of Jesus	Matt. 27:57-66; Mark 15; Luke 23	316
The Death of The Son of God	John 19	318
Jesus is Risen!	Luke 24:1-12; Matt. 28; Mark 16; John 20	320
On the Way to Emmaus	Luke 24:13-35	322
Jesus Appears to His Disciples	John 20,21; Luke 24	324
Jesus Goes Back to Heaven	Acts 1:14; Luke 24:44-53	326
The Holy Spirit is Poured Out	Acts 2:1-41	328
The Lame Beggar is Healed	Acts 3	330
Ananias and Sapphira	Acts 5	332
The First Christian Martyr	Acts 6:8-8:3	334
Philip The Evangelist	Acts 8	336
The Salvation of Saul	Acts 9:1-22; Acts 22	338
A Gentile Believes	Acts 10	340
Peter Delivered From Prison	Acts 12:1-19	342
Paul's First Missionary Journey	Acts 13	344
The Philippian Jailor	Acts 15:36-16:40	346
Paul on Mars Hill	Acts 17	348
Paul at Ephesus	Acts 19	350
Paul at Jerusalem	Acts 21:17-40	352
The Plot Against Paul	Acts 23:12-33	354
Paul on Trial	Acts 24	356
Paul Before Festus and Agrippa	Acts 26	358
Paul's Shipwwreck	Acts 27	360
Paul Arrives at Rome	Acts 28	362

New Testament Stories Continued

The Olive Tree	Romans 11:15-24	364
Obedience to Rulers	Romans 13:1-7	366
God's Field and God's Temple	1 Corinthians 1:10-17	368
The Body of Christ	1 Corinthians 12	370
The Resurrection Hope	1 Corinthians 15	372
The Sufferings of Paul	2 Corinthians 11	374
Paul the True Apostle	Galatians 1-2:5	376
By Faith Alone	Galatians 2:6-4:31	378
Chosen for Holiness	Ephesians	380
Rejoice in the Lord!	Philippians	382
Christ, Our All In All	Colossians 1:9	384
Christ's Return	Thessalonians 1-2; Acts 17	386
Timothy is Chosen	Acts 14 and 16	388
Advice to Timothy	Timothy 1-2	390
A Runaway Slave	Philemon	392
The Great High Priest	Hebrews 8-10	394
Faith Unto the End	Hebrews 11	396
James Writes to the Twelve Tribes	James 1-5	398
Trials and Temptations	Peter 1-2	400
The Apostle of Love	John 1-2-3	402
The Vision of John	Revelation	404

Portraits of Heroes of the Faith

Aaron	406
Abraham	407
Adam	408
Daniel	409
David	410
Elijah	411
Elisha	412
Ezekiel	413
Isaac	414
Jacob	415
Jeremiah	416
Jonah	417
Joseph	418
Joshua	419
Moses	420
Noah	421
Samson	422
Solomon	423

Maps

Holy Land in the time of Christ	424
Missionary Journeys of Paul	425

"Let the earth bring forth grass"   *"And God made two great lights"*

THE BEGINNING OF THE WORLD

"In the beginning God . . . ." These are the very first words of the Bible because in the beginning there was nothing except God. There were no boys or girls, no dogs or bears, no robins or goldfish. There were no roses or elms, no mountains or lakes. There was not even an earth or a sun or a moon. There was nothing — nothing at all — except God.

The heavens and the earth that we see about us God created out of nothing. At first, the earth was without any life, and even without any order. And it was all dark. Then God said, "Let there be light." And there was light, even though there was no sun or moon. God saw that the light was good — just the way He wanted it to be. But he did not want it to be light all the time. So He made the light and the darkness take turns. The light he called "day" and the darkness He called "night." That was the end of the first day.

On the second day, God made the bright blue sky. Below the sky were the waters which still covered the earth. Up in the sky were the waters which would come down as dew, rain, or snow.

On the third day God said, "Let the waters under the heaven be gathered together into one place, and let the dry land appear." And of course it happened just as God commanded. The waters began to form brooks and rivers which ran downhill and emptied into the seas. Great areas of dry ground soon appeared.

"Fill the waters in the seas" *"God made the animals of the earth"*

Again God saw that it was good. Then he commanded the bare land to bring forth grass, plants, and fruit trees. As each plant and tree sprang up, it bore seeds so that more plants and trees of the same kind could grow from it. God saw that all of this, too, was just as He wanted it to be.

On the fourth day God made the sun and the moon and placed them in the sky. The sun was to shine upon the earth by day, and the moon by night. Besides giving light, they would help man keep track of the days, months and years. God also made the billions of twinkling stars.

The next day God created all kinds of creatures to swim about the seas — from the little minnows and sea horses to the enormous whales. At the same time He made the birds — from the tiny humming birds to the huge, soaring eagles. He commanded the sea creatures to multiply and fill the waters, and the birds to fill the sky. Thus the fifth day ended.

On the sixth day God made the other animals: the sheep and cows, the lions and tigers, the snakes and lizards, and many, many others.

The earth was now a beautiful place. The sun was shining in the blue sky. Colorful flowers and tall trees were growing everywhere. Birds were singing, fish were swimming in the waters, and animals roamed the woods and meadows. But there was still not a single man in the whole earth!
(Genesis 1:1-25)

There He put the man   *And Adam gave names to every animal*

THE FIRST MAN AND WOMAN

On the sixth day, after God had created all of the animals, He said, "Let us make man in our image, after our likeness." Then God formed him from the dust of the ground and breathed life into him. This man was a very special creature — different from anything else that God had already made. Because he was made from the dust, he was earthly, like the animals. But, unlike the animals, he was also heavenly, for he had been created in the image, or likeness, of God. He was like God in that he could think and plan, love and hate, and choose to do good. He was also like God in that he was to have dominion, or to rule, over the rest of creation. Yet even though he was so special, he was still just a creature himself. He was like God, but not the same as God. He was to rule creation; but he, in turn, was to be ruled by God.

God put this first man, Adam, in a garden in the land of Eden and told him to take care of it. This garden was even more beautiful than all the rest of God's beautiful creation. The trees that grew there were very pretty and gave delicious fruits for man to eat.

God then said, "It is not good that man should be alone." So He caused all the animals and birds to come to Adam to be named. By giving each one a name which described what the animal was like, Adam showed how much wiser, he

God caused a deep sleep to fall

God brought her to the man

was than the birds and beasts. But after he had seen and named them all, God said, "I will make a helper for him." For among all of God's creatures there was not another one like Adam with whom he could share his happiness.

So God caused Adam to fall into a deep sleep. While he slept, God took out one of his ribs and from it made a lovely woman. When Adam awoke, God brought the woman to him. How surprised and happy he was to have a wife to live with and to love! Both the man and the woman were naked, but they were not ashamed.

At the end of the sixth day, the creation of the world was finished. And on the seventh day God rested from His work of creating. Therefore, He blessed that day and called it holy. And he commanded man also to stop his work on that day and use it to praise Him.

Many years later, when God gave the Israelites the Ten Commandments, He reminded them of this command to keep the Sabbath day holy. "Six days you shall labor and do all your work, "He said; "but the seventh day is the Sabbath of the Lord your God" (Exod. 20:9,11). The reason for this commandment was that "in six days the Lord made heaven and earth, the sea and all that is in them, and rested the seventh day."
(Genesis 1:26-2:25)

Has God said, You shall not eat?

The woman saw the tree was good

THE FIRST SIN

In the beautiful garden where God placed the first man there were two very special trees. One was the tree of life and the other was the tree of the knowledge of good and evil. Before Eve was even created, God had told Adam that he was not allowed to eat the fruit of this tree of the knowledge of good and evil. Everything else, however, was for him to use and to enjoy. In telling him not to eat of the fruit of just that one tree, God wanted to test Adam's love and obedience. He wanted Adam to obey Him just because He, the Lord, had commanded it and not because Adam could see any good reason for doing so. God also warned Adam that if he disobeyed he would surely die. Although Eve was not there when God gave this commandment, she was told about it later.

Some time before this — we do not know when — God had also created the angels in Heaven. He had made them good, too, like everything else. But one day Satan and some other angels sinned against God and were thrown out of Heaven as punishment (II Peter 2:4). Satan was very angry about this and wanted to do something against God. He knew that there was no way to hurt God Himself. So he chose to try to ruin man, who had been made like God.

She took of the fruit of it   *and gave also unto her husband*

So Satan took the form of a snake one day and came up to Eve in the garden. Starting to talk to her, he asked, "Has God said, You shall not eat of every tree of the garden?" The woman replied that they were allowed to eat the fruit of every tree in the garden except the tree of the knowledge of good and evil. If they ate the fruit of that one tree, or even touched it, she explained, they would die.

Then Satan, whom Jesus called the father of lies (John 8:44), lied to Eve. "You will not surely die," he said. "For God knows that in the day you eat of it; then your eyes will be opened, and you shall be as God, knowers of good and evil."

For the first time Eve looked at the tree and its fruit with sinful thoughts in her heart. It was no longer enough for her that she had been created like God. She now wanted to be the same as God. God had given her and her husband all that they needed to be happy. He had even warned them that they would die if they ate the fruit. But Eve believed the lie of Satan rather than the truth of God.

Reaching out her hand in disobedience, she plucked one of the forbidden fruits from the tree and ate it. Then she gave one to her husband to try. And he also disobeyed the command of God and ate of the fruit. God had put Adam to a test and he had failed. By eating the fruit, he had committed the first of many, many sins against God. (Genesis 3:1-6)

They sewed fig leaves together   *She gave me of the tree*

THE PUNISHMENT

As soon as Adam and Eve ate the fruit, a change came over them. For the first time they were ashamed that they were naked. They picked some large fig leaves and sewed them together to make coverings for themselves.

Then, when they heard the Lord walking in the garden, they became afraid. Before, they had enjoyed walking and talking with Him. But now they tried to hide from Him among the trees. How foolish they were to think that trees or anything else could hide them from God!

God called to Adam, "Where are you?" God, of course, knew where Adam was. He only called him to come forward and confess his sin. But Adam replied, "I heard Thy sound in the garden, and I was afraid because I was naked and I hid myself."

The Lord then asked Adam outright, "Have you eaten of the tree which I commanded you that you should not eat of it?" Instead of admitting his wrong, Adam answered, "The woman whom Thou gavest to be with me, she gave me of the tree, and I did eat." So he tried to shift the blame to his wife, and to God for giving him such a wife!

God turned to the woman and said, "What is this that you have done?" Eve would not take the blame either. She, too, passed it on."The serpent deceived me," she replied.

The serpent deceived me   *So he drove out the man*

    Adam and Eve had hoped for greater happiness when they ate the forbidden fruit. But they soon found out that happiness does not come from disobeying God. First, God told the serpent what its punishment would be. From then on it would have to crawl on its belly. Serpents and men would always be enemies and would try to kill each other. God then told the woman that when she gave birth to her children she would have great pain. As for Adam, he would have to work long and hard to get enough food. And finally, both Adam and Eve would die and return to the dust from which they had been taken. The Lord then drove them out of the garden and placed angels and a flaming sword to keep them out.

    This dreadful punishment was not for Adam and Eve alone. Because all men were in Adam and he was acting for all mankind, everyone is just as much to blame for this first sin as if he himself had been there. And because of this, everyone born of Adam comes into the world with a sinful heart — a heart which never chooses good. Only the Holy Spirit can give man a new heart to love God. Everyone, by nature, deserves pain and suffering, toil, and finally death and hell (Rom. 5:12).

    Yet God in His mercy did not leave man without hope. Even while He was telling Adam and Eve what their punishment would be, He gave them a wonderful promise. He told them that Satan would one day be defeated by the seed of the woman — Jesus Christ. (Genesis 3:7-24)

She bore his brother Abel *Cain brought an offering*

THE FIRST MURDER

Outside of the beautiful garden of Eden, life was not nearly as pleasant as it had been. Adam had to work until the sweat poured down his face and his back ached. Sin plagued Adam and his wife. And they could no longer walk and talk with God.

But there was also much to make Adam and Eve happy. One of their happiest moments was when their first son, Cain, was born. They had never seen a baby before, for this was the first one ever to be born! A short time later, Eve had another son, whom they called Abel. As the two boys grew up, Cain began to work in the fields as a farmer, while Abel took care of sheep.

One day Cain brought a gift to God. He gave Him some of the crops which he had raised. His brother Abel brought a gift, too — a lamb from his flock. The Lord was pleased with Abel's offering, but not with Cain's. But why? The Book of Hebrews tells us that "by faith Abel offered to God a more excellent sacrifice than Cain" (Gen. 11:4). So Abel's offering was pleasing to God because his heart was right toward God and Cain's was not. We do not know how God showed that He liked Abel's gift and not Cain's. But somehow He made Cain know. And Cain was very angry.

Cain was angry at God and jealous of his brother. God asked him, "Why do you look so angry?" He warned him to change his ways before it was too late.

Cain rose up and killed him

My punishment is more than I can bear

But Cain only became more hateful. He hated Abel so much that he wanted to to kill him. A little later, when they were in the field together, Cain murdered his brother. There lay Abel before him, dead. And the blood which flowed from his wound soaked into the ground.

Then the Lord called to Cain, saying, "Where is Abel, your brother?" God gave Cain a chance to ask for forgiveness. But Cain only made his sin worse by lying. "I do not know," he replied. "Am I my brother's keeper?" So the Lord said, "The voice of your brother's blood cries to me from the ground." As punishment for this dreadful sin, God cursed Cain and told him that the ground which had soaked up his brother's blood would no longer produce crops for him. From then on, he would have to wander about the earth to try to find enough food to eat.

"My punishment is greater than I can bear," cried out Cain sorrowfully. But he was sorry only for the troubles which had come upon him and not for his sin. He was afraid, too, that those who met him would try to kill him. But God, in His mercy, promised that if anyone did, he would be punished sevenfold. Then Cain went to live far away to the east.

Adam and Eve must have been very unhappy! Their beloved Abel was dead, murdered by his own brother. And now Cain, too, was gone from them. Such dreadful things were happening since they had disobeyed God in the garden! (Genesis 4:1-15)

Make an ark   *Noah . . . a preacher of righteousness*

NOAH BUILDS THE ARK

God soon gave another son to Adam and Eve. This son, called Seth, was given to Eve in place of his godly brother, Abel, whom Cain had murdered. Besides Seth, God also gave Adam and Eve many other sons and daughters.

In the beginning men lived much longer than we do today. Adam, for example, lived to be 930 years old. Seth lived 912 years. And Methuselah, the oldest man of all, lived 969 years. But even though they lived so long, each one finally died. For part of the punishment for Adam's sin was that man should die and return to the dust.

At first, there were some who worshipped and glorified God. And there were also some who were just as wicked as Cain had been. Then, as the worshippers of God began to marry those who followed in the footsteps of Cain, they, too, became very sinful. They forgot about God. They quarreled and fought with each other. They lied and cheated and stole. The whole earth became so wicked that God was sorry that He had ever made man. There was only one man left who still tried to love and obey Him, and to lead his family to glorify God. That was Noah.

One day God commanded Noah to build a huge boat. He told him that because of man's great wickedness He was going to destroy every man and beast and bird with a flood. Only Noah and his family (just 8 people — Noah and

And take of all food that is eaten   *they went in to Noah into the ark*

his wife, their 3 sons and their wives) would be saved, together with the animals in the ark.

    Noah began at once to build the boat, or ark, just the way God had told him to make it. He made it very large: 450 feet long, 75 feet wide, and 45 feet high. It had three stories, and on each floor there were many rooms so that the animals could be kept separated. Then he coated the whole ark inside and out with tar so that it would not leak.

    What a task this was for Noah and his family with their simple tools! Yet because they had faith that God's word would come true, they worked hard to get it done. The other people must have made fun of Noah for building such a big boat when there was no water around. Noah warned them that God would destroy them all with the flood if they did not repent of their wickedness (II Pet. 2:5). But they just laughed at him and went on eating and drinking and making merry.

    When the ark was finished at last, Noah began gathering food. He had to have enough stored away to feed his family and all the different animals for a long, long time. Then God told Noah that it was time to go into the ark. For in seven days the flood would begin. Again Noah obeyed the Lord. As he and his family got ready to enter the ark, God caused the animals to come to him. Two by two they came male and female. One pair of most beasts and birds and creeping things entered the ark. But of certain kinds there were seven. (Genesis 4:25-7:16)

The ark went up *In her mouth was an olive leaf*

THE FLOOD

When the last pair of animals was safely inside the ark, the Lord shut the door. Then Noah and his family waited. For almost a week nothing happened. But then it began to rain. For forty days and forty nights the rain poured down in torrents. At the same time the fountains of the great deep broke loose and gushed over the land.

The people who had made fun of Noah no doubt climbed to the highest points they could find. But it was of no use. Higher and higher rose the waters. The heavy ark was lifted off the ground and began to float. In the lowlands, the tops of the tallest trees were soon covered. Then the low hills disappeared under the water. And finally the high mountains could no longer be seen. All was quiet except for the beating of the rain upon the roof of the ark and the lapping of the water against the sides. Outside the ark there was not a single man or beast or bird left alive. Inside, safe in God's care, were believing Noah and his family, with the animals.

For a long, long time the ark drifted about. Then, at the end of five months, God sent a wind to dry up the waters. Even before the mountains could be seen at all, the ark struck a high peak and rested there.

And Noah went forth   *Noah offered burnt offerings*

    Very slowly the waters went down, down, down. One day Noah opened the window of the ark and let out a large black bird called a raven. This bird never came back. A week later, Noah sent out a dove. She, however, soon came back to the ark. So Noah knew that there was no dry land on which she could rest. Another week passed. Again Noah sent out the dove. This time she returned with an olive leaf in her beak which she had picked from a tree. Noah now knew that at least the trees were uncovered and growing again. A week later he let the dove go again. This time she did not come back.

    After waiting another whole month, Noah took off the top of the ark and looked out. The water was all gone! By this time everyone must have been very eager to leave the ark. But Noah waited almost two more months — until God told him that it was time to leave. Finally, one year and ten days after entering the ark, Noah, his family, and the animals went out. How thankful everyone must have been to feel firm ground underfoot, to breathe the fresh air, and to feel the sun once more!

    The first thing that Noah did was to build an altar. On it he burned some animals and birds as a thank-offering to God. God was pleased with Noah's offering and promised that He would never again destroy the world with a flood. He said that the beautiful rainbow in the sky would forever be a reminder of His promise. (Genesis 6-8)

Let us make brick

Let us build us a tower

THE TOWER OF BABEL

The wicked people had all been destroyed by the flood. Only Noah, his wife, their three sons Shem, Ham, and Japheth and their wives were left to start life over again. God blessed Noah and his sons and said to them, "Be fruitful, and multiply, and fill the earth." God had given Adam and Eve this same command in the beginning. Now that life was beginning over again, He repeated it. For He wanted man to spread all over the earth and rule it.

Children were born to Shem, Ham, and Japheth. They grew up and had more children. So it was not long before there were a great many people in the earth again. Yet though they were many, they all spoke the same language.

This one big family left the mountains where the ark had landed and moved southeast to the beautiful plain of Shinar. There they found good, rich soil for farming. They also found out that from the mud they could make bricks. By baking them in hot ovens, they made them strong. And by using pitch, or tar, to cement them together, they were able to build houses and walls.

After a while, these people had an idea. "Let us build us a city and a tower with its top in the heavens," they said, "and let us make a name for ourselves, lest we be scattered upon the face of the earth." They saw that as their numbers grew, many of them would be moving farther and farther away. They did not want that. They wanted to stay close together.

They quit building the city

So the Lord scattered them abroad

If they built a great city with a high tower, they thought, they would not have to scatter over the face of the earth, as God had commanded. So they set to work. Some baked the bricks. Others carried them to the ones who were laying them carefully in place.

God, however, was not at all pleased. He had commanded them to fill the earth. But they wanted to live and work in one place. And because they all spoke the same language, it was easy for them to do so. If, however, they were made to speak different languages, they would not be able to live so peaceably together, and would be forced to scatter.

So God caused them to start speaking many different languages. Soon they realized that they had to stop building. For when one man called for more bricks, the other worker could not understand him at all. And when another gave directions to a builder, that builder did not know what he was talking about. They could not get any work done when no one knew what the other was saying. What a mixed-up affair this was! They soon were compelled to do what God commanded them to do. They left the unfinished city and tower, which were given the name "Babel," and traveled off in different directions. They had tried to disobey God. But simply by mixing up their language, He put a stop to their sinful plan. And He brought His own plan to pass instead. (Genesis 11:1-9)

He went forth . . . from Ur   *Get up and leave thy father's house*

GOD CALLS ABRAM

God spoke to Abram, who was living in Ur of the Chaldees, saying, "Get up and leave your country and your kinfolk, and come into the land which I will show unto you." (Acts 7:3). Abram did not know which land the Lord was going to show him. But he obeyed. With his wife, Sarai, his father, Terah, and his nephew, Lot, he left Ur and started out toward the land of Canaan. After going almost 600 miles northwest along the mighty Tigris and Euphrates rivers, they finally came to a city which was called Haran. Perhaps they had planned to stop there just a short while to rest. But they stayed for quite some time. In fact, Terah never did leave Haran, but continued to live there until his death at the age of 205.

A second time the Lord appeared to Abram and spoke to him. He told him that he must again move on. As before, the Lord promised to show him a new land. But now He promised Abram other blessings, too. Abram's family, God said, would become a great nation. And through Abram all the peoples of the earth would be blessed. For the Savior promised to Eve in the garden would be born from his family.

It was not easy for Abram to pick up and leave. He was now seventy-five years old — no longer a young man. He had no doubt become comfortably

So Abraham departed *He built an altar unto the Lord*

settled in Haran and had gotten many servants and cattle. Abram, however, trusted God. The Book of Hebrews says, "By faith Abraham obeyed . . . And he went out without knowing where he was going." (Gen. 11:8) Taking his wife, his nephew, Lot, and all their goods and servants, Abram started out again for Canaan, about 400 miles to the southwest. But it was not until he arrived that he learned that this was the land which the Lord had in mind. There, in the city of Shechem, God appeared a third time to Abram, saying, "Unto your seed will I give this land." It would never belong to Abram himself. He would always be a stranger in the land, living in tents. But God had promised that Canaan would some day belong to his children's children.

    At that time, however, Abram did not even have one son, for his wife Sarai had never been able to have any children. How, then, could he have children who would own the land of Canaan? How could they ever become a great nation? And how could the Saviour be born from his family? These were real questions for an old man whose wife had never been able to have children. But Abram had great faith. He believed that if God promised blessings through his children, He could and would bring His promises to pass. In thanksgiving, Abram built an altar there in Shechem and offered sacrifices to the Lord. (Genesis 11:27-12:7)

Say that you are my sister

The woman was taken to Pharaoh

SARAI IN PHARAOH'S HOUSE

Abram had arrived in the land of Canaan, the land which God promised to his children. In all, he had traveled about a thousand miles to get there. That was a long distance, indeed, to come by foot or camel, with flocks of sheep and herds of cattle following slowly behind. But Abram soon was to be driven out of this country to which God had called him. There was a famine in the land, and Abram, who did not own even one small patch of ground, could not find enough food for his large flocks and herds. So once again he gathered together his household and his animals and set out. He decided to go to Egypt and to stay there until the famine was over.

Sarai, Abram's wife, was a beautiful woman, even though she was over sixty-five years old. As they drew near Egypt, Abram became afraid that when the Egyptians saw how beautiful she was, someone would kill him and take her for his wife. So he said to her, "Tell them that you are my sister, that it may be well with me for your sake." It was really true that Sarai was Abram's half sister (Gen. 20:12). But that was only half of the truth, for she was also his wife. And sometimes, as here, telling half of the truth is the same as lying.

Not only did Abram ask his wife to say this, but he also allowed her to break another of God's laws by becoming someone else's wife. Perhaps he did

What have you done to me?

They sent him away

this because he thought that if he were killed, God's promise that his children would be a great nation could not come to pass. But he was wrong in thinking that he had to sin in order to help God fulfill His promises. Abram was a man of great faith. But in this case his faith was weak. He did not believe that God could take care of him.

When they arrived in Egypt, it happened just as Abram expected. The princes of Egypt saw Sarai and told Pharaoh, their king, about her. When she said that she was Abram's sister, Pharaoh took her to be one of his wives. He was very kind to Abram, who he thought was just her brother, and gave him many gifts.

The Lord, however, sent plagues upon the king and his household in order to protect Sarai. Pharaoh soon learned that she was Abram's wife. At once he called Abram to his court. "What is this that you have done to me?" he asked angrily. "Why did you not tell me that she was your wife?" Abram did not reply. He knew that he had done wrong. "Here is your wife," Pharaoh went on. "Take her and go your way." Pharaoh then commanded his soldiers to send Abram out of Egypt at once, with his household and all his goods.

Abram had acted in a faithless way. But God was still faithful. After protecting Abram's wife from evil, He had given her back to her husband. And He had kept Abram alive. (Genesis 12:10-20)

Abram was very rich

There was fighting

ABRAM AND LOT SEPARATE

    The tall camels swayed as they walked. Donkeys and oxen plodded along under heavy loads of food and household goods. Shepherds drove great flocks of sheep before them. Abram was on his way back to Canaan after being sent out of Egypt by Pharaoh. With the gifts which Pharaoh had given him, Abram was now even richer than before he went to Egypt. Yet with all his great wealth, he did not forget God. As soon as he reached Canaan, he worshiped the Lord and offered sacrifices to Him.

    Abram's nephew, Lot, was also rich in flocks and herds. Soon there was not enough grass and water in one place for the animals of both men. Lot's herders and those of Abram began quarreling with each other. They argued who would get the better pastures. And they argued over the brooks and springs. Abram did not like to see such arguing among the servants. Besides, he was afraid that soon he and his own nephew would start quarreling, too. Lot had been with him ever since he left Ur. But now Abram decided that it would be best for them to separate. Then each one would have enough land for his own animals and there would be no more quarreling. "Separate from me," he said to Lot. "If you take the left hand, then I will go to the right. Or if you go to the right hand, then I will go to the left."

Separate yourself from me

Lot chose the plain of Jordan

Abram was very kind. He let Lot have first choice of the land. Actually, Abram was the one who had the right to choose first. He was the older man. And besides, God had promised all this land to him, and not to Lot. But Lot was selfish. He chose the very best land for himself — the rich, green plain near the Jordan River. Saying goodbye to his uncle, he started out for his new home. Lot was pleased with the good land he had chosen. But his selfishness soon brought him much unhappiness. For the people among whom he finally settled, in the city of Sodom, were very, very wicked.

Abram, meanwhile, pitched his tents in the land of Canaan. There God spoke to him again. He told him to look north, south, east, and west, for all of this land — even that which Lot had chosen — would belong to his children. Once more the Lord reminded him that many men would come from his sons. They would be as countless as the dust of the earth. If Abram were to scoop up a handful of dirt, he could not possibly count all the tiny grains even in that one handful. In the same way, said God, Abram's children would be so many that no one would be able to count them. To these children God promised the land of Canaan. "Get up," said the Lord to Abram, "and walk through the land in the length of it and in the breadth of it; for I will give it unto you." (Genesis 13)

So shall your seed be   *Her mistress was despised in her eyes*

ISHMAEL IS BORN

Abram was sitting in his tent one night when God appeared to him in a vision. Three times before this the Lord had told him that he would have a very great family. Yet he still did not have even one child. Did that mean, Abram now asked the Lord, that his faithful servant Eliezer would be his heir? Would Eliezer, rather than one of Abram's own children, receive all of his goods when he died?

"Not Eliezer," the Lord replied, "but a son of your very own will be your heir." He then took Abram outside of his tent. "Look now toward heaven," God said. In the clear, black sky above, Abram saw thousands of stars twinkling brightly. God told him to count them if he could. Abram could not possibly count them all. The Lord said, "So shall your seed be." And Abram believed the promise of God regarding his children.

But ten years after God had first promised children to Abram, he still had no child. Then Sarai had an idea. Since the Lord had kept her from having children, she would give her Egyptian servant, Hagar, to her husband as a second wife. Perhaps she would give birth to the promised child. Abram agreed. He married Hagar, and it was not long before she was expecting a baby.

Abram believed God's promise that he would have a child. But maybe he no longer thought that God could give it to him through his lawful marriage.

Do to her as it pleases you

Return to your mistress

Perhaps he thought that he had to try to get it himself by taking a second wife, Hagar. In so doing, both Abram and his wife showed that their faith was weak. And they also broke God's commandment that a man should have just one wife.

When Hagar knew that she was going to have a baby, she became very proud. She despised Sarai because she had not been able to have any children. Sarai became unhappy. She complained to Abram about the way Hagar was acting. She even blamed him for marrying Hagar when it had been her idea in the first place! Instead of arguing with her, Abram simply told her to do with Hagar whatever she wished. Hagar was, after all, her servant.

Sarai tried to put Hagar in her place. She wanted her to realize that she was still only a slave. Sarai dealt harshly with her. Hagar did not like the way she was being treated. She ran away from Sarai and started back to Egypt. Hot and tired from walking, she stopped to rest beside a spring. There the Lord appeared to her. He told her to return to her mistress and be obedient to her. But he also comforted her by promising that she, too, would have many descendants. For the son whom she would bear would become a great nation.

Hagar returned. And when Abram was eighty-six years old, she gave birth to a son, whom they called Ishmael. This son later became the father of the large tribe of the Ishmaelites. (Genesis 15-16)

And Abram fell on his face   *Abraham ran unto the herd*

ISAAC IS PROMISED

Twenty-four years had passed since God had appeared to Abram in Haran (Gen. 12:1-3). At that time the Lord had promised him many children and a land of his own. Abram was now ninety nine years old and still had no children by Sarai. Nor did he own a bit of land. He was still traveling about, living in tents.

But when God makes a promise, He always keeps it. It may seem impossible to men. It may take a long time to come true. But it is sure to come to pass in God's own good time. Abram believed this, even though at times his faith was weak.

Once again the Lord appeared to him. Abram bowed his face to the ground. The Lord told him that his name would now be "Abraham," which meant "Father of many nations." For he would become the father of nations and kings. That day God made a covenant with Abraham — He promised to be his God and the God of his children. For his part, Abraham was to worship and obey the Lord faithfully. As a sign of this covenant, the Lord commanded Abraham — and his children after him — to circumcise every boy and man in his household, including the servants.

God went on. Sarai's name would now be "Sarah," which meant "Princess." For she would soon give birth to a son, and through him she would become the mother of nations and kings. Abraham laughed. How could such an old couple as they were still have a child? he thought to himself. And what about

He stood by them under the tree   *Sarah laughed within herself*

Ishmael? The Lord replied that He would indeed bless Ishmael. "But," He said, "I will establish My covenant with Isaac, whom Sarah will bear to you at this time next year."

    A short while later, the Lord repeated this promise. One day, when the sun was at its hottest, Abraham was sitting at his tent door. Suddenly he looked up and saw three men standing before him. Abraham quickly arose to welcome them. He offered to get water for their dusty feet and food to strengthen them. When they agreed, he told Sarah to hurry and make some cakes. Then he ran to his herd and picked out a young calf which he had a servant prepare. When the meal was ready, Abraham set it before his guests under the tree and stood beside them while they ate.

    "Where is Sarah, your wife?" One of them asked. "In the tent," replied Abraham. "Within a year she will have a son," He said. Sarah was listening from inside the tent. She laughed to herself when she heard it. Was she not too old now to have children? "Why did Sarah laugh?" asked the man. "Is anything too hard for the Lord?" Then Abraham realized that it was God Himself who was speaking and that the other two were angels. They had all come down from Heaven in the form of men to tell Abraham that his long wait was almost over. Next year Sarah herself would give birth to the promised child! (Genesis 17-18)

Turn in to your servant's house   *Brothers, do not do so with me*

FIRE AND BRIMSTONE FROM HEAVEN

Two dusty travelers arrived at the wicked city of Sodom. It was evening, and Lot was sitting at the gate. When he saw them coming, he got up and politely bowed down before them. "My lords," he said, "pray you, spend the night at my house." In those days there were not many hotels, and unless someone offered these strangers a place to stay, they would have to spend the night in the streets. At first the men refused Lot's kind offer. But Lot knew how evil the people of the city were. He was afraid that the travelers would not be safe on the streets all night. So again he begged them to come to his house. Finally they agreed.

Just as Lot and his guests were about to go to bed, they heard a lot of noise outside. A great crowd of men had gathered around the house and were shouting to Lot to hand the strangers over to them. Lot did not want any harm to come to his guests. Stepping outside, he shut the door behind him and tried to quiet the mob. But they became even more excited and tried to attack Lot himself and break down the door. At that moment, the guests opened the door, pulled Lot inside to safety, and closed it again. Then they caused everyone in the crowd to become blind. Lot's guests could do this because they were angels sent by God, even though they looked just like ordinary men. The blinded men soon grew tired of groping around for the door and went on home again.

Escape for your life!

The Lord rained fire and brimstone

    The angels then told Lot why they had come. The city of Sodom, along with the other cities of the Jordan plain, had become so wicked that God had decided to destroy them all. They told Lot to get his family ready to leave. That very night Lot went to his married children to tell them what the angels had said. But just like the people in the days of Noah, they only laughed at his warning.

    The next morning the angels woke Lot up early. "Hurry," they said. "Take your wife and your two daughters who live with you and leave at once, before you are destroyed with the city." Lot feared what would happen. But he was slow to obey. He found it hard to leave his house, all his goods, and the rest of his family. So the angels took Lot, his wife, and their daughters by the hand and fairly dragged them out of the city. "Now, run for your lives," they commanded them. "And don't look back, but flee to the mountains before you are destroyed."

    As soon as Lot had reached safety, the terrible judgment of God fell upon Sodom and the other cities. Fire and brimstone rained down from heaven upon them, burning everything to ashes — houses, people, animals, trees — everything. Billows of smoke rose to the sky like the smoke of a great furnace. Lot's wife, in disobedience to the command of the angels, turned around to see what was happening. And she became a pillar of salt. (Genesis 19)

Sarah bore Abraham a son   *Sarah saw the son of Hagar mocking*

HAGAR AND ISHMAEL ARE SENT AWAY

The Lord did unto Sarah as He had promised. For Sarah gave birth to a son when she was ninety years old. And Abraham was a hundred years old!

How was it possible for such an old couple to have a baby? God had waited until it was impossible for Sarah and her husband to have a baby in a natural way. And then, in a miraculous way, He sent them Isaac. How happy they were with him! Now they realized that Ishmael, Hagar's son, was not the child through whom God had promised to bless all the nations of the earth (Gen. 12:3). For the Saviour would be born from among Isaac's children, not Ishmael's.

As time went on, Ishmael came to dislike Isaac more and more. One day, when Ishmael was about sixteen, Sarah caught him making fun of Isaac, who was then only two or three. Paul even says that he was "persecuting" him (Gal. 4:29). Sarah decided that Ishmael must leave at once and said to Abraham, "Send away this slave woman and her son: for the son of this slavewoman shall not be heir with my son Isaac."

Abraham felt very sad. He loved Ishmael and did not want to see him leave. But God told Abraham to do as Sarah had asked. The Lord reminded him that He had made His covenant with Isaac, and not with Ishmael (Gen. 17:21). But He also

Abraham sent her away *She gave the lad a drink*

comforted Abraham by reminding him of His promise to make of Ishmael a great nation (Gen. 17:20). This He would do because Ishmael, too, was Abraham's son.

So early the next morning Abraham gave Ishmael and Hagar some bread and a leather bottle of water and sent them away. The boy and his mother wandered about in the hot, dry desert. They drank often from their supply of water until every drop was gone. Soon Ishmael became so thirsty that he could not walk a step further. Hagar helped him lie down in the shade of a scraggly bush. But she could not bear to sit there and watch her son die. She went a short distance away — about as far as you could shoot an arrow — and sat down and cried bitterly.

God called to her from Heaven, "What's the matter with you, Hagar?" He reminded her of the promise He had made the first time He had found her wandering in the desert (Gen. 16:10). Ishmael nation. Then the Lord caused her to see a nearby well. She ran and filled the bottle with the precious water and gave her son a drink. Ishmael soon felt much better and could walk again.

From then on, Ishmael lived in the desert and grew to be a strong hunter. He married an Egyptian girl and became the father of twelve princes, and they also had a great many sons and grandsons. (Genesis 21:1-21)

Stay here with the donkey   *Where is the lamb for the offering?*

ABRAHAM'S FAITH IS TESTED

"Take now your son, your only one — Isaac, whom you love," God said to Abraham, "and go into the land of Moriah; and offer him there for a burnt offering." What do you think Abraham thought about killing his beloved son Isaac, for whom he had waited so long? Should he sacrifice the very one through whom God had promised to bless the nations of the earth?

Abraham's faith had been tested many times before. It was tested when he was called to leave his homeland and his father; when he could not own any of the land which God had promised him, but had to wander about in it as a stranger; when he had to wait so long for Isaac to be born; and when he had to send away his first-born son, Ishmael. But this was the greatest test of all.

Early the next morning Abraham obediently got ready to leave. He ordered his donkey saddled and some wood cut for the fire. Then he and his son Isaac started out. For two days they traveled. We can well imagine what thoughts were going through Abraham's mind as he walked along. During those two days he had plenty of time to change his mind and turn back from sacrificing his son. But he kept on going because he trusted God.

On the third day Abraham saw in the distance the mountain on which God had told him to sacrifice his son. His servants would not understand what he was about to do. He told them to stay with the donkey. "The boy and I are going to

He took the knife to kill his son　　　*Abraham went and took the ram*

worship up there," he said. Abraham took the wood and placed it on young Isaac's back. He himself carried the knife and the live coals to light the fire. Together they slowly began to climb the mountain. Isaac sensed something strange about all this. "Father," he said. "What is it, my son?" replied Abraham. "We have fire and wood. But where is the lamb for the burnt offering?" How could Abraham tell his son now that he was to be the sacrifice? In great faith he answered, "God will provide Himself the lamb."

    At last they reached the spot. Isaac helped his father build an altar of stones and lay the wood in place. Then Abraham tied his son, his only son Isaac, whom he loved, and laid him on the wood. But Isaac — a strong, young boy of about eighteen — did not struggle to get free. He, too, must have believed that God could still fulfill His promises even though he were killed.

    The moment of testing had arrived. Clutching the knife in his hand, Abraham raised it to kill his son. Just then the Lord called from Heaven, "Abraham, Abraham! Do not lay your hand upon the boy. Now I know that you fear God, for you have not held back your son from Me." Joy flooded Abraham's soul. Looking around, he saw a wild ram caught in a bush by its horns. Quickly Abraham cut his son loose and in his place offered the ram as a burnt offering. The Lord had indeed provided His own sacrifice! (Genesis 22:1-19)

He made his camels to kneel down   *Let me drink a little water*

A WIFE FOR ISAAC

It was evening. A caravan of ten camels stopped at the well outside the city of Haran. The travelers made the camels kneel down. Then the tired, dusty, and thirsty riders got off to rest.

The leader of this group of strangers was the oldest of Abraham's servants. He was in charge of all of his master's possessions. Abraham had sent this faithful old servant to the city where his brother Nahor lived to find a wife for his son Isaac from among his own people. Sarah, Isaac's mother, — was already dead. And before Abraham himself died, he wanted to make sure that his son — who was now forty years old — married a woman from his family instead of one of the heathen Canaanites among whom they lived.

The travelers had reached the end of their journey just at the time of day when the young women came to draw water at the well. Abraham's godly servant bowed his head and prayed, "O Lord God, if I ask one of these young women for a drink and she also offers to water my camels, may she be the one whom Thou hast chosen for Isaac." Before the servant had finished praying, a beautiful young woman came to the well, carrying a pitcher on her shoulder. After she had filled her pitcher, the servant went up to her and said, "Please let me drink a little water." At once the young woman let down her pitcher and said, "Drink, my lord." Then she added, "I will draw water for your camels, also." After emptying

The man took a golden ring

Take her and go

her pitcher into the drinking trough, she ran back to the well for more water. Back and forth she went, until all the thirsty camels had had enough to drink. All the while, the old servant was watching this kind, lovely girl. When she had finished, he gave her a gold ring and two gold bracelets. "Whose daughter are you?" he asked. "Is there room at your house for us to spend the night?" "I am Rebekah, Nahor's granddaughter," she replied. "And we have plenty of room and food for you and your camels." Gratefully the servant bowed his head and thanked God for leading him to the family of Nahor, the brother of his master, Abraham.

Rebekah hurried home to tell what had happened. When her brother Laban saw the gold ring and bracelets, he ran back to get this rich, important stranger and bring him home. There Laban unsaddled the camels, fed them, and gave water to the men to wash their dusty feet. But the old servant would eat nothing until he had told Rebekah's family who he was and why he had come. On hearing his story, they said, "This is truly God's doing. Take Rebekah, and let her be Isaac's wife."

The servant thanked God for the success of his trip. Then he unpacked the saddle bags and gave rich gifts of jewelry and clothing to Rebekah and her family. The very next morning Rebekah and her maids mounted their camels and set out for Canaan with Abraham's servants. (Genesis 24:1-51)

Isaac brought her to Sarah's tent   *Isaac prayed to the Lord for his wife*

ESAU SELLS HIS BIRTHRIGHT

Isaac was very happy with the beautiful bride which his father's servant had brought back for him. He took her to the tent of his mother, Sarah, who had died three years before, and she became his wife. Isaac grew to love Rebekah very much and hoped that they soon would have sons and daughters.

But years passed and no children were born to them. God made them wait a long time before giving them children, just as He had done with Sarah and Abraham. But Isaac did not follow his father's sinful example by taking a second wife in order to have children. Instead, he prayed earnestly to the Lord. At last his prayers were answered When he was sixty years old — that is, after he had been married twenty years — Rebekah gave birth to twin boys.

Although these babies were twins, they were as different as they could be. The first-born, whom they called Esau, was covered all over with reddish-brown hair. The other one, whom they named Jacob, was smooth and soft. When they grew older, Esau liked to run and play in the fields, and he became a skillful hunter. Jacob, however, was much quieter and liked to stay near the tents. Esau was Isaac's favorite son because he often brought deer meat for his father to eat. Jacob, on the other hand, was Rebekah's favorite.

Perhaps Rebekah loved Jacob more than Esau because of what God had

Feed me with that red pottage

He did eat and drink

told her about the two boys before they were born. He had said that the twins would become the fathers of two different nations, but that the older would serve the younger. That was a strange promise, for usually the oldest son was the one who became the head of the family when the father died. And he also received the greatest blessings from his father. In this case, that blessing would include all the rich promises which God had made to Abraham and to Isaac. However, God had told Rebekah that this right of the first-born — called the birthright — would one day belong to the younger son, Jacob, rather than to Esau, the older.

Once, after a long day of hunting, Esau came home tired and hungry. Jacob was cooking a thick soup of red beans. "Give me some of that red soup," Esau said to his brother. Now Jacob should have been kind enough to have given the soup to his hungry brother. Instead, he said, "Sell me your birthright today." "What good is the birthright to me?" replied Esau carelessly. Actually, Jacob was trying to buy what God had promised would be his anyway. Instead of taking advantage of his brother's hunger, he should have trusted that God would keep His promise. But Esau was even more to blame. As soon as he swore that Jacob could have the birthright and was given the soup, he hungrily ate it and left. It seemed to make no difference to him that he had sold something as precious as his birthright for one bowl of soup. (Genesis 25:20-34).

And Rebekah was listening *And she put the skins on his hands*

ISAAC IS TRICKED

Isaac was now a blind, old man. Before he died, he wanted to give the blessing of God to his first-born son. Calling Esau to him, he said, "'Take your bow and arrows and go kill a deer. Then fix me a tasty dish so that I may eat, and bless you." Esau left at once to go hunting.

Rebekah overheard what her husband had said to Esau and was very upset. Esau had shown time and again that he cared nothing for the things of God. He had sold his birthright to his brother for a bowl of soup. And he had caused his parents great sorrow by marrying two heathen women. Not only this, but before the twins were born God had said that the younger one should take the place of the elder (Gen. 25:23). Rebekah knew that Esau was not to receive the blessing. But instead of letting God work it out, she used trickery to get it for her favorite son.

Calling Jacob, she told him of his father's plan. "Go to the flock," she said, "and bring me two kids. I shall fix the meat to be tasty. Then you can take it to your father and he will bless you." Jacob was worried. His father would not be able to see him, but he could feel that he was not hairy like his brother. If Isaac should find out who he really was, he might curse him instead of bless him. Rebekah, however, said she would take care of that. So Jacob killed two kids and his mother cooked them. She dressed Jacob in Esau's clothes, which

So he blessed him

I am your son

smelled like the fields, and tied the hairy kid skin over Jacob's smooth arms and neck.

Jacob took the tasty meat to his father's tent. "My father," he called. "Who are you, my son?" "I am Esau, your first-born," lied Jacob. "Sit up and eat this meat, so that you may bless me." Isaac was surprised that his son was back so soon. "Come near so that I may feel if you are Esau," he said. Fearfully, Jacob went close to his father. Isaac felt the hairy kid skins on Jacob's arms and neck. "The voice is Jacob's voice," said Isaac, "but the hands are the hands of Esau."

So Isaac ate the delicious meat. "Come near now and kiss me," he told his son. As Jacob did so, his father smelled the woodsy smell of Esau's clothes. Now completely sure that this was indeed his first-born son, the old man gave Jacob the blessing.

Hardly had Jacob left his father's tent when Esau returned with a deer. Not knowing what had happened, he fixed the meat and took it in to his father. "Who are you?" his father asked in surprise. "I am Esau, your first-born son," he replied. Then Isaac trembled all over. He realized that he had been tricked into giving the blessing to Jacob instead of Esau! But he also remembered that it rightfully belonged to Jacob and he could not take it back. God had stopped him from giving the blessing to Esau. (Genesis 26:34-27:40)

Arise and flee to Laban

God Almighty bless you

JACOB'S DREAM

Esau hated Jacob for cheating him out of the blessing which he thought was his. "My father is old and will soon die," he thought to himself. "Then I will kill my brother Jacob."

One of the servants heard of Esau's wicked plan and told Rebekah. At once she called Jacob to her and told him that his life was in danger. "Now therefore, my son," she said, "obey my voice; and arise and flee to Laban, my brother, in Haran. Stay with him for a few days, until your brother is no longer angry with you. Then I will send for you."

Rebekah did not tell her husband, Isaac, about Esau's plan to murder Jacob. Perhaps she thought he would not even believe that his favorite son could be so wicked. Or perhaps she did not want to worry him. In any case, she gave Isaac a different reason, though a true one, for sending Jacob away. She told him that if Jacob should marry a heathen woman as Esau had done, it would be more than she could bear. Remembering how his own father, Abraham, had gone to such trouble to get him a wife, Isaac agreed. He called Jacob to him and said, "You shall not take a wife of the daughters of Canaan. Go to your uncle Laban in Haran and take a wife from among his daughters." Then Isaac added: "May God Almighty bless you, and make you fruitful, and multiply you.

And he dreamed, and behold, a ladder   *He set it up for a pillar*

And may He give the blessing of Abraham to you and to your children, that you may inherit the land in which you are a stranger."

So Jacob started out on his long trip. One evening, after a long, tiring day of walking, he lay down on the ground as usual to go to sleep. For a headrest he used a large stone. While he slept, he had a wonderful dream. He saw a ladder set on the earth which reached all the way to Heaven. Angels were going up and down the ladder, and at the top of it stood God Himself. Then the Lord spoke. He first repeated to Jacob the promises which He had given many times to Abraham and Isaac. Then He added, "Behold, I am with you and will keep you everywhere that you go and will bring you again into this land." Jacob awoke. What a comfort it was to Him to know that God was with him, even though he did not deserve His love! "How fearful is this place," he said. "This is none other than the house of God and this is the gate of Heaven."

Early the next morning Jacob set his stone headrest on end and poured oil on it as a reminder of the wonderful vision. And he named the place Bethel, which means "House of God." And Jacob made a promise to God, saying, "If God will be with me, and will keep me in this way that I go, so that I come to my father's house in peace — then shall the Lord be my God." (Genesis 27:41-28:22)

Where are you from? *Jacob watered the flock of Laban*

THE TRICKER IS TRICKED

As Jacob set out again for his uncle Laban's in Haran, he was no longer lonely or afraid. He knew that God was with him and would take care of him.

After many days of travel, Jacob came to a well in a field. Three flocks of sheep were lying near the well, waiting to be watered. But before water could be drawn for the animals, the large stone over the mouth of the well had to be taken off. Jacob went up to the shepherds and asked, "Where are you from?" "From Haran," they replied. That was where his uncle Laban lived! "Do you know Laban?" he asked. "Yes, we do," they answered. "Here comes his daughter Rachel with his sheep."

Jacob was so happy that God had led him safely to his relatives that as soon as Rachel reached the well, he rolled away the heavy stone all by himself and watered her sheep. If Rachel was surprised at this, she must have been even more surprised when the stranger came up and kissed her! Then Jacob told her that he was her cousin, the son of Rebekah.

Rachel hurried home and told her father, Laban. At once Laban returned to the well to get his nephew and take him home. How much there was to talk about! Almost a hundred years had passed since Laban's sister Rebekah had left to become Isaac's wife. And now here was her son!

He took Leah his daughter

Did I not serve you for Rachel?

Jacob stayed with Laban and took care of his sheep. After a month, Laban could see that his nephew was a very good shepherd. He wanted Jacob to keep on working for him and asked what his wages would be. Now Jacob had come to love Laban's beautiful daughter, Rachel. So he replied, "I will work for you for seven years for Rachel, your younger daughter." That suited greedy Laban very well.

Jacob served his uncle faithfully, and the years flew by because he loved Rachel so much. At the end of the seven years, Laban gave a wedding feast for his nephew. But then he played a mean trick. That night, instead of giving Jacob his beloved Rachel, Laban gave him her older sister, Leah. Because a veil covered most of Leah's face, Jacob did not find out till the next morning what Laban had done. Jacob, who had tricked his blind, old father, had now been tricked by his uncle! Angrily he went to Laban. "What is this you have done to me?" he demanded. "Did I not serve you for Rachel?"

Laban replied that it was not proper to let the younger daughter marry before the older one. Of course, he did not tell that to Jacob seven years before. But now he said, "We will give you Rachel also if you will work seven more years for me." To this Jacob agreed. Perhaps he felt in his heart that this was God's punishment to him for his own trickery. So after a week he married Rachel, too, and began seven more years of work for his uncle. (Genesis 29:1-28)

Give me my wives and my children   *Jacob has taken away all*

JACOB FLEES FROM LABAN

For fourteen years Jacob worked for his uncle Laban in order to win his two wives, Leah and Rachel. During that time the Lord blessed Jacob's work and Laban's flocks grew very large. But Jacob himself still had no sheep or goats of his own. Yet he had a large family to support: his two wives, their two maids, and now eleven sons.

Jacob wanted to return to Canaan. He longed to see his father and mother again. And besides, he wanted to start working for himself. "Give me my wives and my children, for whom I have served you," he said to Laban, "and let me go." But his greedy uncle, knowing that he had gotten rich because of Jacob, said, "I will pay you whatever you ask if you will stay on." Jacob replied that if he could have all of Laban's spotted sheep and goats, including any that would yet be born, he would stay. Now since the sheep were usually white and the goats a brownish-black, Jacob was not asking for much — only for the unusual animals. So Laban agreed.

But of the next lambs and kids that were born, many were spotted. These, then, became Jacob's. When Laban saw how many animals Jacob was getting, he broke his agreement and decided to pay him with different animals the next time. But again most of the new lambs and kids were Jacob's. Ten times Laban broke his agreements with Jacob. But each time Jacob got the most. At the end of

Jacob stole away   *You would have sent me away empty*

six years, he had large flocks and herds, as well as many servants. By this time, however, Laban was very jealous of him. His sons, too, grumbled, saying, "Jacob has taken away all that was our father's!"

Then the Lord said to Jacob, "Return to the land of your fathers and I will be with you." Jacob now wanted to leave more than ever. But he was afraid that if he did not go secretly, his uncle might stop him. So once, when Laban was away for a few days, shearing his sheep, Jacob saw his chance to slip away. The tents and household goods were packed up and the flocks and herds gathered together. Then Jacob and his family mounted their camels and off they started. They traveled as fast as they could, but such a large caravan could not make very good time.

After three days, Laban heard that Jacob had fled. At once he and some of his relatives set out after him. Without flocks and children, Laban was able to travel faster than Jacob, and in a week he caught up with him. But because God had warned him in a dream not to harm Jacob, Laban only scolded him for having fled secretly. Jacob, however, was angry with Laban for chasing after him. He reminded him of how faithfully he had served him for twenty years. "But unless God had been with me," he rebuked Laban, "you would have sent me away empty. So Laban returned in peace and Jacob continued on his way. (Genesis 29:30-31:55)

Esau comes to meet you   *They passed over the ford*

JACOB MEETS ESAU AGAIN

Jacob had escaped from Haran safely. But now he had another worry. After twenty years would his brother Esau still be angry with him for cheating him out of the blessing? Jacob sent some messengers on ahead to tell Esau that he was coming home and to find out if he was still angry. They soon returned with the news that Esau was already on his way to meet him with four hundred men.

Jacob was terrified. He divided all his animals and servants into two groups, hoping that if Esau should attack one, the other would be able to escape. Then he prayed earnestly. "O God," he said, "I am not worthy of the least of all Thy mercies." He recalled how he had gone to Haran twenty years earlier with only his staff in his hand. And now he was returning with wives and children, servants, and a countless number of animals. Since the Lord had blessed him so greatly in the past and since He Himself had commanded him to return to Canaan, Jacob pleaded, "Save me, I pray Thee, from the hand of my brother."

Jacob then got a good-will present ready for Esau. He gathered goats, sheep, camels, cattle, and donkeys into separate droves — 580 animals in all! These he sent on ahead, one drove at a time. As each drove met Esau, the servant in charge of it was to tell him that the animals were a present from Jacob. In this way, Jacob hoped to turn away Esau's anger.

Esau embraced him

Who are these with you"

    That night Jacob helped his family and the rest of his animals and servants to cross over the Jabbok River. But he himself stayed on the northern bank to pray. Soon a man came and began to wrestle with Jacob. All night long they wrestled. When the man saw that Jacob was holding on, He touched Jacob's hip, making him lame. Then, as it was beginning to get light, the Man said, "Let me go." But by this time Jacob realized that he was wrestling with God Himself in a human form. He answered, "I will not let Thee go, except Thou bless me." All his life Jacob had trusted more in his own cleverness than in God. But now he understood that he needed God's blessing above all else. And he would not let go until God blessed him. So after changing Jacob's name to Israel, which meant "A prince with God," the Lord blessed him, and Jacob let go.

    Morning had come. Limping because of his lame hip, Jacob crossed over the river. In the distance he saw Esau and his men coming! Trembling, Jacob went toward him, bowing low seven times. Then Esau, whose mind God had changed, ran up to Jacob and kissed him. The twin brothers wept at being together again. And Esau was amazed at all Jacob's children and possessions. He also asked why Jacob had sent him such a generous present. His brother replied, "If I have found grace in your sight, then receive my present." So Esau accepted the gift, showing that he no longer desired to kill Jacob. (Genesis 32-33)

And Jacob set a pillar on her grave   *He made a coat of many colors*

JACOB'S FAVORITE SON

When Jacob had tricked Esau, his mother Rebekah had told him to flee to her brother Laban until Esau got over his anger. She had hoped that she could send for him soon. But instead of staying with his uncle for a short while, Jacob stayed for twenty years. Then he returned to Canaan, but it was eleven years more before he finally reached Hebron, where his old father, Isaac, was living. By that time, Rebekah had died. So after Jacob left home, he never saw his mother again. Perhaps this was part of God's punishment to them both for having tricked blind, old Isaac into giving the blessing to Jacob instead of Esau.

Shortly before Jacob reached his father in Hebron, something very sad happened. His favorite wife Rachel died while giving birth to her second son. Jacob buried her near Bethlehem and set up a stone to mark her grave.

Counting this new baby, whom he called Benjamin, Jacob now had twelve sons. His wife Leah had borne Reuben, Simeon, Levi, Judah, Issachar, and Zebulun. His other wife, Rachel, had given him Joseph and Benjamin. Dan and Naphtali were his sons by Rachel's maid, and Gad and Asher, his sons by Leah's maid. These twelve were the beginning of the twelve tribes of Israel.

Of all of his sons, Jacob's very favorite was Joseph, Rachel's first — born. Jacob should have remembered how much trouble was caused when he was

Your sheaves bowed down to my sheaf   *Shall I bow down to you?*

young because his own father had played favorites with Esau. But instead, when Joseph was a lad of seventeen, Jacob gave him a beautiful, brightly colored coat with long sleeves. None of his brothers had one like it. And they hated Joseph when they saw that their father loved him so much more than the rest of them. In fact, they could not even speak kindly to him.

Then Joseph had a dream which made his brothers hate him even more when they heard it. "We were tying sheaves (or bundles) of grain in the field," he told them excitedly. "And then my sheaf stood upright and your sheaves stood around mine and bowed down to it." His brothers understood at once that the meaning of the dream was that they themselves would bow down to Joseph. "Do you think that you are going to rule over us?" they asked angrily.

Later, Joseph had another dream very much like the first one. This one he told to both his brothers and his father. "In my dream," he said, "the sun and the moon and eleven stars bowed down to me." The sun and moon, of course, referred to his father and mother, and the eleven stars to his brothers. This dream, too, made his brothers angry. Even his father scolded him. "Shall I and your mother and your brothers indeed bow down to you?" he asked. But his father thought about the dream again and again. He wondered if it could really be foretelling something that would happen someday. (Genesis 35; 37:1-11)

They plotted to slay him   *They stripped Joseph of his coat*

SOLD AS A SLAVE

One day Jacob said to his son Joseph, "Your brothers are feeding the flocks in Shechem. Go see if everything is all right with them and bring me word again." Jacob probably did not realize how much his other sons hated Joseph. If he had, he would not have sent him on such a dangerous errand.

Joseph obediently set out alone in search of his brothers. When he finally reached Shechem, he looked and looked but he could not find them anywhere. Seeing Joseph wandering about, a man asked him, "What are you looking for?" When Joseph told him, he replied, "I heard them say, 'Let us go to Dothan.'" So off Joseph went toward Dothan until at last he saw his brothers and their flocks in the distance. When they saw him coming, wearing his beautiful coat, they said to each other, "Here comes the dreamer. Let us kill him and throw him into a pit. We will say that some wild animal has eaten him. And we shall see what will become of his dreams."

But Reuben, the oldest brother, wanted to save Joseph. "Let us not shed his blood," he said, "but just throw him into the pit." He hoped that later on he could get Joseph out secretly and send him home to his father. The brothers knew that in that lonely place no one would ever hear Joseph call for help and that he would slowly die of hunger. So they agreed. When Joseph came near, they roughly grabbed hold of him, tore off his coat, and threw him into a dry

They sold Joseph *Joseph is no doubt torn to pieces*

well nearby. And then they sat down to eat as if nothing had happened. Joseph called and called to them, but they paid no attention to him. (Gen. 37:14-24)

Just then some Ishmaelite merchants came riding along on their camels. They were on their way to Egypt to sell the costly spices in their packs. Seeing these traders, Judah, one of the brothers, had another idea. Would it not be better, he suggested, to sell Joseph to these merchants than to let him die? In this way, they would not be to blame for their own brother's death, and yet they would still be rid of him. Again the brothers agreed. They hauled Joseph out of the well and sold him to the merchants for twenty pieces of silver. The merchants then took Joseph and rode away with him to far-off Egypt.

Reuben was away while his brothers were selling Joseph. When he returned to the well to pull him out, he was horror-struck to find his brother gone What could he ever tell his father? The brothers, however, were not planning to tell their father that they had sold Joseph. Killing a goat, they dipped Joseph's beautiful coat in its blood and sent it back home. Their father would then think that Joseph had been eaten by a wild animal. When Jacob saw his son's coat stained with blood, he cried out, "Joseph is without doubt torn to pieces." For a long, long time Jacob mourned for his son. (Genesis 37:12-36)

Potiphar bought him   *He served him*

THROWN INTO PRISON

After many weary days of travel, the camel caravan arrived in Egypt with young Joseph. There the Ishmaelite merchants were able to sell him to a rich, important soldier named Potiphar. This man was a high officer of King Pharaoh, the captain of his guard. Thus Joseph, the favorite son of his father, became a slave in a faraway land. But the Lord had not forgotten him. In fact, He had brought him to Egypt for a very special purpose. To get Joseph ready for the great work which He would soon have for him to do, God first gave him some experience in Egyptian business.

Joseph's master did not put him to work in the fields, but rather, inside his own house. The Lord blessed Joseph greatly, and Potiphar noticed that everything that this slave did was done well. Joseph was soon promoted to waiting upon Potiphar himself. Here, too, Joseph pleased his master so much that he put Joseph in charge of everything he owned — all the servants, his house, and even the animals and fields. Potiphar did not have to bother himself about a thing at home. And because the Lord continued to bless Joseph's work, Potiphar became even richer than before.

Joseph was now a very handsome young man and, as head servant over his master's house, he was probably dressed in fine robes. Potiphar's wife began to like him. One day she came up to him and tried to get him to kiss her and love

He left his robe and fled   *Joseph's master put him in prison*

her. Joseph, of course, refused. He even rebuked her by saying, "My master has put me in charge of everything. There is none greater in this house than I. Neither has he held back anything from me except you, because you are his wife. How, then, can I do this sin against him and against God?" But this shameless woman was not persuaded by Joseph's words. Day after day she coaxed him to love her. But Joseph would not give in.

One day Joseph went into the house alone to attend to some work. When Potiphar's wife saw that no other servants were around, she grabbed hold of Joseph's robe and begged him to lie with her. This was too much for Joseph. He tried to get away, but she would not let go of his robe. He finally managed to wriggle out of it and quickly ran out of the house, leaving his robe in her hands. Now Potiphar's wife was angry with Joseph. And to explain how she had his robe, she decided to make up a story. She pretended to cry out as if she needed help. In a moment her servants rushed in. "The Hebrew servant, Joseph, tried to make love to me," she lied. "But when I cried out he left his robe with me and fled."

When her husband returned home, she told him the same lie. Instead of listening to Joseph, who had served him so faithfully, Potiphar believed his wife. He became very angry at his servant and threw him into prison. (Genesis 39:1-20)

Why do you look so sad today?   *I took the grapes and pressed them*

THE BUTLER AND THE BAKER

As captain of the king's guard, Potiphar had a prison in his own house, and he himself had charge over it. In this dungeon the king's prisoners were kept. Here, too, Potiphar put Joseph because of the lie which his wife had told about him.

At first, Joseph's feet were chained to the dungeon wall (Psalm 105:18). But God soon caused the keeper of the prison to like Joseph and to be kind to him. When the keeper noticed what a good man he was, he put him in complete charge of all the other prisoners. Just as God had raised Joseph to be head servant over Potiphar's house, so now He raised him to be head over all the prisoners. One day Pharaoh's chief butler, or cupbearer, and his chief baker made the king very angry. He had them thrown into prison, the very prison where Joseph was. Since Joseph was in charge of all the prisoners, these two important officers of Pharaoh's court were also put in his care. He visited them every day and soon came to know them quite well.

One morning Joseph found them both looking very troubled. "Why do you look so sad today?" he asked them kindly. "We have each dreamed a dream, and here in prison there is no one who can explain our dreams to us," they replied. "Men cannot explain dreams," said Joseph, "only God can. Tell me what they are." He was sure that God would tell him their meaning.

The birds ate them   *He gave the cup to Pharaoh*

So the chief butler said to him, "In my dream I saw a vine that put forth three branches. These branches blossomed and then bore bunches of ripe grapes. Pharaoh's cup was in my hand. I took the grapes and squeezed them into Pharaoh's cup and gave the cup to the king." Joseph at once explained the dream to him. "The three branches are three days," he began. "In three days Pharaoh will once again make you his chief butler and you will give him his cup of wine as you used to do. But when you are back in favor, tell Pharaoh about me and get me out of this house. For I have not done anything that they should put me in this dungeon."

Hearing that the meaning of the butler's dream was a happy one, the baker also told Joseph his dream. "I had three baskets on my head," he said, "with all kinds of baked goods for Pharaoh in the top one. And the birds came and ate out of the basket." Again Joseph knew the meaning. "The three baskets are three days," he explained. "In three days Pharaoh will have you hanged on a tree and the birds shall eat your flesh."

It happened just as Joseph had foretold. Three days later Pharaoh gave a great feast because it was his birthday. The butler was taken back to court and he again gave Pharaoh his cup of wine. But the baker was hanged. Joseph, however, was left in prison, for the butler forgot to tell Pharaoh about him.
(Genesis 39:20-40:23)

I remember my fault today   *Seven other cows came up after them*

PHARAOH'S DREAMS

For two more years Joseph was kept in the dungeon because the chief butler forgot to tell Pharaoh, king of Egypt, about him. Then something happened which reminded the butler of the Hebrew slave who had told him the exact meaning of his dream.

One morning King Pharaoh was very troubled. He called in his magicians and wise men and told them about two very strange dreams which he had had that night. He wanted to know what they meant, for he was sure that they were foretelling something he must know. But not one of the magicians or wise men could explain the meaning of his dreams.

All this time, the chief butler was standing by, listening. Suddenly he remembered Joseph. The butler said to the king, "Pharaoh was angry at the chief baker and me and put us in prison. While we were there, each of us dreamed a dream in the same night. A young Hebrew slave who was in prison with us explained the meaning of our dreams, and it happened just as he said. I was made chief butler again, but the baker was hanged." Then Pharaoh commanded them to call Joseph. His servants hurried to the prison to get him. But Joseph could not appear in the king's court looking like a prisoner. First he had to shave himself and put on different clothes. Then he was led before Pharaoh.

Seven ears, dried up and thin

Look for a man who is wise

"I have dreamed a dream," Pharaoh said to Joseph, "and no one can tell me what it means. I have heard that you can explain the meaning of dreams." "Not I," replied Joseph humbly, "but God will give you the answer." So Pharaoh began. "In my dream," he said, "I stood on the bank of the Nile River. First, I saw seven beautiful, fat cows come up out of the river and feed in the meadow. And then seven ugly, thin cows — such as I have never seen in all Egypt, came up after them. The thin cows ate up the fat cows, but they stayed just as thin as before. Then I awoke. But when I fell asleep again, I had another dream. In it I saw seven ears of grain grow up on one stalk. Then seven thin ears, withered, and scorched by the east wind, sprang up after them and ate them up.

Joseph replied to the king, "Both of Pharaoh's dreams mean the same thing, and God is showing Pharaoh what He is about to do. The seven fat cows and the seven plump ears both mean that there will be seven years of great plenty in the land of Egypt. The seven thin cows and the seven thin ears mean that seven years of famine will follow. The famine will be so hard that the years of plenty will be forgotten." After explaining the dream, Joseph continued, "Now let Pharaoh find a wise man who will gather into storehouses one — fifth of all the food of those good years. Then there will be enough food during the seven years of famine and the people will not die of hunger." (Genesis 41:1-36)

He put a gold chain about his neck *They cried before him, Bow the knee*

JOSEPH BECOMES GOVERNOR

Pharaoh was pleased with Joseph's explanation of the two dreams and also with his advice to find a wise man to gather in food during the good years. He asked the men of his Court, "Where can we find a wiser man than this?" Then turning to Joseph, he said, "Since God has showed you all of this, there is none so wise as you are. You shall be the ruler of all the land of Egypt. Only I will be greater than you."

Pharaoh then took his signet ring from his hand and put it on Joseph's finger. With that ring, Joseph could give the king's approval to any laws he thought were needed. Pharaoh also commanded his servants to dress Joseph in fine linen robes and to put a chain of gold around his neck. Joseph was given a handsome chariot to ride in. Only Pharaoh's was finer. As he rode through the streets, servants ran before him calling to the people, "Bow the knee." And everyone kneeled down as this great ruler passed by. It would not do, however, to have a man with a foreign name ruling over the proud Egyptians. So Pharaoh gave Joseph an Egyptian name. He also gave him an Egyptian woman to be his wife.

The Lord had caused Joseph to suffer many things. But always He had His good purposes in doing so. He had let Joseph be sold to Potiphar as a slave. But as Potiphar's head servant, Joseph had learned much that was useful to him as

Grain like the sand of the sea   *Go to Joseph*

governor of Egypt. God had also allowed him to be thrown into prison for a sin he had not committed. But because he was able to explain the butler's dream there, he was later called on to explain Pharaoh's dreams. And so, when Joseph was only thirty years old, God suddenly raised him from being a slave in prison to being ruler over the mighty land of Egypt.

The first seven years after Joseph became governor were indeed years of plenty. Joseph chose officers in each city to gather into barns one-fifth of the grain which grew in the fields around those cities. When those barns were filled, new barns were built. At first, the officers kept track of how much food was brought in. But after a while they gave up because there was so much.

Then, just as Joseph had said, the seven years of plenty were ended and the years of famine started. The people of Egypt began to suffer hunger and cried to Pharaoh for bread. But Pharaoh said to them, "Go to Joseph." So the people went to Joseph, and he opened the barns and sold them grain.

Not only did little or nothing grow in Egypt during those years, but the crops also failed in other countries. These people had not known that the famine was coming and had not saved up any food. So when they heard that there was bread in Egypt, they, too, came to Joseph to buy grain. (Genesis 41:37-57)

Joseph's brothers bowed down *You are spies*

JOSEPH'S BROTHERS COME TO EGYPT

Joseph, the governor of Egypt, sat in his splendid chair and waited for his servants to bring in the next group of those who wished to buy grain. Ten men entered and bowed low before him. Joseph knew them at once. They were his brothers. But they did not recognize him. The last time they had seen him he was only a boy of seventeen. Now he was a full-grown man, shaved and dressed like an Egyptian. Besides, they never expected to find him the governor of Egypt! When Joseph saw his brothers bowing before him, he thought of the dreams which he had had as a boy. In them, you remember, his brothers' sheaves and the sun, moon, and eleven stars had bowed down to him. Now those dreams were coming true!

"Where are you from?" Joseph asked them roughly, pretending not to know them. "From the land of Canaan to buy food," they replied humbly. "You are spies," he said to them. "No, no," they answered. "We are all the sons of one man. We are not spies." "Yes, you have come to spy out the weakness of this country," insisted Joseph. "Your servants are twelve brothers," said the men. "The youngest is with our father, and the other one is no more." "We shall see if your words are true," replied Joseph. "One of you will go back home to get your brother and the rest will be kept here in prison." Then he had them all locked up.

Three days later he sent for them again. This time he was not quite so

We are truly guilty *He bound him before their eyes*

harsh. "One of you shall stay here in prison. The rest may take grain back to your hungry families. But bring your youngest brother to me to prove that you are speaking the truth and you shall not die."

Joseph had been speaking to them through an interpreter, as if he did not understand their language. Now the brothers began talking among themselves. "We are truly guilty concerning our brother," they said, speaking of how they had sold Joseph as a slave years before. "When he begged us, we would not hear. Therefore this trouble has come upon us."

Joseph understood every word they said. He was so moved that he began to cry and quickly left the hall so that his brothers would not see his tears. For he was not treating them roughly just to get even with them. Not at all. He wanted to help them become better men than they had been when they had sold him as a slave. For the moment, they seemed truly sorry that they had been so cruel to him. But he wanted their change of heart to be deeper and more lasting. He was not yet ready to tell them who he was.

When Joseph returned to the hall, he commanded his guard to tie up Simeon and take him back to prison. But the rest were sent home. Joseph ordered his servants to fill all of their sacks with grain and to put each man's money in the mouth of his sack. (Genesis 42:1-25)

He saw his money

My son shall not go with you

THE BROTHERS COME A SECOND TIME

The nine brothers strapped their sacks of grain onto their donkeys and started back to Canaan. Simeon had to stay in prison until they brought Benjamin back. On their way home, one of the brothers opened his sack of grain to feed his donkey. There, in the mouth of the sack, he found his bag of money! He and his brothers were afraid. They wondered what God was doing to them.

When they arrived home, they told Jacob how harshly the Egyptian ruler had treated them. They also told him that they had to take their youngest brother back to Egypt, for if they went without him they would die as spies. Jacob, however, refused. "My son shall not go down with you," he said. "For his brother Joseph is dead and he is left alone." If anything should happen to Benjamin, too, he felt, his sorrow would be so great that he would die.

Later, as the brothers were emptying their bags of grain, each one found his money in the mouth of his sack. What could this mean? Would the ruler accuse them all of stealing?

It was not long before the grain which they had brought from Egypt was almost all gone. Jacob said to his sons, "Go again and buy us a little food." Judah replied, "If you will send our brother Benjamin with us, we will go. But if you will not send him, we will not go down. For the man said unto us, "You shall

We have brought it again

He brought Simeon out to them

not see my face unless your brother is with you." Jacob was greatly troubled He was afraid to let Benjamin go. But if he did not, they would all die of hunger. Finally he agreed that there was no other choice. But at least they should do all they could to win the favor of the ruler. They must take him a present of spices, honey, and nuts, and twice as much money, in case there had been some mistake the first time. Then Jacob sent them off with the prayer that God Almighty would cause the ruler to show them mercy.

    The brothers arrived in Egypt and appeared before Joseph. He was pleased to see that they had brought Benjamin with them. He ordered his head servant to take them to his own house, for he wished to have dinner with them at noon. When the brothers learned that they were being taken to the ruler's house, they were afraid. They wondered if he was going to make them all his slaves because of the money which they had found in their sacks. Before entering Joseph's house, they explained to the head servant how their money had been mysteriously returned to them. They had brought it back again, with other money to buy more grain. The servant assured them that everything was all right. He brought Simeon from prison and gave them water to wash their feet. When he told them that they were to have dinner with the ruler, the brothers were puzzled. Why should they be so honored by this strange governor? (Genesis 42:26-43:25)

Is this your younger brother?

Benjamin's was five times as much

JOSEPH'S SILVER CUP

When Joseph returned home for dinner, his eleven brothers bowed low before him and gave him their present. Still pretending to be a stranger to them, Joseph politely asked about their father. Then turning toward Benjamin, he said, "Is this your younger brother?" "Yes, it is," they replied. Joseph looked at him tenderly. Because he and Benjamin both had the same mother, Joseph was much closer to him than to any of his other brothers. "God be gracious to you, my son," he said. Again Joseph began to cry. He left the room quickly and went where he could weep without their knowing it. Then he washed the tears from his eyes and returned to the room.

It was now time for dinner. Joseph, the great ruler, sat at a table by himself. He seated his brothers at a separate table according to their age — the oldest first, then the next, and so on. This surprised them. How could the Egyptian know the order of their ages? When the food was served, Joseph had his servants give Benjamin five times as much as the others. And they ate and drank and had a good time in the governor's house that day.

The brothers had indeed changed greatly. But Joseph wanted to put them to one more test. He commanded his head servant to fill all of their sacks with grain and to put every man's money back in his sack as he had done before. In

Why have you rewarded evil for good?   *The cup was found in Benjamin's sack*

the mouth of Benjamin's sack he was also to put Joseph's silver cup.

    Early the next morning the eleven brothers started home with thankful hearts. Their sacks were full, the ruler had treated them kindly, Simeon had been freed from prison, and no harm had come to Benjamin! But hardly had they left the city when they saw the governor's servant riding full-speed toward them. As soon as he overtook them, he said in a stern voice, "Why have you paid back evil for good and stolen my master's silver cup?" The brothers were amazed! "Why does my lord say these words?" they asked him. "We brought back from Canaan the money which we found in our sack. Why then should we steal silver or gold from your lord's house?" They were so sure that none of them had stolen it that they said, "The person with whom the cup is found shall die and the rest of us will be my lord's slaves." The servant replied, "The one with whom the cup is found will be my servant. The rest shall be blameless." The men quickly set their sacks on the ground and the Egyptian began the search. First he looked in the sack of Reuben, the oldest. Not finding it there, he looked in Simeon's next. Then down the line he went until he came to Benjamin's sack. He felt around in the grain and pulled out Joseph's cup! The brothers were thunder-struck! How had it gotten there? They all tied their sacks back on their donkeys and returned to the city, for they could not go home without Benjamin. (Genesis 43:25-44:13)

We are my lord's servants   *Let your servant speak a word*

JOSEPH MAKES HIMSELF KNOWN

Greatly troubled, the eleven brothers returned to the ruler's house with the head servant. They could not understand how the ruler's silver cup had gotten into Benjamin's sack. But they felt that God had caused this trouble to come upon them as punishment for the cruel way they had treated Joseph years before. They bowed to the ground before the governor, and Judah said, "We are my lord's slaves, both we, and he also with whom the cup was found." Joseph replied, "No, only the one with whom the cup was found will be my servant. The rest of you may go in peace to your father." Joseph wanted to see if his brothers would take this chance to save themselves and leave Benjamin in Egypt as a slave.

Judah stepped forward and began to speak. He reminded the ruler of how he had told them that they could not come to Egypt again unless they brought their youngest brother back with them. Judah said that their father did not want to let him go for fear that harm would come to him. If they went home now without him, their father would die of sorrow. "Now therefore," pleaded Judah, "let me stay instead of the boy, and let the boy go back with his brothers. For how shall I go back to my father without him?"

It was enough! Joseph could see now that his brothers were no longer the same cruel men who had thrown him into a pit and then sold him as a slave.

I am Joseph   *And he fell upon Benjamin's neck*

Then, they had caused their father great sorrow by making him think that his favorite son was dead. But now they refused to leave Egypt without Benjamin. Judah was even willing to become Joseph's slave in Benjamin's place rather than to cause his father more grief.

    Joseph could control himself no longer. He ordered all of the Egyptians out of the room and then began to weep aloud. When he could again talk, he said to his brothers in their own language, "I am Joseph." At first the brothers could not believe it. Then they were greatly frightened as they realized that Joseph had them in his power and could punish them in any way he wanted. But Joseph had no desire to punish them. "Come near to me," he said kindly. "Do not be sorrowful, nor angry with yourselves that you sold me here. For God sent me before you to save your lives. There have been two years of famine and there will be five more. Hurry, go back to my father and tell him that his son Joseph is ruler over all the land of Egypt. Tell him to come down with his children and children's children, his flocks and his herds and all that he has. And you shall live near me in the land of Goshen and I will give you food."

    Then he threw his arms around Benjamin and kissed him. They both cried for joy. He also kissed all of his other brothers and wept over them. After that they talked for a long time. (Genesis 44-45)

Joseph is yet alive *Joseph went up to meet his father*

JACOB GOES TO EGYPT

Pharaoh was very pleased when he heard that Joseph's brothers had come to Egypt. Because he was so grateful to Joseph for having saved Egypt from starvation, he said to him, "Tell your brothers to go back to Canaan and bring their father and their families to live here in Egypt with you." So Joseph sent his brothers off at once, with wagons to carry the women and children, and plenty of food for the way.

As soon as the brothers reached home, they told their father the exciting news: "Joseph is still alive, and he is governor over all the land of Egypt!" Impossible! thought Jacob. Had not Joseph been torn to pieces by wild animals? He could not believe it. But then, when his sons told him all that Joseph had said, and when he saw the wagons, he replied, "It is enough. Joseph, my son, is yet alive. I will go and see him before I die."

Jacob began the long trip to Egypt with all of his family and his possessions. But something still troubled him. Was it all right to leave Canaan — the land which God had promised to give them — and go live in another country? One night the Lord answered Jacob in a vision. "Fear not to go down into Egypt," He said. "For there I will make of you a great nation. I will go down with you, and I will also surely bring you up again." Comforted by these words, Jacob continued his trip.

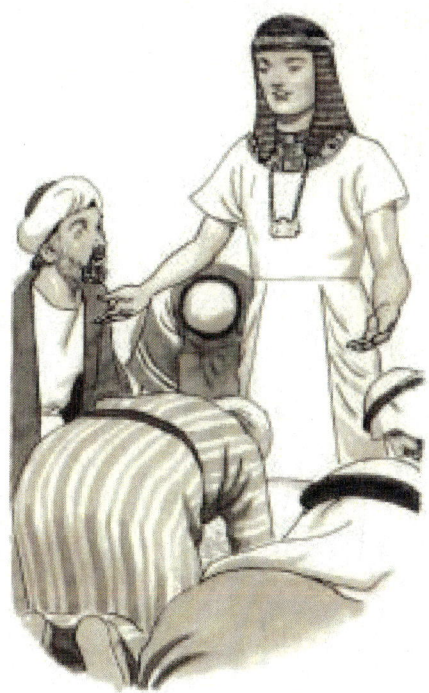

Do not bury me in Egypt *God meant it for good*

When Joseph heard that his father was coming, he got into his chariot and rode out to welcome him. What a happy meeting it was! Jacob had never expected to see his favorite son alive again. Now here he stood before him, the grand ruler of Egypt! Joseph ran and threw his arms around his dear father and wept for a long time. "Now I can die in peace," said the old man, "since I have seen your face."

Pharaoh gave Joseph's family the rich land of Goshen in which to live. They were happy there, and Jacob lived on for seventeen more years near his son Joseph. But they still thought of Canaan, not Egypt, as their home. Therefore, just before Jacob died, he said to Joseph, "Swear to me that you will not bury me in Egypt. But bury me with my fathers in the land of Canaan."

After their father died, the brothers were afraid that Joseph would now try to punish them for having sold him as a slave. Joseph wept when he learned of their fears. Had he not shown them these last seventeen years that he had truly forgiven them? He said to them kindly, "Do not be afraid. You meant it for evil, but God meant it for good in order to save the lives of many people."

Joseph and his family stayed on in Egypt long after the famine was over. But just before Joseph died, he reminded them that one day God would take them out of Egypt back to the Promised Land. (Genesis 45:16-50:26)

And they made their lives bitter

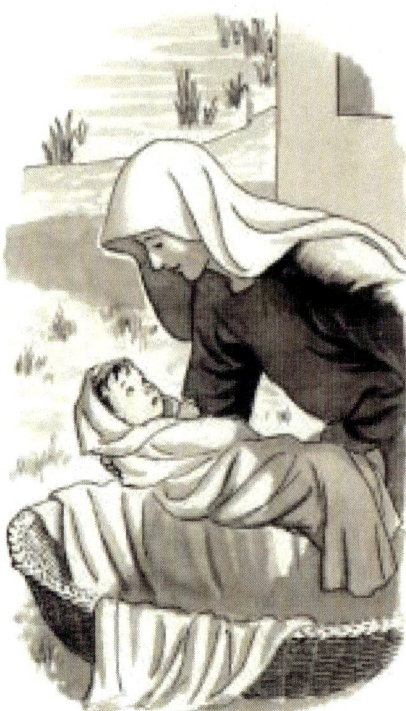
She put the child in it

A BOAT IN THE BULRUSHES

Joseph and all of his brothers died in Egypt. Their children and their children's children grew up and died, and still the Israelites lived in Egypt. God blessed them there, just as He had promised Jacob He would do (Gen. 46:3). They had many, many children and they spread all over the land of Goshen. In fact, they became so numerous that the Egyptians were worried. King Pharaoh said to his people, "Behold, the children of Israel are more and mightier than we. If there is a war, they may take sides with our enemies and fight against us."

This king did not know how Joseph had saved Egypt from the dreadful famine. So he was not kind to the Israelites as other kings had been. Instead, he made them work very hard as slaves. They had to make bricks, build cities, and work in the fields. All the while taskmasters stood over them with whips to make them work faster. But God was with His people, and the harder the Egyptians made them work, the more they grew in number.

Then Pharaoh tried to get the nurses who helped the Hebrew women when they were having their babies to kill every boy baby as soon as he was born. When this cruel plan did not work, Pharaoh commanded all of the Egyptians to throw into the Nile River every son that was born to the Hebrews.

About this time a beautiful baby boy was born to a man and his wife of the

She saw the child

Take this child and nurse it

tribe of Levi. They already had a girl and another little boy. But they loved this child, too, and did not want him drowned. Until he was three months old, his mother kept him hidden in the house. But then she could do so no longer. So she gathered some reeds, or bulrushes, from the river's edge and wove a little basket. This she daubed with tar so that no water could leak into it. Then she laid her precious baby in the covered basket and put it in the river among the reeds where it would not drift away. Only God could save her child now.

Soon Pharaoh's daughter came down to the river with her maids to wash. While she was bathing, she saw the strange little boat and sent one of her maids to get it. Carefully the princess opened the basket, and just then the baby started to cry. The princess felt sorry for him. "This is one of the Hebrews' children," she said tenderly.

Miriam, the baby's older sister, had been watching from a distance. Now she came close and asked the princess, "Shall I go and call a Hebrew nurse for you?" "Yes, go," replied Pharaoh's daughter. Miriam ran home quickly and brought back her mother. "Take this child and nurse him for me," the princess said to her, "and I will pay you for it." The happy mother took her baby home. She could still take care of him, and now the king would not drown him. (Exodus 1-2:9)

Moses was taught in all wisdom   *He killed the Egyptian*

MOSES FLEES TO MIDIAN

Pharaoh's daughter gave the baby which she had found in the basket the name of Moses. For a few years the princess paid Moses' mother to take care of her own son. During that time his mother taught him about the only true God. For she knew that when he went to live with the princess, he would not hear about the Lord again.

When Moses was old enough to leave his mother, he was taken to the Egyptian court. Pharaoh's daughter adopted him for her own son, and so he was treated like a little prince. He went to school in the palace and was taught all that the wise men of that day knew (Acts 7:22).

Both Moses' training by his mother and his studies in the palace were part of God's plan to get him ready for a great work. The children of Israel had lived in Egypt almost four hundred years and had suffered greatly under the whips of the cruel taskmasters. The only comfort they had was God's promise to both Abraham (Gen. 15:13, 14) and Jacob (Gen. 46:4) that He would surely take them back to Canaan. And now through God's wonderful working, the very one who was to lead them out of Egypt — Moses — was being brought up by the Egyptians themselves!

Moses could have kept on living like an Egyptian prince. But he did not feel it was right when his fellow Israelites were suffering so much as slaves.

Who made you a judge over us?   *Moses stood up and helped them*

When he was forty years old, he went out to see how his people were getting along. He became very sad when he saw how hard they had to work. Then, when he saw an Egyptian beating one of them, Moses grew very angry. After looking around to make sure that no one was watching, he killed the Egyptian and buried his body in the sand.

The next day he went out again and saw two Israelites fighting with each other. "Why are you hitting your brother?" he asked one of them. But the Israelite just snarled back, "Who made you a prince and a judge over us? Are you going to kill me the way you killed the Egyptian?" Moses was afraid. Somehow, his killing of the Egyptian had been discovered! Soon even Pharaoh heard about it and sought to kill him. So Moses ran away to Midian, a dry wasteland east of Egypt.

One evening Moses sat down by a well to rest. Seven young women — all of them daughters of a priest named Jethro came and began to draw water for their flocks. But soon some rough shepherds arrived and started to chase the girls away, just as they did every day. Moses jumped up and drove off the shepherds. Then he drew water for the girls' flocks. When they got home earlier than usual, they told their father about the kind Egyptian who had helped them. Their father sent for Moses at once and asked him to stay with them. Moses lived with the priest for a long time. He even married Zipporah, one of his daughters. (Exodus 2:10-22)

Now Moses kept the flock of Jethro *Behold, the bush burned with fire!*

THE BURNING BUSH

At his mother's knees, Moses had learned about God. In the palace school, he had learned the wisdom of Egypt. Now, in the wilderness of Midian, he was to learn to be humble and patient. For Moses, the Egyptian prince, became a lowly shepherd and took care of the flocks of Jethro, his father-in-law. And during the forty long years that he stayed with Jethro, he learned to wait patiently until the Lord called him.

Then one day, as Moses was tending his sheep on Mount Horeb, he saw a bush on fire. But as he stood there watching, it did not burn up! He started toward it, but God called out of the fire, saying, "Do not come here. Take off your shoes, for the place where you are standing is holy ground. I am the God of Abraham, Isaac, and Jacob." In wonder and awe Moses took off his shoes and hid his face. "I have seen the troubles of My people in Egypt," God went on. "And I have come to deliver them and bring them up to a good land. I will send you to Pharaoh, that you may bring forth My people out of Egypt."

Moses did not feel fitted for such a task. "Who am I," he replied, "that I should go to Pharaoh and bring forth the children of Israel out of Egypt?" God, who so often chooses weak and lowly people to do His work, promised, "Surely I will be with you." Then Moses asked, "When I come to the children of Israel,

And it became a snake *I am slow of speech*

who shall I say sent me?" "Tell them that the Lord God of Abraham, Isaac, and Jacob sent you, and that He will bring them out of Egypt. Then go to Pharaoh and ask to take the Israelites on a three days' journey into the wilderness to sacrifice to Me."

Moses still held back. "They will not believe me," he objected. "What is that in your hand?" God asked. "A rod," replied Moses. "Throw it on the ground," commanded God. Moses threw his shepherd's staff on the ground and it became a long snake. He fled from it in fear. "Now pick it up by the tail," said God. When Moses obeyed, the snake changed back into a rod. Then God gave Moses a second sign so that the Israelites would believe that he had been sent by God. He commanded Moses to put his hand into his coat and take it out again. When he did, it was white with leprosy! "Do it again," said God. He did, and this time the leprosy was all gone.

Then Moses objected again. "O my Lord," he said, "I am slow of speech and cannot talk well."The Lord answered, "I will teach you what you will say." But still Moses did not want to go." O my Lord," he begged, "send someone else, I pray Thee." Now God was angry and said, "I will send your brother Aaron with you and he will speak for you." So at last Moses started back to Egypt, with his staff in his hand. (Exodus 3-4:17)

Who is the Lord? *So the people were scattered*

NO STRAW FOR BRICKS

Moses had not gone very far on his way to Egypt when he met his older brother, Aaron, whom God had sent to him. Moses told his brother how the Lord had appeared to him in the burning bush and had said that He was going to use both of them to bring the Israelites out of Egypt.

The two brothers returned at once to Egypt and gathered together the elders of Israel. They told them that their slavery in Egypt was almost over. Then they showed them the signs of Moses' rod turning into a snake and his hand becoming leprous. The people bowed their heads in thanksgiving and worshipped the Lord. They had thought God had forgotten them, but now they knew that He had heard their cries of sorrow after all.

Soon afterwards, Moses and Aaron entered the splendid palace and said to the mighty Pharaoh, "The Lord God of Israel has said, Let My people go that they may worship me in the wilderness." They were not asking for much, only for permission to make a three-day trip in order to worship the Lord. But the king replied scornfully, "Who is the Lord, that I should obey His voice? I do not know the Lord, neither will I let Israel go." Moses and Aaron pleaded some more, but Pharaoh only accused them of trying to free the Israelites from their work. Then Pharaoh called his task-masters and the Israelite officers who had been set over their own people. "From now on," he commanded them, "you shall give them no

The officers of Israel were beaten

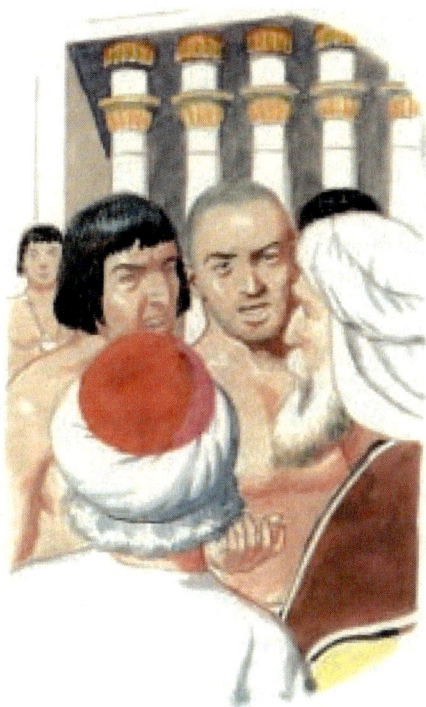

And they met Moses and Aaron

more straw to make bricks. Let them go and gather straw for themselves. But they must still make the same number of bricks each day. It is because they do not have enough work to do that they are crying, "Let us go and sacrifice to our God."

The taskmasters and officers went out and told the people about Pharaoh's impossible order. The next day the people scattered throughout the land to gather the short stubble that was left in the fields after the grain had been cut. But, of course; that took them so long that they did not have enough time to make the same number of bricks. Then the officers were beaten because the people had not finished their work. When they went to ask Pharaoh's mercy, he only answered sternly, "Get back to work. You shall be given no straw, but you must still deliver the same number of bricks."

The officers left discouraged. God had promised to deliver them, but now they were worse off than before. Outside the palace they met Moses and Aaron and complained to them. God had warned Moses that Pharaoh would refuse to let the people go. He had also promised him that He would bring His people out with mighty miracles. Moses, however, now complained to the Lord that He had not kept His promise. God replied, "Now you shall see what I will do to Pharaoh, and you shall know that I am the Lord your God." (Exodus 4:27-6:8)

Aaron's rod swallowed up their rods　　　　*Let my people go*

WATERS TURNED TO BLOOD

When Moses complained to God that He had not delivered His people from slavery as He had promised, the Lord replied, "Say to the children of Israel, 'I am the Lord, and I will bring you out from under the burdens of the Egyptians with a stretched out arm.'" Moses obeyed. He went to the Israelites and told them that God was soon going to deliver them. But they would not listen to Moses. Ever since they had had to work so much harder by getting their own straw, they had lost faith in God's promises.

But God was still faithful to His chosen people. He told Moses to go again to Pharaoh and ask him to let the children of Israel go into the wilderness in order to worship Him. Moses replied, "If the children of Israel will not listen to me, how then shall Pharaoh hear me?" God answered that it was true that even after He had shown His power through many miracles, Pharaoh would still stubbornly refuse to let the people go. But then, said God, "The Egyptians shall know that I am the Lord when I stretch forth my hand upon Egypt and bring out the children of Israel from among them."

So Moses and Aaron again went to the palace and asked Pharaoh to let the people go. Pharaoh replied, "Show me a miracle first." Moses told Aaron to

All the waters turned to blood

And all the Egyptians dug

throw down his rod. He did, and it changed into a long snake which crawled over the marble floor. Pharaoh called for his magicians and commanded them to do the same. When each of them threw down his rod, it turned into a snake, too. Aaron, however, had the greater power, for his snake swallowed up the others. But Pharaoh paid no attention to the miracle, and he would not listen to Moses.

After this refusal of Pharaoh, God caused the first of ten dreadful plagues to come upon Egypt. In the morning, when the king and his servants came down to the edge of the Nile River, they found Moses and Aaron waiting for them. Aaron said to Pharaoh sternly, "Because you will not let God's people go, I will strike this river with my rod and change the water into blood." Then Aaron lifted up his rod and struck the water. Instantly it turned into blood. Pharaoh again commanded his magicians to copy Aaron's miracle. And again they did as he had done. But God's plague was no small thing. Not only did the main river turn into blood, but also every side stream and canal and pool. All the fish died and the river soon began to smell because of the rotting fish. The people could not drink the foul water. So they tried to dig around in the ground near the river to find some fresh water. Yet for seven days all the waters of Egypt were blood. But Pharaoh still would not let God's people go. (Exodus 6-7)

Aaron stretched out his hand   *. . . into your kneading troughs*

FROGS, LICE, AND FLIES

Again the Lord sent Moses and Aaron to ask Pharaoh to let the Israelites go. Moses warned the king that if he refused, God would send frogs upon all the land. But the king would not listen. So Moses said to Aaron, "Stretch forth your rod over the canals and rivers and ponds and cause frogs to come up upon the land of Egypt." Aaron obeyed. At once frogs began hopping out of the river and swarming over the land. They entered every house they came to. They hopped right up the marble steps of Pharaoh's palace. They went into the kitchen and jumped into the troughs where the bakers were mixing dough for bread. They hopped into Pharaoh's bedroom and up onto his bed. Everywhere the Egyptians turned, there were those horrible frogs!

Pharaoh's magicians were also able to make frogs come up out of the water, but they could not take them away. Pharaoh called for Moses and Aaron and said, "Pray to the Lord to take away the frogs, and I will let the people go sacrifice to Him." So Moses prayed to God, and all the frogs that were in the fields and villages and houses died. Only those still in the water were left alive. The people gathered up the dead frogs into great piles. And the land began to smell from rotting frogs. But when this second plague was over, Pharaoh hardened his heart and would not let them go.

Pharaoh was given no warning of the next plague. In obedience to God's

They gathered them together in heaps

There came a swarm of flies

command, Aaron struck the dust of the land, changing it into millions of tiny, biting insects called lice. Pharaoh's magicians again tried to do the same thing. This time they failed and they had to admit that it was God's doing. But Pharaoh hardened his heart and would not let the people go.

Then God sent Moses to meet Pharaoh by the edge of the river. Moses told him, "The Lord says, 'If you will not let My people go, behold, I will send swarms of flies upon you and upon all your people. But there will be no swarms of flies in the land of Goshen among My people, so that you may know that I am the Lord of all the earth.'" The next day, when the stubborn king still refused, God sent the flies to plague the Egyptians. They buzzed about their heads. They crawled all over their bodies and in their food. Yet not a fly bothered the Israelites. Unable to stand it any longer, Pharaoh called for Moses and Aaron and said, "Go, sacrifice to your God in the land." But Moses insisted that they go away into the wilderness to sacrifice, as God had commanded. Because the Egyptians worshipped bulls as gods, he said, they would probably stone the Israelites if they saw them sacrificing their sacred animals. Pharaoh finally agreed, and then begged Moses to get rid of the flies. So Moses prayed to the Lord and He took away the flies. Not one remained. But again Pharaoh hardened his heart and would not let the Israelites go. (Exodus 8)

The cattle of Israel are not dead   *Moses sprinkled it up toward heaven*

DEAD ANIMALS, BOILS, AND HAIL

Once more God sent Moses to ask Pharaoh to let the children of Israel worship Him in the wilderness. He told the king that if he should refuse this time, God would kill many of the animals of the Egyptians by means of a serious sickness. But not one of the animals belonging to the Israelites would die. The next day, after the stubborn king still refused, many of the Egyptians' cattle became sick and in a short while were dead. Horses, too, and donkeys, camels, and sheep died in great numbers, so that the land was filled with their bodies. Pharaoh sent some servants to Goshen to see how many animals the Israelites had lost. They came back with the amazing news that not a single cow or sheep or camel there had died. This should have been proof to Pharaoh that the God of the lowly Israelite slaves was Lord of all the earth. But Pharaoh only hardened his heart and would not let God's people go.

Next, God commanded Moses and Aaron to go again to Pharaoh. Without any warning, Moses took handfuls of ashes from the furnace and threw them up into the air. As Pharaoh watched, the ashes turned into clouds of fine dust which caused painful boils to break out upon all the Egyptians. Even the magicians suffered from them. Before, they had tried to copy God's plagues. But now this new plague was upon them, too. So Moses, the servant of God, won out

Moses stretched forth his rod

The hail struck both man and beast

completely over these servants of Pharaoh. But the king still would not bow before the Lord, nor would he let the people go.

    Another time Moses came to the palace early in the morning and demanded that Pharaoh let the Israelites go. Because of Pharaoh's stubbornness, said Moses, God was going to send even greater plagues upon Egypt, that Pharaoh might learn that there was no one like Him in all the earth. Then Moses warned, "Tomorrow God will send a hailstorm such as Egypt has never known. Therefore, bring home all the animals and servants that are in the fields. For the hail will kill every man and beast that is left out in the open." Those Egyptians who had come to fear the Lord's doings wisely obeyed Moses' warning. But others paid no attention to it and left their animals and servants in the fields. The next day Moses stretched forth his rod toward heaven. The sky grew black. Lightning, like balls of fire, ran along the ground, and the thunder rolled. Large hailstones began falling from the sky, killing every man and animal that was in the open. The hail beat the flax and barley to the ground and even broke down trees. But in Goshen, where the Israelites lived, there was no hail. In great fear, Pharaoh again called for Moses and begged him to pray to God to stop the storm. Even though Moses knew that the king still would not fear the Lord, he did pray, and the thunder and hail stopped. But once more Pharaoh hardened his heart. (Exodus 9)

Let the men go

They were driven out from Pharaoh

LOCUSTS AND DARKNESS

The Lord said to Moses, "Go in to Pharaoh, for I have hardened his heart, and the heart of his servants so that I might show these My miracles before him and so that you may tell your sons and your sons' sons the great miracles which I have performed in Egypt."

"So Moses and Aaron again came before Pharaoh and asked sternly, "How long will you refuse to humble yourself before the Lord? Let His people go, that they may serve Him. For if you do not," they warned, "tomorrow He will bring locusts such as Egypt has never seen. They will cover the land and eat up everything green that the hail has left." Without even waiting for a reply, Moses and Aaron turned and walked out of the palace.

Then Pharaoh's servants pleaded with the king to let at least the men of Israel go, for Egypt was being destroyed by these plagues. At last Pharaoh gave in. He called Moses and Aaron back and told them that the men could go away to worship, but not the women and children. In that way, Pharaoh was sure that his valuable slaves would not leave Egypt for good. Moses, however, still insisted that they all had to go men and women, grown-ups and children, flocks and herds. The king again refused and had Moses and Aaron driven out of the palace.

Then God told Moses to stretch his rod over Egypt. When he did so, God

They ate every herb of the land   *And Moses stretched forth his hand*

caused a strong east wind to start blowing. It blew all that day and all that night. The next morning it brought the locusts Never before had so many locusts come upon Egypt. They were so thick upon the ground that the Egyptians could not walk without crunching them under their feet. They ate every blade of grass and every leaf that had not been destroyed by the hail. Soon there was not a green plant or tree left in all the land of Egypt.

Now Pharaoh was really alarmed. He quickly sent for Moses and Aaron and confessed, "I have sinned against the Lord your God and against you. Now therefore forgive my sin only this once and beg the Lord your God to take the locusts away." So Moses went out and prayed to the Lord. And God sent a strong west wind which carried the locusts out of Egypt into the Red Sea. Not a single one was left. Then Pharaoh showed that it was not really his sin that had troubled him, but only God's punishment for his sin. For as soon as the punishment was over, Pharaoh hardened his heart and would not let the people go.

Now God commanded Moses to stretch forth his rod again toward heaven. Moses obeyed, and a thick darkness — so thick that it could almost be felt — settled over the land. It was so dark that the Egyptians would not move from their houses. They could not even see anyone in the same room. Yet in the land of Goshen, among God's people, there was light. (Exodus 10:1-23)

Go away from me *He went out in a great anger*

MOSES' LAST WARNING TO PHARAOH

For three days the thick darkness lasted. The Egyptians sat in terror and waited for this unnatural blackness to be lifted. Finally Pharaoh called for Moses. "You may all go and serve the Lord," he told him, "But your flocks and herds must stay behind." Pharaoh well knew that God wanted all of the Israelites, with all of their animals, to go away into the wilderness to sacrifice to Him. But the king was always trying to cheat God. At first, he did not want them to take time off from their work at all. Then he told the Israelites that they could sacrifice in Egypt, but not in the wilderness. Next, he wanted to let just the men go, but not the women and children. Now he was trying to keep back the flocks and herds. But Moses was firm. All of God's demands had to be granted by the king. Besides, they needed some of their animals as burnt-offerings.

The stubborn king was furious. "Get out of here," he ordered Moses. "If you see my face again, you will die." "You are right," replied Moses."I will never see your face again. But I warn you that at midnight, the Lord will go throughout Egypt, killing all the first-born in the land, from the first-born son of Pharaoh, even to the first-born of the maid that grinds the grain, and all the first-born of the animals. There shall be a great cry throughout all the land of Egypt, but

And the two side posts with the blood   *The people bowed and worshipped*

not one of the first-born of the Israelites will die." Then Moses said, "Your servants will come and bow down to me and beg me and all my people to get out. After that, I will go." In holy anger, Moses left the palace for the last time.

Then Moses called together the elders of Israel and said, "Tell the people that each family of you must take a lamb from the flock. It must be a year-old male that is perfectly healthy. Kill the lamb, catching the blood in a bowl. Then dip a hyssop plant in the blood and strike the two side posts and the upper door post of your house with the blood. None of you shall go out of your house until morning. For the Lord will go through the land to kill the first-born of the Egyptians. But when He sees the blood on your doorposts, He will pass over your house and will not kill your first-born. Meanwhile, roast the lamb and eat it. You must eat it in a hurry, with your shoes on and your staff in your hand. This day shall be a special feast day which you must keep every year after you come to the Promised Land. When your children will ask what this feast means, you will say, 'It is the Passover of the Lord, who passed over the houses of the children of Israel in Egypt, when He killed the Egyptians.' "

When the elders told the people God's command, they bowed their heads in thanksgiving and worshipped the Lord. (Exodus 10-12)

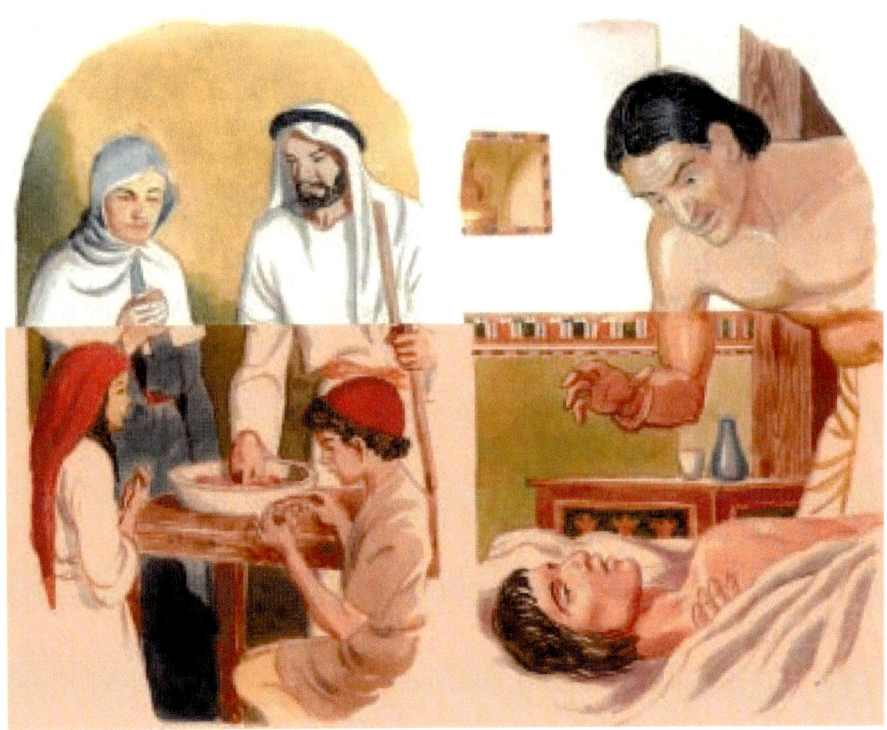

Eat the flesh in that night   *And Pharaoh rose up in the night*

THE PASSOVER

What excitement and bustle among the Israelites! The father in each family picked out the lamb for the Passover Feast. He killed it and sprinkled its blood on the doorposts of his house. Then, while the lamb was roasting, the family quickly gathered together the few possessions which they would be able to carry on their backs or on their donkeys and camels. When the lamb was cooked, they sat down to eat, with their shoes on and their staff in their hand, all ready to go at a moment's notice.

At midnight, the last and most dreadful of the ten plagues began. The Lord went through the land, as Moses had warned, and killed the first-born child in every Egyptian home. Pharaoh's oldest son lay dead. The first-born of his chief officer was dead. The first-born of the maid who ground the grain and of the prisoner in the dungeon had died. The first-born of all their cattle were dead, too. All of the Egyptians, from the greatest to the lowliest, rose up in the night and wept, for there was not an Egyptian home that did not have a dead child in it.

But in Goshen, the Lord had passed over the homes of the Israelites, which had been sprinkled with the blood of the Passover lamb. This lamb pointed forward to the true Passover Lamb, Jesus Christ. For just as the first-born of the Israelites were saved from sudden death by the blood of that lamb, so all

They asked of the Egyptians jewels   *A mixed multitude went with them*

believers are saved from hell by the blood of Jesus, which was shed on the cross.

In great fear, Pharaoh sent his servants to Moses and Aaron in the middle of the night. They bowed low before them and begged them to take the Israelite people with all their cattle and leave at once.

The long-awaited moment had arrived! The Israelites gathered up their last minute things. They even packed their bread pans with the dough in them. Then they asked their Egyptian neighbors for gold and silver jewelry and fine clothing, as Moses had told them to do. The Egyptians were now so glad to get rid of these people that they gave them anything they wanted. So the Israelite slaves left the country like a victorious army loaded down with riches.

It was a tremendous multitude that left Egypt that night. There were 600,000 Israelite men, plus all the women and children. In addition, there were others who were not Israelites but who wanted to go along with them. Moses had been so timid when, from the burning bush, God had first called him to lead the Israelites out of Egypt. Now he was in charge of over two million people, besides all the flocks and herds! But the Lord who had called him had also fitted him for the task. For the many miracles which God had performed through him had not only made the Egyptians tremble, but had also strengthened Moses' faith and made him very brave. (Exodus 12:29-13:22)

They were very much afraid *The waters were a wall to them*

A PATH THROUGH THE SEA

Not long after the Israelites had left, Pharaoh and his servants said to each other, "What is this that we have done, that we have let Israel go from serving us?" So soon after God had punished them with the death of their first-born, their hearts were again hardened against Him. They were sorry, now, that they had let their valuable slaves leave and decided that they must be brought back again. So the king commanded his soldiers to make ready their chariots. The riders mounted their war horses. And Pharaoh's powerful, well-trained army set out after the Israelites.

The Lord, meanwhile, was leading His people toward the Red Sea. By day He went before the slow-moving crowd in a pillar of cloud, and by night in a pillar of fire. When the Israelites came to the shore of the sea, they camped there. Suddenly, they saw great clouds of dust to the north. Terror filled their hearts as they realized that it was Pharaoh's army. They looked around. To the east lay the sea. They could not flee that way. To the south and west, mountains blocked their escape. From the north, the hated Egyptians were coming. They were trapped! Instead of trusting the Lord, who had proved His great power through the ten plagues, they cried out to Moses, saying, "It had been better for us to serve the Egyptians than to die here in the wilderness." Then Moses replied in great faith, "Fear not. Stand still and see the salvation of the Lord. For the

He took off their chariot wheels

The waters covered the chariots

Egyptians whom you have seen today you will never see again."

As night came on, the children of Israel watched and waited. The pillar of cloud, which had been going before, now moved behind and came between them and the Egyptian army. On the Egyptian side it was a dark cloud. But all night long it glowed brightly for the Israelites. Then Moses stretched out his rod over the sea and the Lord caused a strong east wind to blow. Soon a broad path of dry land appeared in the midst of the sea. At Moses' command, the whole multitude of the Israelites, with all their animals, started bravely along the path. To the right and to the left of them the waters were heaped up like high walls.

When the Egyptians saw that the Israelites were crossing the sea in safety, they dashed in after them. But toward morning God took off their chariot wheels, and the chariots hardly moved. "Let us flee from the Israelites," they shouted, "for the Lord is fighting for them." The Egyptians turned around and tried to escape. But by that time the Israelites had reached the opposite shore and Moses again stretched forth his rod. The walls of water broke and rushed over the path. All the Egyptian chariots and horsemen were buried beneath the waves. Not one was left.

So, by this great act of power, the Lord saved His people from their enemies and brought judgment upon the wicked and stubborn Egyptians. (Exodus 13:17-14:29)

The quails came and covered the camp   *It bred worms, and stank*

BREAD FROM HEAVEN

The children of Israel looked back across the Red Sea, through which they had just passed on dry ground. Everything was peaceful now. Only the bodies of the dead Egyptians which the tossing waves were casting up on the shore were a proof that their miraculous escape had not been a dream. The people marveled at the wonderful way the Lord had saved them, and they sang a beautiful song of praise to Him.

But the Israelites' faith in God's love and power did not last long. After traveling three days into the wilderness without finding a brook or spring, they grumbled against Moses instead of asking God to give them water. Another time, they were growing weak from hunger. "We wish we had died in Egypt," they complained, "where we had plenty of meat and bread." Did they not remember how they had suffered under the Egyptians? Had they forgotten the mighty miracles of their God? Moses rebuked the people, saying, "Your murmurings are not against us, but against the Lord. However, He has heard your murmurings. This evening you shall eat meat, and in the morning you shall be filled with bread."

That very evening a huge flock of quails flew into their camp, covering the ground. The people ran and caught them, and everyone had plenty of meat to eat that night.

They gathered it every morning   *Take a pot and put manna in it*

    The next morning the Israelites found little, round, white things all over the ground. "This," said Moses, "is the bread which the Lord has given you to eat. Let every man gather what he needs for the day. But do not keep any of it until tomorrow." The people busily went about picking up this bread, which they called manna. It tasted very good, like wafers made of honey. Most of the people used theirs all up that day, for they believed Moses' word that God would send more the next day. Others, however, kept some over. The next morning they found that their bread was full of worms. Moses was angry at these people for not obeying.

    Every morning God sent fresh manna from Heaven. And every morning the people gathered what they needed early, for when the sun grew hot, the manna on the ground melted. On the sixth day, Moses said, "Gather twice as much today. For tomorrow is the Sabbath, the day of rest, and God will send no manna." Those who obeyed found that the manna which they kept over for the Sabbath did not become wormy. But others had gathered enough for only one day. When they went out on the Sabbath to gather their manna, they did not find one small piece. They had to go hungry that day because of their disobedience.

    Six days a week, for forty years, God sent this bread from Heaven. Later, when the tabernacle was built, Moses commanded Aaron to put some of it in a golden pot in the ark of the covenant (Heb. 9:4). There it reminded the Israelites year after year of God's loving care for His people. (Exodus 14:30-16:36)

Give us water   *And Moses did so before the elders*

THE ISRAELITES' FIRST BATTLE

The Lord continued to lead His people on through the wilderness by means of the pillar of cloud. When the cloud moved forward, the Israelites broke up camp and followed it. When the cloud stopped, they stopped, too, and pitched their tents. At one place where they camped, called Rephidim, the people could find no water. Once more they seemed to forget how wonderfully God had been taking care of their needs. They grumbled against Moses and demanded, "Give us water to drink." "Why do you grumble against me?" he replied. He was not God, that he could cause water to spring up out of the ground. But the people would not listen. "Why have you brought us up out of Egypt to kill us and our children and our cattle with thirst?" they asked. Greatly troubled, Moses prayed to the Lord. "What shall I do with this people?" he asked sorrowfully. "They are almost ready to stone me." "Go on ahead of the people," replied God, "and take with you some of the elders and the rod with which you struck the river. I will be with you there upon the rock. You shall strike the rock, and water shall come out of it, that the people may drink."

Moses and the elders walked ahead to the rock. While the elders stood by as witnesses, Moses lifted his rod and struck the rock hard. Water gushed out over the dry ground. It was not just a trickle, but a great stream — enough to

Aaron and Hur held up his hands

Joshua defeated Amalek

satisfy the thirst of over two million people, with all their animals. Because of the Israelites' faithless grumbling, they had deserved only punishment from God. But the Lord, who is "slow to anger and plenteous in mercy" (Ps. 103:8), once again gave His thankless people what they asked for.

While the weary Israelites were still resting from their journey, a rough band of men began to attack them. They were the men of Amalek. Moses called Joshua, a brave, young Israelite, and said to him, "Choose out men, and go out to fight with the Amalekites. Tomorrow I will stand on the top of the hill with the rod of God in my hand." At once, Joshua gathered together a small army and the next day they went out to wage war against the attackers. Meanwhile, Moses, Aaron, and another man named Hur climbed a high hill from which they could see the fighting. Whenever Moses held up his rod — thus calling on the power of God, as he had done when he brought the plagues upon the Egyptians — the Israelites drove back the Amalekites. But when he let it down, the Amalekites were stronger. Moses tried to hold his arms up all the time, but they grew so tired that he had to let them drop. So Aaron and Hur found a large stone for him to sit upon. Then the two men stood beside him, one on each side, and held up Moses' arms until the sun went down. In this way God gave the victory to Joshua. (Exodus 17)

You shall set "bounds"   *Moses brought forth the people*

GOD GIVES THE TEN COMMANDMENTS

Thunder began to roll. Flashes of lightning streaked across the morning sky. A thick cloud settled upon the top of Mt. Sinai and the trumpet of God sounded loudly. The Israelites, who were camped at the foot of the mountain, trembled with fear. This was the great day in which the Lord Himself was coming down upon the mountain. He was going to give them His Law, so that they might know how to live and worship in a way that was pleasing to Him. For although the Israelites were God's own special people, chosen above all the nations of the earth, they no longer served Him as faithfully as Abraham, Isaac, and Jacob had done. So before God brought them to their new home in Canaan, He wanted to teach them His Law.

Three days before this, the Lord had told Moses how to get the people ready for this great occasion. They all had to wash their clothes. Mt. Sinai had to be fenced off so that no one could go up or even touch the holy mountain. Any man or beast that went past the fence would be stoned to death or shot through with an arrow.

Now, at the sound of the trumpet, Moses brought the people forth to the foot of the mountain to meet with God. All of Mt. Sinai was quaking and was smoking like a great furnace, for the Lord had come down upon it in fire. Then the

Mount Sinai was smoking

Do not fear

voice of God thundered from the mountain, saying "I am the Lord your God, who brought you out of the land of Egypt, out of the house of bondage." With these words God taught the Israelites that they should obey His Law out of thankfulness for what He, their God, had done for them. He then gave them part of that Law, the Ten Commandments: "1) You shall have no other gods before me," He said. "2) You shall not make any graven image, to bow down to it or serve it. 3) You shall not take the name of the Lord your God in vain. 4) Remember the Sabbath day, to keep it holy. 5) Honor your father and your mother. 6) You shall not kill. 7) You shall not commit adultery. 8) You shall not steal. 9) You shall not bear false witness against your neighbor. 10) You shall not covet anything that is your neighbor's."

The people were terrified at hearing God speak to them. They drew back from the mountain in fear and begged Moses to stand between God and themselves. "But let not God speak with us," they cried, "or we will die." "Do not fear," Moses told them, for God did not want to frighten His people. He was showing them His great power and majesty so that they would obey Him.

Then God called Moses up into the mountain in order to give him many more laws. Leaving Aaron and Hur in charge of the people, Moses climbed the mount and disappeared into the thick cloud. (Exodus 19-20)

... and made it a molten calf *He saw the calf and the dancing*

THE GOLDEN CALF

For forty days and forty nights Moses stayed up on Mt. Sinai without eating or drinking. During this time God wrote the Ten Commandments upon two tables of stone and gave Moses many other laws.

The Israelites, meanwhile, were growing tired of waiting for Moses. They went to Aaron and said, "Make us gods to go before us; for as for this Moses, we do not know what has become of Him." Aaron was not a strong leader. Instead of stopping the people from committing such a great sin, he went right along with them. "Break off your golden earrings," he said to them, "and bring them to me. Aaron melted down the earrings which the people brought and made a calf, such as they had seen the Egyptians worship. The people shouted joyously, "These are your gods, O Israel, who brought you up out of the land of Egypt." They sacrificed burnt offerings to it and held a great feast. After eating and drinking, they began to sing and to dance in a shameful way. Just forty days after God had commanded them not to bow down to images, they were worshipping a golden idol!

On top of the mountain God said to Moses, "Go down, for the people have made a calf of melted gold and have worshipped it. Now let Me alone, that I may consume them." Moses hurried down the mountain, carrying the two tablets of stone. When he arrived at the camp and saw the people wildly dancing around

He threw the tablets out of his hands

Now put off your garments

the golden calf, he, too, became filled with holy anger. He threw the tablets and smashed them to pieces in the sight of the people. Then he burned the calf and ground it to a fine powder. He sprinkled the powder in the brook and made the Israelites drink it.

Moses turned to his brother, Aaron, and sternly rebuked him for causing the people to sin. Then, upon the command of God, he sent the men of the tribe of Levi through the camp to kill all those who had persuaded the people to disobey the Lord. That day three thousand men were killed with the sword!

After getting rid of the calf and these sinful leaders, Moses turned to the Lord to ask His forgiveness. God told Moses to continue the journey. He would send an angel on before them, but He Himself would no longer go with these disobedient people. When the Israelites heard this, they were very sorrowful and took off all their jewelry as a sign of mourning. Moses begged God not to send them on to Canaan if He would not go along with them. At last the Lord agreed to go. The people had sinned greatly against Him by worshipping the calf. But when they showed true sorrow for their sin, He graciously promised to lead them. Again He called Moses up to the mount to give him the Ten Commandments written on two stone tablets. Thus He showed that He had again acknowledged the Israelites as His own people. (Exodus 32-34; Deut. 9, 10)

The court round about the Tabernacle

THE TABERNACLE

On Mount Sinai the Lord said to Moses, "Let the children of Israel bring Me an offering and let them make Me a place of worship, that I may dwell among them." This place of worship, however, could not be a temple of stone. Instead, it had to be a tent-church which could be packed up and carried along whenever the Israelites moved on.

When Moses came down from the mount, he told the Israelites what the Lord had commanded. Many materials were needed to build this tent-church, or Tabernacle, as it was called. So Moses said, "Whoever is of a willing heart, let him bring an offering to the Lord." The people gladly brought their gifts, such as gold, silver, brass, jewels, linen, and skins. In fact, they soon were bringing so much that Moses had to tell them to stop.

Then certain of the people, to whom the Holy Spirit gave special wisdom, started work. They sawed long boards and poles and covered them over with gold. They wove fine, white linen curtains and embroidered blue, purple, and scarlet cloth. Every little detail of the Tabernacle and its furniture had to be made exactly as God had commanded Moses, for it was a type of the sacrifice of Jesus Christ. For about six months these people worked hard, resting only on the Sabbath. At last they finished, and Moses commanded the Tabernacle to be set up.

The golden altar in the tent

The ark

All around the Tabernacle were the tents of the Israelites. But it was hidden from view by white linen curtains which were high enough so that none could look over them. If Aaron, the high priest, wished to go into the Tabernacle, he would push aside the blue, purple, and scarlet curtain at the east end and step into an open court. Directly in front of him would be a large, brass altar for burnt offerings. On past this, there was a huge brass laver, or wash bowl. Beyond this, towards the rear of the courtyard was the Tabernacle itself. Three sides of the Tabernacle were boards covered over with gold, and four different coverings were spread over the outside of these walls and across the top to form the tent.

If Aaron should step past the beautiful curtain across the entrance of the Tabernacle, he would come into the first room, called the Holy Place, which was lighted only by a golden lamp stand on the left side. Opposite him he would see a beautifully embroidered curtain, or veil. In front of it would be the golden altar of incense and on the right, the golden table of show bread. Only once a year could he go beyond the veil into the second room, called the Holy of Holies. There he would see only the ark, a gold chest containing the Ten Commandments and the pot of manna. Above the ark the glory of the Lord shone continually. In this way God showed the Israelites that, although He is everywhere at all times, He was now in the midst of His people in a very special way. (Exodus 35-40)

Take the blood and sprinkle it   *Kill the goat of the sin offering*

THE DAY OF ATONEMENT

The Tabernacle, you remember, was divided into two rooms: the Holy Place and the Holy of Holies. Every day the priests came into the Holy Place to burn incense upon the golden altar and to fill the golden lamp stand with oil. And each Sabbath day they replaced the bread on the table of show bread with twelve fresh loaves. But no one except the high priest was allowed to go past the veil into the Holy of Holies, and he could go there only once a year, on the great Day of Atonement. For in that room the glory of God shone continually above the ark. By thus forbidding the people to come into His holy presence, God taught them how sinful they were.

Every day lambs or bulls were sacrificed in front of the Tabernacle for the sins of the people. But special sacrifices were also offered once a year, on the Day of Atonement. All that day the people thought about their sins and asked God's forgiveness. They did no work, nor did they eat or drink anything.

While the people were sorrowing for their sins, the high priest performed the sacrifices. First he had to offer a sacrifice for his own sins and those of the other priests. For even the priests sinned daily against God. He killed a young bull in front of the Tabernacle and carried some of its blood into the Holy of Holies. There, he sprinkled it once upon the mercy seat, or cover of the ark, and

Aaron shall lay both his hands *The veil was torn into two pieces*

seven times on the floor in front of the ark.

Now he was ready to make a sacrifice for the people. Two goats were brought to him. He killed one of them and also sprinkled its blood on the mercy seat and the floor of the Holy of Holies. Then he went outside again. Laying both of his hands upon the head of the live goat, he confessed over it all the sins of the Israelites. With these sins upon it, the scapegoat was then led far away into the wilderness, never to return. This act pictured how one day Jesus would become a scapegoat by having the sins of believers placed upon Him. After that, the high priest burned two rams on the altar as a sign of the surrender of the priests and the people to the Lord.

These sacrifices, performed year after year, were in themselves useless, for it was not possible that the blood of bulls and goats should take away sins." (Heb. 10:4). But they reminded the people of their sins and taught them to look forward to the perfect Sacrifice and High Priest, Jesus Christ. Because Jesus was without sin, He did not first have to make a sacrifice for His own sins, as the sons of Aaron did. Nor did He have to make His sacrifice every year. But when He died on the cross, He made the one perfect sacrifice for the sins of all believers. At His death, the veil in the Temple was split from top to bottom, showing that the way into God's presence was now open to all believers, not just to the high priest once a year. (Leviticus 23:27-44)

Miriam and Aaron spoke against Moses *And the three came out*

MIRIAM IS PUNISHED

Moses' task as leader of the Israelites was not an easy one. Not only did the people murmur against him time and again, but even his own sister, Miriam, and his brother, Aaron, rebelled against him. They both held positions of great honor among the people: Miriam was a prophetess, and Aaron was the high priest. But Miriam was still not satisfied. She was jealous that her younger brother Moses was so important. And she stirred up Aaron to feel the same way. Such jealousy was a sin against the Lord. For they did not appreciate the high positions in which God had placed them. And they forgot that Moses had not even wanted his position, but had been given it by God.

Miriam and Aaron could not point to anything wrong in the way Moses was ruling. So they found fault, instead, with the fact that his wife was not an Israelite. Later, they revealed the real reason for their complaint when they asked, "Has the Lord indeed spoken only by Moses? Has He not spoken also by us?"

Moses was always quick to defend the honor of the Lord. But now he did not even try to speak out in his own defense. The Lord, however, did so for him. He called Moses, Aaron, and Miriam to come at once to the Tabernacle. When they were gathered there, He came down in the pillar of cloud and

Behold, Miriam became leprous *Do not lay the sin upon us*

stood at the door of the tent. Then He began to speak from the cloud. In a stern voice, He told Miriam and Aaron that He spoke to the prophets only in dreams and visions. But Moses was greater than the prophets, for He, the Lord, spoke with him face to face. "Why then," He asked "were you not afraid to speak against my servant Moses?" With that, the Lord departed.

When the cloud was lifted from the Tabernacle, Miriam discovered that her skin had become a dead white. She was covered all over with the dreadful disease known as leprosy! Aaron was horrified to see his sister a leper. He also realized that he, too, could have received the same punishment. "Alas, my lord," he said to Moses, "I beg you, do not lay the sin upon us, in which we have done foolishly, and in which we have sinned. Let her not be like one dead."

Instead of being angry with his brother and sister for rebelling against his leadership, Moses was kind and forgiving. He prayed, "Heal her now, O God, I beseech Thee." And the Lord did restore Miriam so that her skin was normal again. But He commanded her to be shut out of the camp for seven days because of the unclean disease which she had. What a humbling punishment for Miriam! Not satisfied with the honor which God had already given her, she had proudly sought to be equal with Moses. Now, instead of gaining greater honor, she became an outcast for a whole week, not worthy to have a place among the lowliest of the Israelites. (Numbers 12)

You take too much upon you *Korah gathered all the congregation*

KORAH, DATHAN, AND ABIRAM

One day three men strode boldly up to Moses and Aaron. They were followed at a short distance by 250 others — all of them important and respected men. You take too much upon you, snarled the three men. "Why do you lift yourselves up above the congregation of the Lord?"

Korah, the leader of the group, was a Levite. His tribe was the one which God had set apart to take charge of the Tabernacle and its furniture. But they were not allowed to sacrifice animals or offer incense, for God had appointed only Aaron and his sons to these duties. But Korah was jealous of Aaron and thought that he had as much right to the priesthood as Aaron did. The other two men, Dathan and Abiram, were of the tribe of Reuben — Jacob's first-born. They thought, therefore, that as children of the oldest son, they, rather than Moses, should be allowed to rule the people.

Moses was very upset at this rebellion. "Tomorrow," he said, "the Lord will show who are His and who are holy." He commanded them all to appear before the Tabernacle the next day with censers of burning incense. Then he tried to reason with Korah and the other Levites. By desiring to be priests, he said, they were, in fact, rebelling against the Lord. For they were despising the privilege He had given them of caring for the Tabernacle. And they were trying to take over a position which He had given to Aaron. But Korah would not listen.

Dathan and Abiram stood in the door   *They went down alive into the pit*

    The next day, he and the 250 princes, each carrying a censer, assembled in front of the Tabernacle. Crowding around them were great numbers of the people, whom Korah had persuaded to rebel against Moses and Aaron. Then the Lord commanded Moses to warn all the people to get away from the tents of Korah, Dathan, and Abiram. Moses hurried to their tents and exclaimed, "Depart, I beg you, from the tents of these wicked men." The people pushed back in fear and watched. Dathan and Abiram came out of their tents and stood defiantly at the door, with their families around them. Then Moses said, "If these men die the common death of all men, then the Lord has not sent me. But if the earth opens her mouth and swallows them up, then you shall understand that these men have provoked the Lord." No sooner had Moses spoken than the ground under the tents of Korah, Dathan, and Abiram split wide open and all of them — men, women, and children — plunged screaming into the gaping hole. Then the earth closed over them again. The Israelites who were standing near fled in terror. Meanwhile, a fire blazed forth from the pillar of cloud and destroyed the 250 princes who were offering incense.
    By this sudden and terrible judgment, the Lord showed the people that Korah, Dathan, and Abiram were the ones who had taken too much upon themselves, and that Moses and Aaron were the rightful leaders of His people. (Numbers 16)

They carried it between two men   *The cities are great and walled up to heaven*

SPIES INTO CANAAN

When the Israelites finally arrived at the southern border of the Promised Land, the Lord said, "Send men, that they may spy out the land of Canaan." So Moses picked out a ruler from each of the twelve tribes and sent them off to see what kind of land Canaan was and how hard it would be to capture.

Forty days later the twelve spies returned. Two of them were carrying a staff with one huge cluster of grapes hanging from it. The others brought pomegranates and figs. "The land flows with milk and honey," they exclaimed, "and this is the fruit of it. Nevertheless, the people who live in the land are greater and taller than we; the cities are walled and very great; and we have seen giants there." The people broke into an uproar. But Caleb and Joshua, two of the spies, stepped forward and said, "Let us go up at once and possess the land, for we are well able to overcome it." But the other ten men replied, "No, no, we are not able to go up against the people, for they are stronger than we."

How disappointed the Israelites were! That night they cried and cried. "Would that we had died in Egypt or in this wilderness!" they moaned. "Why has the Lord brought us to this land, to fall by the sword?" They were through with Moses and Aaron. They would choose a captain to lead them back to Egypt!

When Moses and Aaron heard of this, they fell on their faces, and Joshua

Only rebel not against the Lord

The Cannanities defeated them

and Caleb tore their clothes in grief. Had these confused people no faith in God's promise that He would give them this land? Had they forgotten how wondrously He had freed them from the mighty Egyptians? Caleb and Joshua spoke to them, saying, "The land is an exceeding good land. If the Lord delights in us, then He will bring us into this land. Only rebel not against the Lord." But the excited people picked up stones to throw at them. Only the sudden appearance of the glory of the Lord in the Tabernacle stopped them.

The Lord then told Moses that since these rebellious people had refused to trust Him, they must now turn back to the wilderness, to wander there for forty years. Except for Caleb and Joshua, He said, every one of the adults — twenty years old and over — would die in the wilderness without ever seeing Canaan. After that, He would give the Promised Land to their children.

When the people heard of their punishment, they wept bitterly. Then, early the next morning they appeared before Moses. They had changed their minds. They were ready to go up and take the land. But Moses said to them, "Do not go up, for the Lord is not among you. The day before, they were afraid to attack with God's help. Now, they felt brave enough to attack without His help, and off they started. But they were not brave. They were foolish and disobedient. And their army was badly beaten by the Canaanites. (Deut. 1:19-46; Numbers 13, 14)

Neither is there any water to drink

Hear now, you rebels

THE DEATH OF MOSES

For forty long and weary years the Israelites wandered about in the hot, barren wilderness. Almost all of those who had not believed that God could bring them into Canaan had died, as God had said they must. Their children were now grown men and women. But like their parents, they often showed little faith in God. For example, when they could find no brook near their camp at Kadesh, they did not ask the Lord for water. Instead, they complained to Moses and Aaron, "Why have you made us to come up out of Egypt, to bring us to this evil place? It is no place of seed, or of figs, or of vines, or of pomegranates; neither is there any water to drink."

Moses brought their complaint to the Lord. God told him to take Aaron's rod and gather the Israelites before a certain rock. Then he should speak to the rock and it would bring forth water. Moses gathered the people before the rock. But this time he had lost all patience with them. In hot anger he cried out, "Hear now, you rebels, must we bring forth water out of this rock?" Then, instead of speaking to it, he struck it twice with his rod. Water did indeed pour forth out of the rock. But God was not pleased with the way Moses had acted. He said to him, "Because you did not believe in Me, to sanctify Me in the eyes of the children of Israel, therefore you shall not bring this congregation into the land which I have given them."

He laid his hands upon him

The Lord showed him all the land

How disappointed Moses was! He pleaded with the Lord to let him cross over the Jordan River and see the land. But God replied, "Speak no more to Me of this matter. You shall not go over the Jordan." Moses did not murmur against God. He believed firmly that God's judgments are always just, and no one ever receives a greater punishment than he deserves.

Even in his disappointment, Moses was concerned about his people. He asked God to choose a man to lead the Israelites into Canaan in his place. So the Lord picked Joshua, one of the two faithful spies. Moses laid his hands upon the younger man and said to him: "Be strong and of good courage, for you must go with this people into the land. And the Lord will go before you. He will be with you. He will not fail you, nor forsake you. Fear not."

Later, as the Israelites neared Canaan, the Lord commanded Moses to climb Mount Nebo, a high peak east of the Jordan River. When Moses reached the top, he looked out over the Promised Land. "This is the land," said the Lord, "which I swore unto Abraham, Isaac, and Jacob. I have caused you to see it with your eyes, but you shall not go over into it." So Moses died there on the mountain. And the Israelites wept for their great leader for thirty days. (Numbers 20-27; Deuteronomy 30-31-32-34)

Take up the ark of the covenant   *The seven priests carrying the seven trumpets*

JERICHO IS TAKEN

The first city which the Israelites came to after they crossed over the Jordan River was Jericho. This was also the best fortified of all the cities of Canaan. The king of Jericho had heard of how the Lord had brought the Israelites out of Egypt. And he was afraid. He commanded all the gates of the city to be shut tight. No one could come in or go out. He posted guards along the city walls and ordered his soldiers to get ready.

While Joshua must have been wondering how the Israelites could take such a walled city, the Lord said to him, "See, I have given Jericho into your hand." He then told Joshua exactly what he must do. The city would be theirs not by their own strength, but by the power of God. They had only to obey His command and wait for His mighty acts.

Joshua called the priests at once. "Take up the ark of the covenant," he commanded. "Let seven priests carry seven trumpets of rams' horns and go before the ark of the Lord." He ordered most of the soldiers to go first with their swords and shields. They were followed by the seven priests with their trumpets. Then came the four priests carrying the ark upon their shoulders. Last of all came the rearguard. Quietly they started marching around the walls of the city. No one said a word. Only the priests blew on their trumpets. The people of Jericho looked down in scorn at this strange sight.

The wall fell down flat

The people went up into the city

After the Israelites had marched all the way around the city once, they returned to their camp for the night. The next morning early they started up again. Silently they walked around Jericho. Only the sound of trumpets and the tramping of feet could be heard. Then back to camp they went again. For six days they did the same thing while the people of Jericho watched and wondered.

On the seventh day the Israelites began at daybreak. Around the walls they marched once, then twice, then again and again until they had encircled the city seven times. Then the priests gave a long blast on their trumpets and Joshua cried out, "Shout, for the Lord has given you the city." The Israelites gave a mighty shout, and the walls of Jericho came crashing down as if knocked over by an unseen hand. From all sides the Israelites rushed into the city over the piles of stone and killed every man, woman, child, and animal. Only the family of Rahab was saved, because she had helped Joshua's spies. God was giving Canaan to His people. But they had to destroy all the heathen of the land so that they would not be tempted by them to turn away from the Lord and worship false gods. The silver, gold, brass, and iron of Jericho, however, had to be brought to the treasury of the Lord. No one was allowed to keep any of it for himself. After that, Joshua commanded his men to set the city on fire. (Joshua 6)

They fled before the men of Ai   *Tell me now what you have done*

ACHAN'S SIN

The victory at Jericho showed clearly that God was with Joshua even as He had been with Moses. The Israelites were encouraged to believe that they could take the next city, Ai, just as easily. First, however, Joshua wisely sent spies there to look the town over. When they returned, they reported that it was but a small city. Only two or three thousand soldiers were needed to capture it. So Joshua sent them off, certain that they would have no trouble. But the Israelites were badly beaten. Thirty-six of them were killed, and the rest fled before the men of Ai.

The people were overcome with fear. Joshua could not understand what had gone wrong. This was their first real battle in Canaan, and they had lost. He and the elders fell down before the ark and prayed all day. Joshua told God that when the rest of the Canaanites heard of their defeat, they would surround them and wipe them out. Surely He had not brought them all the way to Canaan to be destroyed there! Then God replied that they had been defeated because they had sinned against Him. Someone had stolen some of the goods from Jericho which He had said must be brought into the treasury. They were His people, to be sure, but He would not be with them unless they obeyed His commandments. Even though just one man and his family had disobeyed Him in this, Israel would not be able to overthrow their enemies until those wicked

Behold, it was hidden in his tent   *And all Israel stoned him with stones*

ones had been punished.

Early the next morning, Joshua called all the people together. He cast lots upon the tribes, families, and households in order to find out who was the cause of their trouble. At last God showed Joshua that the guilty man was one named Achan.

All the time that the lots were being cast, Achan had remained silent, hoping that he would not be discovered. But he should have known that he could not hide from God. "My son," said Joshua to him, "give glory to the Lord God of Israel, and make confession unto Him, and tell me what you have done." Achan could hide his sin no longer. He confessed that at Jericho he had taken a handsome Babylonian coat, some silver, and some gold and had buried everything in the ground under his tent. Joshua sent messengers to Achan's tent. They dug and found the goods just where Achan had said they were. Then they took them back and laid them out before Joshua and all the people.

At Joshua's command, the people took Achan, with his sons, his daughters, his tent, his sheep, donkeys, oxen, and all that he had to a nearby valley. There they stoned him and his family to death and burned them and all their goods. Thus the Lord taught His people that He would set them on high above all the nations of the earth if they would obey His commands. But if they disobeyed, they would be defeated by their enemies, as at Ai. (Joshua 7)

The number of those who lapped *Gideon heard the telling of the dream*

WITH TORCH AND TRUMPET

Gideon sent out a call to arms. A great horde of Midianites had swept into Canaan from across the Jordan. They had come to steal or destroy the crops and cattle of the Israelites, just as they had often done before. Thirty-two thousand Israelite soldiers answered Gideon's call and gathered around him to fight the Midianites. That sounds like a good-sized army, but their enemy had four times as many soldiers.

Yet the Lord said to Gideon, "The people that are with you are too many for Me to give the Midianites into their hands." If the Israelites defeated the Midianites, said the Lord, they would boast that they had done it in their own strength. He commanded Gideon to send home every soldier who was afraid. That day 22,000 men, frightened by the sight of an enemy as numerous as grasshoppers, started out for home. That left Gideon with only 10,000 men. But God said to him, "There are still too many." He told Gideon to take them down to the edge of the water and let them drink. Three hundred of the men scooped the water up in their hand and drank. All the rest got down on their knees. Then God told Gideon that he would save Israel with the three hundred who lapped the water out of their hand. The rest he must send home. Three hundred against 135,000! Only a miracle of God could give Gideon the victory.

The sword of the Lord, and of Gideon   *Every man's sword against his fellow*

    Although Gideon did not speak a word of complaint, the Lord knew what he was thinking. He told him to go down to the enemy's camp that night with his servant. When he heard what the Midianites were saying, he would have greater courage to fight against them. Gideon did so and overheard a man telling a fellow soldier about a dream he had had. "A cake of barley bread," he said, "tumbled into the army of Midian and knocked over the tent." His friend replied, "This is nothing else but the sword of Gideon, for into his hand God has delivered Midian."

    Gideon and his servant hurried back to their soldiers. If the Midianites themselves believed that Gideon would win, how could he doubt it? He quickly gave his orders. They were to divide up into three companies. Each man was to carry a torch hidden under a pitcher, and a trumpet. Quietly, in the still, black night, they spread out around the camp of the enemy. At a given signal, every man broke his pitcher on the rocks, held his torch high, and blew loudly on his trumpet. Then they all shouted, "The sword of the Lord, and of Gideon!" The Midianites awoke. They saw their camp surrounded by blazing torches and blaring trumpets. There must be millions of Israelites, they thought. In their terror and confusion, they began fighting and killing each other. Many others were trampled to death as they fled in panic. Gideon called back the other Israelites whom he had sent home, and together they chased after the Midianites until they had destroyed them all. (Judges 6:33-7:25)

And see where his great strength lies   *To shave off the seven locks of his hair*

SAMSON AND DELILAH

As long as the Israelites served the Lord, He blessed them. But as often as they turned away from Him to worship false gods, He gave them over to their enemies. Once, when they cried out to Him because the Philistines were oppressing them, He raised up a man named Samson to save them. God promised to be with him as long as he did not cut his hair. When Samson obeyed, God made him so strong that he could kill 1,000 Philistines at one time.

The Philistine rulers soon learned that they could not take Samson by force. So they planned to do it by trickery. Each of them promised Delilah, the Philistine woman whom Samson loved, eleven hundred pieces of silver if she would find out the secret of his great strength. She agreed to try. When he came to visit her, she teased him to tell her what made him so strong. Samson said that if he should be tied with seven green twigs, he would be as weak as other men. The next time he came, she tied him with seven green twigs while he was asleep. Some Philistines were hiding nearby ready to seize him. But when she woke him, saying, "The Philistines are upon you, Samson," he sprang up, snapping the twigs as if they were threads, and escaped.

Two more times she pleaded with him to tell her his secret, and two more times he lied to her and thus escaped being captured. But Samson sinned in

The Philistines took him *He bowed himself with all his might*

playing such a dangerous game with the strength God had given him to save Israel. When he saw what Delilah was trying to do, he should have kept away from her. But he did not. Time after time she coaxed him until finally he gave in and said, "If my head is shaven, then my strength will go from me."

Now she knew that he had told the truth. She called for the Philistines to come once more. Then as Samson slept with his head on her lap, a man stole into the room and shaved off all his hair. There was no real strength in his hair, but when he disobeyed God's command, the Lord left him. This time when Delilah woke him, he thought that he could escape as before, but now his strength was gone. The Philistines caught him and put him in prison. There they put out his eyes and made him grind grain like a donkey.

The Philistines were so overjoyed at having captured the mighty Samson that they gave a great feast to thank their fish-god, Dagon. They brought out blind Samson to make fun of him and set him between the two pillars which held up the roof. Samson had come to realize his great sin. He prayed, "O Lord God, strengthen me only this once and let me die with the Philistines." God answered his prayer. Grasping the two pillars, Samson bowed forward with all his God-given strength. The pillars cracked and gave way. The roof crashed down, killing Samson, but also thousands of Philistines. (Judges 16)

Orpah kissed her mother-in-law

Do not beg me to leave you

RUTH

Elimelech was hungry. His wife, Naomi, and their two sons were hungry, too, for there was a famine in the land. At last they decided to leave their home in Bethlehem and go live in the heathen land of Moab until the famine was over.

But all did not go well in their new home. Elimelech soon died, leaving Naomi with their two sons. Then, shortly after these sons each married a young woman of Moab, they died, too. Poor Naomi was now left in a strange land with only her two daughters-in-law. She longed for her home in Bethlehem, and as soon as she heard that the famine there was over, she decided to go back.

The two young Moabite women started out with their mother-in-law, but she urged them to leave her and go back. At last one of them, named Orpah, agreed to return. She kissed Naomi tenderly and started back home. The old woman turned to Ruth, her other daughter-in-law, and said, "Behold, your sister-in-law has gone back to her people, and to her gods. You go back, too." But Ruth would not be persuaded. She loved Naomi too much to let her go back alone. More than that, she had come to trust the Lord God of Israel and wanted to be with His people. In great faith she replied to Naomi: "Do not beg me to

She came and gleaned in the field

A full reward be given you

leave you, or to return from following after you. For where you go, I will go;" Naomi saw that she could not change Ruth's mind. So the two women went on to Bethlehem.

    They arrived there at the beginning of barley harvest. As the reapers cut the grain and tied it into bundles, there were always some stalks which they missed or dropped. According to Moses' law, they had to leave these stalks for the poor. So Ruth went to the barley fields to glean, or pick up these stalks that were left. By God's providence she began in the field of a rich man named Boaz. Boaz was very good to Ruth because of all she had done for Naomi. He had heard how she had left her parents and homeland to come live with her mother-in-law in a strange land. He said to her kindly, "A full reward be given you by the Lord God of Israel, under whose wings you have come to trust."

    The Lord did give her a full reward. For Boaz soon saw that her virtue and kindness were more than an outward show. He fell in love with her and married her. Boaz and Ruth were very happy together and soon they had a son, named Obed, who became the grandfather of King David. Thus it was from the family of the Moabite woman Ruth that Jesus Christ, "the son of David," was born.
(Ruth 1-4)

It is no good report that I hear *The Lord called Samuel*

SAMUEL, THE PROPHET OF GOD

Eli was both high priest and ruler of Israel. He was a godly man and had served the Lord well. But now that he was old and almost blind, he had turned most of his duties over to his sons, Hophni and Phinehas. These sons, however, were very, very wicked. When the people complained to Eli about them, the old priest scolded them, saying "My sons, it is no good report that I hear." But because he had never been strict enough with them when they were young, they did not obey him now. They kept right on in their wicked ways and even caused the people to sin in their worship of the Lord.

Besides Eli's sons, there was also a boy named Samuel who helped Eli in the Tabernacle. He had been there ever since he was three years old. In spite of all the wicked things that were going on around him, Samuel had grown up "in favor both with the Lord, and also with men."

One night, as he and Eli were sleeping in their rooms near the Tabernacle, Samuel was awakened by a voice calling him. Thinking that it was Eli, he ran to him and said, "Here I am." But the old priest replied, "I did not call. Lie down again." Somewhat puzzled, Samuel went back to bed. Soon he heard the voice again, calling, "Samuel." A second time he hurried to Eli's bed. But again Eli said, "I did not call, my son. Lie down again." The lad was even more puzzled. He was

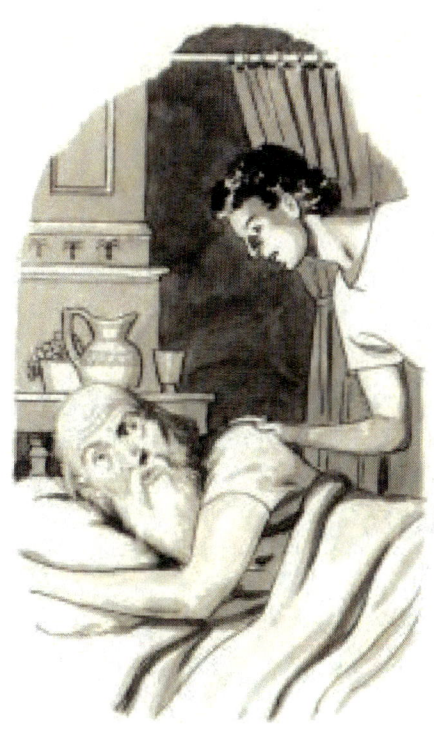
Here I am

It is the Lord

sure he had heard a voice. After Samuel had gone back to bed, the same thing happened a third time. Now Eli realized that God Himself was calling Samuel. He had not thought of this at first because it had been a long, long time since the Lord had spoken to His people. "Go lie down," he said to his young helper. "If He calls you again, say, 'Speak, Lord, for Thy servant is listening.'"

Samuel went back to bed and waited. Then the Lord appeared to him in a vision and said, "Samuel, Samuel." This time he replied, "Speak, for Thy servant is listening." God then told Samuel that He was going to punish Eli's sons and sons' sons because of their great wickedness. He would take the priesthood away from them, and all of them would die before they reached old age. What dreadful news! Samuel did not dare to go back and tell Eli what God had said. He lay there quietly in bed until it was light. Then he got up and opened the doors of God's house, as he did every morning. Eli called him, though, and made him tell everything God had said to him. When Samuel had finished, Eli replied, "It is the Lord: Let Him do what seems good."

This was the first time that Samuel spoke as a prophet, that is, that he spoke to others for God. From then on God often talked to Samuel, and he became known in all Israel as the prophet of the Lord. (I Samuel 2:12-4:1)

They ran and brought him *How shall this man save us?*

SAUL BECOMES KING

The Israelites crowded around Samuel to see him choose their first king. As he began casting lots, they watched breathlessly. First, the tribe of Benjamin was chosen, then the family of the Matrites, and finally Saul, the son of Kish. But where was he? No one could find him anywhere.

God had already told Saul that he would be the first king of Israel. Because he was shy and somewhat fearful of the difficult task before him, he had hidden himself among the baggage while the lots were being cast. But the Lord told Samuel where he was, and Samuel sent some men to bring him back. When the people saw this fine-looking man who stood head and shoulders above the crowd, they shouted joyously, "Long live the king!" Some, however, only made fun of him, saying, "How shall this man save us?" Samuel then sent the people back home. Saul, too, returned to his farm, for it was not yet time for him to begin to rule.

Some time after this, the Ammonites attacked the city of Jabesh-Gilead. The people of the city knew they could never win against such a strong enemy. So they offered to surrender. The Ammonites agreed, but only if they could put out the right eye of every man of Jabesh-Gilead. Not only would that be a terrible disgrace, but the men would never again be able to use a bow and arrow in battle. They asked the enemy for seven days to see if they could get help from the rest

His anger was kindled greatly   *They made Saul king*

of Israel. If not, they would surrender, and the Ammonites could put out their right eyes. The Ammonite king was so sure of his own strength that he foolishly agreed.

At once, messengers hurried from Jabesh to Saul's town. Saul was just returning from the fields with his oxen when he heard the dreadful news. At that moment the Holy Spirit came upon him, and he was filled with anger at the Ammonites' cruel demand. He cut up two oxen and sent the pieces throughout Israel with the words, "Whoever does not come forth after Saul and after Samuel, so shall it be done to his oxen." So 330,000 soldiers flocked to Saul. With this army, he knew he could defeat the Ammonites. He sent the messengers back to Jabesh-gilead, saying, "Tomorrow, by the time the sun is hot, you will be rescued." That very night Saul started marching to Jabesh with his army. He arrived there early in the morning, before the sun was up, and made a surprise attack upon the Ammonites, who were camped around the city. The Israelites fought hard. By noon the enemy was completely defeated, and Jabesh-gilead was saved!

After such a great victory, Saul became a hero. Now all the people were ready to recognize him as king. The prophet Samuel had ruled the people faithfully for many years. He would still pray for them and show them God's will. But he now turned the leadership over to Saul, the first king of Israel.
(I Samuel 10:17-12:25)

Come and let us go over   *Come up to us*

JONATHAN'S BRAVERY

One time, when the Philistines invaded the land of Israel with a large army, most of King Saul's soldiers became so afraid that they left him. Some hid in caves, while others fled across the Jordan River. Only 600 men of Saul's once powerful army remained. And because the Philistines had not allowed the Israelites to make any swords or spears, these men had only farming tools, clubs, and bows and arrows to fight with. Only King Saul and his son, Prince Jonathan, had swords. What hope of victory was there for such a small, frightened, and unarmed band of men?

But Jonathan did not despair. They were few and unarmed, but the Lord was on their side. So one day he said to his armor-bearer in great faith, "Come, and let us go over to the Philistines' garrison. It may be that the Lord will work for us. For He can save either by many or by few." Without telling his father, King Saul, where he was going, Jonathan slipped out of the Israelite camp, followed closely by his faithful armor-bearer. No one saw them go.

As they crept closer and closer to a Philistine outpost on a rocky cliff, Jonathan whispered to his servant, "We will show ourselves to these men. If they say to us, 'Wait until we come to you,' we will not go up to them. But if they say, 'Come up to us,' then we will go up, for the Lord has delivered them into our hand." Jonathan and his servant suddenly stepped into plain view of

They fell before Jonathan   *Number now, and see who is gone*

the Philistine guards. Surprised to see two Israelites so close, they shouted down, "Come up to us." That was the sign Jonathan was waiting for. At once, he and his armor-bearer fearlessly scrambled up the steep slope on their hands and knees. The Philistines began to fall down dead before Jonathan. The ones that Jonathan left, his armor-bearer killed. In no time, twenty Philistines had fallen.

Such an unexpected blow threw the Philistines into a panic. True, only two men had attacked. But they did not know how many more Israelites might be right behind them. At that moment, God added to their terror by causing the earth to rumble and shake.

Meanwhile, from their lookout, Saul's watchmen noticed great confusion among the Philistines. When they reported it to the king, Saul wondered if some of his own men were fighting them. He ordered his soldiers to be counted to see if any were missing and found to his surprise that his own son Jonathan and his armor-bearer were gone! Quickly gathering his little band together, Saul rushed over and attacked the Philistines, who were already fighting among themselves in their confusion. When the Israelites who had been serving in the Philistine army saw Saul and his men arrive, they too, began fighting the Philistines. And those who had been fearfully hiding in caves hurried out to join the battle. All together, the Israelites chased after the frightened enemy and defeated them. (I Samuel 18:15-14:23)

He took Agag . . . alive

I have done the commandment

SAUL DISOBEYS GOD

"Go and strike Amalek," Samuel told King Saul, "and utterly destroy all that they have." The Amalekites had long been enemies of God's people. They had attacked them in the wilderness as they were coming up out of Egypt (Exod. 17) and had waged war on them many times since then. Now the Lord wanted Saul to punish them by completely destroying them all, and all their sheep and cattle as well.

At once, Saul gathered together an army and marched south to where the Amalekites lived. Saul and his men attacked, and soon they had killed every man, woman, and child, except Agag, the king. They also killed many of the sheep and cattle, but saved some of the best of them. God, however, had commanded them to destroy every single thing.

That night God spoke to Samuel. He told the old prophet that He was going to take the kingdom away from Saul because he had disobeyed His command to destroy the Amalekites completely. Samuel was angry and also very disappointed to hear that Israel's first king had turned away from the Lord so soon. He prayed all night to ask the Lord's mercy on Saul. But it was of no use. Early the next morning he set out to find Saul and give him God's message.

When Saul saw God's prophet coming toward him, he went up to him and said shamelessly, "I have performed the commandment of the Lord." Samuel

To obey is better than sacrifice   *And it tore*

replied sharply, "What then is the meaning of the bleating of sheep and the lowing of oxen which I hear?" Saul foolishly tried to push the blame onto his soldiers, saying, "The people spared the best of the sheep and of the oxen to sacrifice to the Lord your God."

That was a poor excuse for Saul to give. He himself had set a bad example for the soldiers by taking King Agag alive. Further-more, as king, he was to blame for not stopping his men from disobeying God. Most important, however, he should have known that sparing the animals, even for something as holy as sacrifices, was still a sin, since God had commanded them to destroy everything. So Samuel rebuked Saul sternly, saying: "Does the Lord have as great delight in burnt-offerings as in obeying His voice? Behold, to obey is better than sacrifice. Because you have rejected the word of the Lord, He has also rejected you from being king."

"Saul said that he was sorry he had sinned. But it seems that he was more worried about what the people thought of him than what God thought. For he asked the prophet to go worship the Lord with him so that it would not appear as though Samuel was displeased with him. Samuel refused. As he turned to walk away, Saul grabbed his robe to hold him back, and the robe tore. "As you have torn my robe," said Samuel, "so the Lord has torn the kingdom of Israel from you this day, and has given it to a neighbor of yours, who is better than you." (I Samuel 15)

Choose a man for yourselves   *Who is this uncircumcised Philistine?*

DAVID AND GOLIATH

The Israelite soldiers watched fearfully from the top of the hill as Goliath again strode down from the Philistine camp into the valley between the two armies. Then he looked up at them and bellowed, "Choose a man for yourselves, and let him come down to me. If he is able to kill me, then we will be your servants. But if I kill him, then you will be our servants. I defy the armies of Israel this day." Every morning and every evening he challenged the Israelites this way. But no one dared to fight against him, not even King Saul or his general. For Goliath was a giant, dressed in brass armor from head to foot and carrying a huge sword and a spear as big as a weaver's beam.

One day a young shepherd named David came to the Israelite camp to see his three oldest brothers. While he was talking with them, Goliath again appeared and began roaring his usual insults up to the Israelites. And as usual, the Israelites trembled and fled. But David cried out, "Who is this uncircumcised Philistine, that he should defy the armies of the living God?" He was filled with a holy anger at this heathen and offered to fight the giant himself. When King Saul heard about David, he sent for him. David said bravely, "Your servant will go and fight with this Philistine." At first, Saul only shook his head. David was only a youth and never had fought in a war. But David told the

Saul armed David with his armor

He took a stone and slung it

king how he had killed a lion and a bear while tending sheep. Then he said, "The Lord that delivered me out of the paw of the lion, and out of the paw of the bear will deliver me out of the hand of this Philistine." At last, the king agreed. But he insisted that David wear his armor to protect him. David tried it on. But he could hardly move about with it on and took it right off again. He chose, instead, his shepherd's staff and his sling. Then, picking out five smooth stones from the river bed, he went forward to meet Goliath.

When the mighty giant saw this unarmed youth coming out to fight him, he was furious. He cursed David and threatened to feed his body to the beasts and birds. David, however, was not afraid. He shouted back, "You come to me with a sword and spear and shield. But I come to you in the name of the God of the armies of Israel, whom you have defied!" Then David took one of the stones from his shepherd's bag and put it in his sling. He whirled it around his head several times and let it fly straight at Goliath. The Lord caused the stone to go deep into the forehead of the giant. Goliath toppled forward and crashed to the ground. David ran up to him, drew the giant's own sword, and cut off his head. With a shout of joy, the Israelites rushed down the hill and chased after the terrified, fleeing Philistines. (I Samuel 17)

David played with his hand   *And Saul threw his spear*

SAUL'S HATRED OF DAVID

King Saul had many spells of madness after the prophet Samuel told him that God had rejected him. For the Holy Spirit had left Saul, and an evil spirit often came to trouble him. However, whenever David played soothing music for him on his harp, Saul was comforted and felt better again for a while.

At first Saul had liked this young shepherd. After David had killed Goliath, Saul had taken him into his court and had put him in charge of many soldiers. Though young, David had proved himself a very wise and brave leader. But one day, when he and Saul were coming back from battle, women welcomed them, singing, "Saul has killed his thousands, and David his ten thousands." Saul became very jealous when he heard them giving more praise to David than to himself. What now, he thought, would keep David from taking his throne away from him?

This time, as Saul watched David's fingers plucking at the harp-strings, he was not comforted by the music. Instead, hateful thoughts crowded into his mind. Suddenly he seized his spear and threw it at David, who leaped out of the way just in time. The spear whizzed past him and stuck into the wall.

After that, Saul tried every way he could think of to get rid of David. He put him in charge of a thousand soldiers and often sent him out against the Philistines, hoping that he would be killed in battle.

Michal let David down through a window   *There was an image in the bed*

But David always returned safely, and was even a greater hero. Saul demanded that David give proof of having killed a hundred Philistines in order to marry his daughter Michal. David killed two hundred, instead. It turned out that the more Saul tried to harm David, the more David came to be loved by the people. When Saul realized that the Lord had left him and was now with David, he hated David even more bitterly.

One day, as David was playing his harp to comfort the king, Saul again threw his spear at him. As before, David narrowly escaped being killed by jumping out of the way. That very night, Saul sent some soldiers to guard David's house and to kill him in the morning. Since the house was on the city wall, David's wife, Michal, was able to let her husband down through the window, and he escaped.

To give him more time to get away, she then played a trick on her father. She put an image in David's bed and covered it up well. The next morning, when Saul's soldiers came in to get him, she told them that he was sick, perhaps even showing them the form in his bed. When they reported this to Saul, the king angrily commanded them to bring bed and all so that he could kill him. But by the time they returned and discovered that there was only an image in the bed, David was far, far away. When Saul learned that he had been tricked, he hated David even more. (I Samuel 18-19)

The men of David said to him

My lord the king

DAVID SPARES SAUL'S LIFE

David escaped from King Saul's Court and fled to the wild, lonely stretches of Israel. There he hid in caves like an outlaw, with his band of six hundred faithful followers. For, although David had always served the king faithfully, Saul hated him so much that he was determined to kill him.

Once, Saul and three thousand of his bravest soldiers chased after David to a rocky place where only wild goats could live. Saul left his soldiers for a while and went alone into one of the many caves that honeycombed the hills. It happened to be the very cave in which David and his band were hiding! But the cave was large and dark, and David and his men were way in the back. So Saul did not realize how close he was to the man he was hunting.

David's men were overjoyed. They whispered to him that God had given Saul into his hands. It would be an easy thing now to kill him. David quietly crept closer and closer to the king. But all he did was cut off a piece of his robe. Even then, he was sorry he had done that much. For Saul was still his king, set over him by God. And any sin against the Lord's anointed was a sin against the Lord Himself. After all the times that Saul had tried to murder him, David still would not hurt him, nor would he let his men lay their hands on him.

See the skirt of your robe

You are more righteous than I

Shortly after Saul left the cave, David went out and called after him, "My lord the king!" Saul wheeled around and saw David standing near the cave where he had just been! David humbly bowed low and said, "Why do you hear man's words, saying, David wants to harm you? Behold, this day the Lord delivered you into my hand in the cave. But I would not put forth my hand against you, for you are the Lord's anointed." Then, holding up the piece of Saul's robe, he went on, "Moreover, my father, see this piece of your robe in my hand. I cut off the skirt of your robe, but did not kill you. Yet you hunt after my life to take it. The Lord judge between you and me. But my hand shall not be upon you.

Saul was so deeply moved by David's words that he wept. For the moment, he was ashamed of the way he had been treating his faithful servant. "You are more righteous than I," he confessed, "for you have returned good for the evil which I have done to you. The Lord reward you for what you have done this day." Then he continued, "I know well that you will surely be king. Swear now, therefore, that you will not destroy my sons after me." When David promised that he would not, Saul returned home. But David stayed in the wilderness, for he feared that Saul would again seek to kill him. (I Samuel 24)

Absalom prepared himself a chariot, horses   *He took him and kissed him*

DAVID IS BETRAYED

Absalom, King David's son, was a handsome young man. In fact, there was no one in all Israel as handsome as he. Whenever he rode by in his gorgeous chariot with fifty servants running before him the people no doubt thought him to be a splendid prince.

But even though he was so splendid looking, he was not a bit proud at least, so the people thought. Why, every day he stood at the palace gate watching the king's judges settling arguments. Usually there were not enough of them to judge all the cases. So Absalom comforted these disappointed people and told them that if he were only king, there would be justice for all. And when anyone tried to bow down to him, Absalom kissed him, instead, as if he were his equal.

All of this was part of Absalom's clever, but sinful plan to become king in place of his father, David. By putting on such a show of splendor and friendliness, and by making the people think that they would be treated more justly if he were king, Absalom succeeded in stealing the hearts of many Israelites. As soon as he had won the favor of enough people, he went to Hebron and unlawfully had himself declared king over Israel, even though David was still the rightful king.

A messenger sped from Hebron to Jerusalem to tell King David the news. The king was broken-hearted to learn that his own son had betrayed him!

Carry back the ark of God

Defeat the advice of Ahithophel

But now there was no time to lose. Absalom would soon be marching on Jerusalem and would kill them all. The king decided to flee at once with his wives and children, and those soldiers and servants who were still faithful to him. It was a sorrowful company that hurried out of the city gates. David was in the lead, walking barefoot. He and all of his followers were also weeping and had their heads covered to show their grief.

A short distance outside of Jerusalem, David stopped and let the whole company pass on before him. In the crowd, he saw the Levites and two priests with the ark of God. "Carry the ark back to the city," he commanded them. David felt that if God no longer wanted him to be king, then he had no right to take the ark with him. But if God should give his throne back to him, he would see the ark again in the Tabernacle at Jerusalem, where it belonged.

Then a messenger caught up with David and told him that one of his wisest advisers, Ahithophel, had gone over to Absalom's side. That was a dreadful blow to David, for now Absalom was even more to be feared with wise Ahithophel to advise him. David prayed, Lord, turn the advice of Ahithophel into foolishness." A few moments later, David met his faithful old adviser Hushai, who wanted to flee with him. But David sent him back to Jerusalem to join himself to Absalom's staff of advisers. For David trusted the Lord would use Hushai to defeat the advice of wise old Ahithophel. (II Samuel 15)

Why did you not go with David?   *I will pursue after David*

THE ADVICE OF HUSHAI

    David's faithful adviser Hushai had hardly gotten back to Jerusalem when Absalom, the king's wicked son, rode triumphantly into the city. No one lifted a sword to stop him.

    Hushai hurried to the palace to greet Absalom. "Long live the king!" he said. Absalom was surprised. "Why did you not go with your friend David?" he asked him. Hushai replied, "No, but whom the Lord and this people choose, his will I be. As I have served in your father's presence, so will I be in your presence." Absalom felt very pleased and proud, thinking that another of his father's servants had come over to his side. For the young prince did not dream that David had sent Hushai to defeat the advice of Ahithophel.

    So far, everything seemed to be going well for Absalom. But wise Ahithophel knew that as long as David was alive, Absalom was not safe on the throne. Absalom had a large army, but it was not well trained. David's followers, on the other hand, were mighty men of war. And if given time, David could probably get a larger army together. Absalom must act swiftly. "Let me now choose out 12,000 men," Ahithophel said to him, "and I will pursue after David this night and attack him while he is weary. The people with him will flee in fear, and I will kill the king only."

    Absalom and his servants thought that this was a good idea. But the prince then sent for Hushai. After all, a wise ruler must listen to different

We will draw it into the river

The advice of Hushai is better

advisers! When Hushai heard Ahithophel's suggestion, he knew that it would mean sure defeat for David. So he persuaded Absalom to do differently, saying, "The advice that Ahithophel has given is not good at this time." He explained that David and his men were all fearless fighters and were now as angry as a bear robbed of her cubs. If any of Absalom's men were killed, word of the bloodshed would spread, and even the bravest of Absalom's followers would become afraid. Therefore, he advised Absalom to wait until he could gather together an army as numerous as the sand on the seashore. Then Absalom himself should go forth at the head of his troops. If David was camping in the open country, they would fall upon him like the dew, and destroy every last man. If, however, he had fled to a walled city, Absalom's huge army could put ropes around the walls and drag the whole city into the river.

The proud young prince, puffed up at the thought of leading a tremendous army to victory, replied, "The advice of Hushai is better than the advice of Ahithophel." When Ahithophel heard that his suggestion was turned down, he went home and hanged himself. Absalom, meanwhile, gathered together his army and went forth against David. But Absalom was killed and his forces defeated. Thus, through the advice of Hushai, the Lord overthrew the rebellious prince and brought David, His own chosen one, back to Jerusalem as rightful king. (II Samuel 16:15-19; 17:1-14)

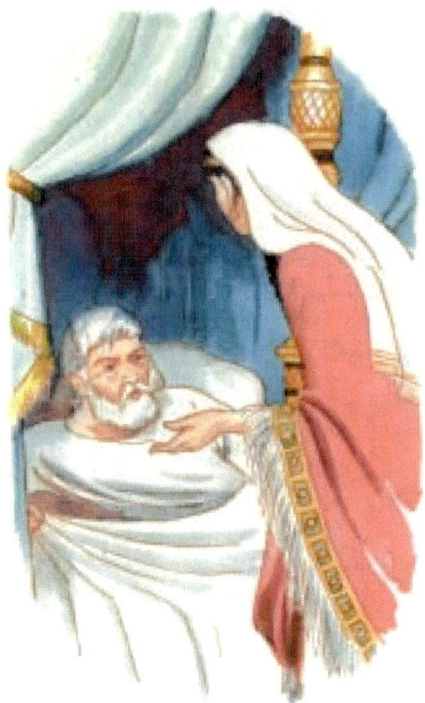

Go in unto King David　　　　*Behold, Adonijah is reigning*

ADONIJAH TRIES TO BECOME KING

King David had ruled over Israel for almost forty years. During that time he had built up a great and strong kingdom. But now he was old, and so weak that he could not even leave his bed. Everyone wondered, "Which of David's sons will be king after him?"

Adonijah, the oldest of the king's living sons, would normally be the next king over Israel. But David chose his younger son Solomon to be king after him because the Lord Himself had commanded it. However, Adonijah said, "I will be king." With the help of a general and a priest, he made plans to begin ruling even before his aged father died. He invited most of his brothers and many of David's servants to a great feast in order to have himself declared king. But he did not invite his brother Solomon, for he did not want him to know that he was trying to take the throne away from him.

A godly prophet called Nathan heard of what was going on. He hurried to Bathsheba, David's wife and the mother of Solomon, and told her that Adonijah was trying to become king without David's knowing anything about it. He urged her to go and remind David that he had promised the throne to Solomon.

Bathsheba went at once to the king's bedroom and bowed before him. "My lord," she began, "you swore by the Lord your God that Solomon, my son, would reign after you. And now, behold, Adonijah reigns." Before she had finished

The people came up after him *Caught hold on the altar*

talking with her husband, Nathan arrived. After bowing low before David, the prophet asked, "My lord, O King, have you said that Adonijah shall reign after you? For he has called all the king's sons and the captains of the army, and Abiathar the priest. And, behold, they are eating and drinking before him and saying, 'Long live King Adonijah!'"

Old King David was alarmed. His former strength of mind returned to him, and he took quick action. First, he assured Bathsheba that he would keep his promise to her. Next, he ordered his trusted servants to put young Solomon upon his own royal mule and take him outside the city. "Anoint him there king over Israel," commanded David. "And blow the trumpet, and say, 'Long live King Solomon!' Then he shall come and sit upon my throne; for he shall be king in my place."

David's servants obeyed. As they returned triumphantly into the city, crowds of happy people followed, playing on pipes and shouting, "Long live King Solomon!" Adonijah and his guests were just finishing eating when they heard the trumpets and shouting. What could it all mean? At that moment a messenger arrived and reported that David had already made Solomon king. Even now Solomon was sitting on the throne, he added. Adonijah's guests became frightened and quickly scattered. The prince himself fled to the Tabernacle and caught hold of the horns of the altar. He felt safe there and would not leave until Solomon promised that he would not kill him for trying to become king. (I Kings 1)

Convey them by sea in floats

Stonecutters in the mountains

THE TEMPLE

The sound of axes rang through the forest on the slopes of Mt. Lebanon in Syria. Mighty cedar and fir trees toppled and crashed to the ground. Workmen then dragged these huge, fallen timbers down to the Mediterranean Sea, where they tied them together to make large rafts. They floated these rafts along the coast to the port of Joppa. From this seaport, other workers brought the timbers to Jerusalem.

For there, at Jerusalem, King Solomon was building a Temple for the Lord. For 480 years the Israelites had worshipped God in the tent-church known as the Tabernacle. But now that they were settled in the land of Canaan and had peace from their enemies, it was time to build a permanent house of worship. Solomon had made an agreement with Hiram, king of Tyre, to supply all the wood which was needed. For no finer trees could be found than those which grew on Mt. Lebanon. And no workers were more skilled in cutting timber than King Hiram's. In return, Solomon gave Hiram tremendous amounts of wheat, barley, oil, and wine each year.

While the cedars and firs were being chopped down in Lebanon, 80,000 Canaanites were working in the mountains around Jerusalem, cutting huge stones for the Temple. Another 70,000 of them hauled these heavy building materials to Jerusalem. But before they did so, every stone and timber was cut to exactly the right size and shape. As a result, not a hammer or axe or chisel could be heard

Neither hammer, nor axe, nor tool   *Their wings touched one another*

where the Temple was going up. The work was done as quietly as possible.

The Temple was built on the same general plan as the Tabernacle. There was the court, the altar of burnt-offerings, the laver, the Holy Place, the Holy of Holies, and so forth. But since this building did not have to be carried around, it was built of wood and stone rather than of wood and curtains.

First, there was a great court where the people gathered. A little higher was the court where the priests offered the sacrifices on a huge brass altar. The laver in which they washed themselves was a great brass basin, resting upon twelve brass oxen. There were also ten smaller basins, five on each side of the court. Directly in front of the Temple stood two tall brass pillars, richly decorated.

Inside the Temple, everything — the floors, walls, ceiling, and all the furniture was made of fine, carved wood, covered over with gold. The altar of incense stood before the veil, just as in the Tabernacle. But instead of only one golden lamp stand and one golden table of show — bread, there were ten of each, five on one side of the Holy Place and five on the other. In the Holy of Holies stood two golden cherubims, fifteen feet high, one on either side of the ark. They were facing forward, and their outspread wings, which met over the ark, also touched the side walls.

It took Solomon seven years to complete the building of this splendid Temple. (I Kings 5-7; II Chronicles 2-4)

She came with a very great train   *A great throne of ivory*

THE QUEEN OF SHEBA'S VISIT

One day a long train of swaying camels filed into Jerusalem, laden down with heavy packs. The Queen of Sheba had arrived to visit King Solomon. She had heard reports that the Lord had given Solomon such great wisdom that he was wiser than all other men. She had also heard that the Lord had given him such great wealth that he was richer than all other kings of the earth. She could not believe that any man could be as wise and as rich as people said he was. She wanted to see for herself. So she had traveled from her kingdom in Arabia northward along the hot, dusty way to Jerusalem.

The Queen was led into the great hall where the king received his visitors. There she saw Solomon, dressed in costly robes and sitting on his gorgeous throne. On each of the six broad steps leading up to the throne she saw two carved lions, one on the right side, and one on the left. The throne itself was made of ivory, covered over with the finest gold. Two more carved lions stood beside the throne, one on each side.

The Queen bowed before Solomon. Then she began asking him hard questions to see how wise he really was. But no matter how difficult the question was, Solomon was always able to answer it. There was not one question which she asked that he could not answer. No wonder, thought the Queen, that kings and important persons came from all the countries round about to hear his wise sayings!

The half was not told me *The Queen of Sheba gave King Solomon*

Then Solomon showed his royal visitor around his splendid palace. She marveled to see the expensive cedar wood which was as common as sycamore. Gold was everywhere. On the walls of the palace hung two hundred large gold shields and three hundred smaller ones. All the cups and plates were made only of gold, for silver was as common in Jerusalem as stones. She also saw strutting peacocks and chattering monkeys, which had been brought from faraway lands. The Queen was amazed, too, at the number of nobles and important officers in Solomon's court. Why, there were so many that every day thirty oxen, one hundred sheep, and great quantities of deer, poultry, fine flour, and meal were needed to feed them.

Overcome by the splendor of Solomon's court and by his great wisdom, the Queen said at last, "It was a true report that I heard in my own land of your acts and your wisdom. However, I did not believe the words until I came and my eyes had seen it. And behold, the half was not told me. Happy are the men," she went on, "who stand continually before you and who hear your wisdom. Blessed be the Lord your God who delighted in you, to set you on the throne of Israel."

Then the Queen unpacked her saddle bags and gave Solomon precious stones, spices in abundance, and much gold. Solomon, in turn, gave the Queen many costly presents before she and her servants returned to Sheba. (I Kings 10:4; II Chronicles 9)

Make his heavy yoke lighter   *I will add to your yoke*

THE KINGDOM IS SPLIT

Solomon ruled Israel for forty years. After he died, his son Rehoboam became king in his place. But the tribes of Israel did not go to the capital city of Jerusalem to honor the new king, but rather to the city of Shechem.

As soon as King Rehoboam and his advisers arrived, the people crowded around him. They complained that his father, Solomon, had put too heavy a yoke upon them. For forty years they had been paying extremely high taxes to supply the needs of the king's magnificent court. And they had been working very hard building the Temple, palaces, and strongholds. They did not want to keep on bearing such heavy burdens for Solomon's son. "Make his heavy yoke which he put upon us lighter," they said, "and we will serve you." Rehoboam told them to come back again in three days and he would give them his answer.

The young king first asked the wise, old men who had been his father's advisers what they thought he should do. They replied that if he should lighten their load, these tribes would serve him forever. Rehoboam then asked the advice of the younger men with whom he had grown up. His thoughtless, young friends answered that instead of making the people's burdens lighter, he should show his power by making them even heavier. The proud king liked this advice better than the older men's. So when the people returned on the third day for their answer, Rehoboam said to them roughly: "My father made your

Rehoboam got up into his chariot *You shall not fight your brothers*

yoke heavy, but I will add to your yoke. My father punished you with whips, but I will punish you with scorpions" (that is, whips with metal hooks on the ends).

When the people heard this harsh answer, they became angry. They were not going to serve such a cruel king, they decided, and off they started for home. Rehoboam did not seem to realize how serious the revolt was. He still thought he ruled over all twelve tribes until he sent his chief tax-collector after the scattering crowd. The people were so furious that they stoned the officer to death. Then Rehoboam the king hurried quickly into his chariot and fled to Jerusalem.

Once there, Rehoboam gathered together an army to fight against the northern tribes and force them to recognize him as king. But a prophet of God warned him, saying, "You shall not fight against your brothers, for this is the Lord's doing." Because Solomon had turned away from God for a time, toward the end of his life, the Lord Himself had told him that He was going to take these ten tribes away from his son. Although Rehoboam had not shown himself a wise leader, he now obeyed God's command and sent his troops home again.

Meanwhile, the ten northern tribes chose their own king a man called Jeroboam. From that day, the land was divided into two kingdoms: Israel in the north, under Jeroboam; and Judah in the south, under Rehoboam. (I Kings 12)

I alone remain a prophet of the Lord

They cried aloud and cut themselves

THE TEST ON MT. CARMEL

Elijah, the prophet of God, stood fearlessly on top of Mt. Carmel. Opposite him stood Ahab, the wicked king of Israel, with 450 prophets of the false god Baal. A great crowd of Israelites pressed around them.

"How long are you going to limp between two choices?" Elijah asked the Israelites sternly. "If the Lord is God, follow Him. But if Baal, then follow him." The people did not answer a word. If some of them felt in their hearts that they had sinned in worshipping Baal, they did not dare to confess it for fear of the king. Elijah went on, "I, even I only, remain a prophet of the Lord, but Baal's prophets are 450 men."

Elijah then asked for two bulls. "Let the prophets of Baal," he said, "choose one bull for themselves and cut it in pieces and lay it on wood and put no fire under it. I will do the same with the other bull." Then he turned to the prophets and said, "You call on the name of your gods, and I will call on the name of the Lord. And the God that answers by fire, let Him be God."

The prophets of Baal cut up one of the bulls and laid it upon the altar. Then they began calling out, "O Baal, hear us." When nothing happened, they began dancing around the altar, shouting loudly, "O Baal, hear us." Still nothing happened. The whole morning they whirled around and around, calling to their

Pour on the burnt sacrifice   *Then the fire of the Lord fell*

god. But, of course, it was of no use, for there was no such god in Heaven. At noon, Elijah began making fun of them. "Cry aloud," he mocked, "for he is a god. Perhaps he is talking or is on a journey or is asleep and must be wakened." The prophets, stung by these jeering words, danced and shouted even more wildly. They even cut themselves with swords until their blood gushed out. But still no answer came from Baal.

    At last, Elijah said to the Israelites, "Come near to me." The people crowded around him. He took twelve stones, one for each of the twelve tribes, and built up again an old altar which had been there. Next, he dug a trench around it. He put wood on the altar and laid the pieces of the bull on the wood. Then he commanded some men to pour four barrels of water over the altar. They did it once, then twice, then three times, so that the sacrifice, the wood, and the ground around the altar were all completely soaked, and the trench was full of water.

    When everything was ready, Elijah calmly prayed, "Lord God of Abraham, Isaac, and of Israel, let it be known this day that Thou art God in Israel, and that I am Thy servant. Hear me, O Lord." At once, in answer to Elijah's prayer, fire flashed down from Heaven, burning up the soaked sacrifice, wood, stones, and dust, and licking up the water in the trench. The people fell upon their faces in fear and cried out, "The Lord, He is God! The Lord, He is God!" (I Kings 18:20-39)

All the earth sought his wisdom *It was all grown over with thorns*

SOLOMON'S WISDOM

David's son Solomon was Israel's wisest king. Even princes and rulers traveled long distances "to hear his wisdom, which God had put in his heart" (I Kings 10:24). Many of his wise sayings along with some by other wise men — have been kept for us in the Book of Proverbs. The purpose of the book is to teach wisdom to both young and old.

Wisdom begins with the fear of the Lord (1:7). Since God Himself is the fountain of all truth, only those who seek to know Him and to obey His wise commandments will find true wisdom. Such wisdom is more precious than rubies or silver or gold (3:14, 15).

These proverbs deal with children and parents, storekeepers and kings, wise men and fools. They deal with anger, pride, laziness, lying, and riches. Let us, then, look at some of them.

Solomon tells us that the man who works his land diligently and takes good care of his flocks will have plenty of bread, and enough goats' milk (27:23-27; 28:19). But the one who will not work will go hungry (19:15). Another proverb tells of how the writer passed by the vineyard of a lazy man. Instead of neat rows of healthy grapevines, he saw that thorns and thistles were choking out the plants. Moreover, the stone wall which was supposed to keep the animals out of the vineyard was broken down. Because the owner preferred to sleep

Go to the ant *He that loves him punishes him*

rather than to weed his vineyard or repair his wall, said this wise man, hunger would soon come upon him like a robber (24:30-34). Still another advises: "Go to the ant, you lazy man. Consider her ways and be wise." For even the tiny ant, who has no ruler to tell her what to do, gathers food in the fall so that she will be able to eat in the winter (6:6-11). A lazy man, however, turns on his bed like a door on its hinges (26:14). He has all kinds of excuses why he cannot work, but in the end he will go hungry.

As for the training of children, Solomon writes: "Train up a child in the way he should go, and when he is old, he will not depart from it" (22:6). He knew that even when children are very young, they must be taught how to behave and then be punished if they disobey. "Correct your son," he adds, "and he shall give delight to your soul. But a child left to himself brings his mother to shame" (29:17, 15). Some people think that it is mean to spank a child. But God, through King Solomon, says just the opposite: "He that spares the rod hates his son. But he that loves him punishes him when necessary" (13:24). For, as another proverb says, "If you beat him with a rod, he will not die, and you will deliver his soul from death" (23:13, 14). Such training is not only good for the child, but it also brings happiness to the parents. For "a wise son makes a glad father," says Solomon, "but a foolish son is the heaviness of his mother" (Proverbs 10:11)

I will not leave you   *And Elijah took his cloak and struck*

ELIJAH GOES TO HEAVEN

Elijah, the fearless, old prophet of the Lord, walked along the dusty road to Bethel with his young helper, Elisha, at his side. He had asked Elisha not to come with him this time. He knew that something very wonderful was going to happen to him, and he wanted to test Elisha. But Elisha knew about it, too, and refused to be left behind. As they drew near to Bethel, a group of prophets came out to meet them. "Do you know," they said to Elisha, "that the Lord will take away your master from you today?" "Yes, I know it," he replied. Probably none of them knew just how it would happen, but the Holy Spirit had told all of them — Elijah, Elisha, and many other prophets that Elijah would be taken away that very day.

Both at Bethel and the next city he came to, Jericho, Elijah again tried to persuade his young servant to stay behind. But Elisha only replied, "As the Lord lives, and as your soul lives, I will not leave you." At Jericho, a group of fifty prophets again asked Elisha if he knew that the Lord was going to take away his master that day, and again Elisha replied, "Yes, I know it."

At last the two prophets reached the Jordan River not at a shallow place, but where the water flowed deep. The prophets from Jericho watched at a distance to see how they would cross. Elijah took off his cloak, rolled it up,

My father, my father!

The spirit of Elijah rests on Elisha

and struck the river with it. At once, the waters parted, and the two men crossed over on dry land.

On the other side, Elijah said to his servant, "Ask what I shall do for you before I am taken away." Knowing that very soon he was to take over Elijah's difficult work, Elisha replied, "Let a double portion of your spirit be upon me." "If you see me when I am taken from you," replied Elijah, "it shall be so." Elijah well knew that only God could give his helper the Holy Spirit. But he felt that if God gave to Elisha what he gave to no other man — the privilege of seeing him being taken away. He would also give Elisha the double portion he asked for.

Then, as the two men were walking along, a blazing chariot of fire drawn by fiery horses suddenly swooped down between them. It caught up Elijah, the mighty warrior of the Lord, and carried him off in a whirlwind to Heaven. Elisha saw him go and cried out, "My father, my father!" He then looked down at his feet and saw that Elijah's cloak had dropped from his shoulders. He picked it up and returned to the Jordan. Rolling up the cloak, he struck the river with it, just as Elijah had done. The waters again parted, and he crossed back on dry ground. When the fifty prophets, who were still waiting there, saw Elisha perform this same miracle, they bowed low before him and said, "The spirit of Elijah rests upon Elisha." (II Kings 2:1-15)

On whom do you trust?

Do not speak in the Jew's language

HEZEKIAH'S FAITH IS REWARDED

A mighty Assyrian army was all around Jerusalem. The city gates were tightly shut, and the people watched in fear from the top of the wall. Three Assyrian officers came to the wall and called up to King Hezekiah's servants, asking in mocking words who would help them against the great king of "Assyria. Hezekiah's servants replied, "Speak to us in the Syrian language, for we understand it. And do not speak to us in the Jews' language." They were afraid that if their people on the wall heard the threats of the Assyrians, they would soon become discouraged. But the Assyrian officers only shouted more loudly, so that all could hear and understand: "Do not let Hezekiah fool you. For he shall not be able to deliver you. Neither let Hezekiah make you trust in the Lord. Has any of the gods of the nations delivered his land out of the hand of the king of Assyria?" The people trembled. They knew that nation after nation had fallen before the might of Assyria. Their sister kingdom of Israel, to the north, had already been carried away captive. And all the other walled cities of Judah had been taken. Only Jerusalem remained. But they said nothing, for Hezekiah had commanded them not to answer.

When good King Hezekiah heard about the enemy's boasting words, he put on sackcloth and went to the Temple to pray. He asked the prophet Isaiah to pray, also. Isaiah comforted the king and told him that God would send news to

Hezekiah spread it before the Lord *Behold, these were all dead bodies*

frighten the Assyrians. So Hezekiah did not surrender the city.

The Assyrian officers went to report to their king, Sennacherib, who was fighting with his army southwest of Jerusalem. Just then, Sennacherib received word that the dreaded king of Ethiopia was marching against him. Since he could not attack Jerusalem just now, he hoped to frighten Hezekiah into surrendering. So he sent more messengers to him with a letter, which said, "Let not your God fool you, saying, 'Jerusalem shall not be given into the hand of the king of Assyria.' Behold, you have heard what the kings of Assyria have done to all the lands by destroying them utterly. And shall you be delivered?"

At this second threat, Hezekiah again went to the Temple and prayed to God. He admitted that the Assyrians had destroyed all the other countries and had thrown their gods into the fire. But their gods were only wood and stone. "Now, therefore, O Lord our God," he prayed, "save us from his hand, that all the kingdoms of the earth may know that Thou art the Lord."

God replied through Isaiah that He had heard how Sennacherib had mocked His name. Therefore, He would put a ring in his nose and a bridle in his mouth and would lead him back to Assyria like a wild animal. That very night He sent an angel to kill 185,000 of the Assyrian soldiers. When Sennacherib awoke the next morning and saw most of his army dead, he returned to Assyria in disgrace, and Jerusalem was saved. (Isaiah 36-37; II Kings 18-19)

Give me your vineyard *The men witnessed against Naboth*

NABOTH'S VINEYARD

King Ahab looked down from his summer palace in Jezreel upon a lovely vineyard just outside the palace walls. What a nice place for a garden, he thought to himself. He went to the owner of the vineyard, a farmer called Naboth, and said, "Give me your vineyard, that I may have it for a garden of herbs. And I will give you a better vineyard for it, or, if you wish, I will pay you for it." Naboth, however, refused. This land had belonged to his family ever since Canaan was divided up among the tribes. He would not sell it now, or even exchange it for another one.

Disappointed, Ahab turned and went into his palace. Like a spoiled child who cannot have his way, he lay down on his bed with his face to the wall and would not eat. His wife, Jezebel, came and saw him sulking on his bed. "Why is your spirit so sad," she asked him, "that you will not eat?" When Ahab told her about the vineyard, she asked scornfully, "Do you now govern the kingdom of Israel?" According to her sinful way of thinking, if Ahab was king, he could have anything he wanted. If he was too weak-willed to take it, she would get it for him herself.

Jezebel sat right down and wrote some letters to the rulers of the city. She signed Ahab's name to them and sealed them with his seal. Ahab must have known that she was up to some mischief when she asked him for his seal.

Arise, take possession of the vineyard   *Have you killed, and also taken?*

But he did not stop her. Perhaps he felt that he could not be blamed for any evil she did.

In the letters, Jezebel commanded the rulers of the city to set Naboth before the people and to have two lying men come forward and say that he had cursed God and the king. The punishment for such a crime was death by stoning.

The rulers of Jezreel did not disobey these cruel orders. As soon as they had the false witnesses state that Naboth had cursed God and the king, the people carried him out of the city. There they stoned him to death, and dogs came and licked up his blood from the ground. When the rulers reported to Jezebel that Naboth was dead, the queen went to her husband and said, "Arise, take possession of the vineyard, for Naboth is dead."

Ahab joyfully went to the vineyard. But who should meet him there but Elijah, the prophet! "Have you killed and also taken possession?" Elijah asked him sternly. Jezebel had, indeed, given the orders. But in the eyes of the Lord, Ahab was as much to blame for Naboth's death as she was. "In the place where dogs licked the blood of Naboth," Elijah went on, "dogs shall lick your blood. Every man-child of yours will be destroyed. And the dogs shall eat Jezebel by the wall of Jezreel." This was a dreadful punishment, but a fitting one for this most wicked king of Israel, and for his even more wicked wife, Jezebel.
(I Kings 21)

The driving is like Jehu's   *Is it peace, Jehu?*

AHAB'S FAMILY IS DESTROYED

King Ahab "did more to provoke the Lord God of Israel to anger than all the kings of Israel before him" (I Kings 16:33). He caused the death of Naboth and stole his vineyard. He worshipped idols and even built a temple for Baal. And he allowed his heathen wife, Jezebel, to kill many of God's prophets. As punishment for such great wickedness, Elijah told Ahab that all of his sons and sons' sons would be destroyed, and Jezebel would be eaten by dogs.

About fourteen years later, Elisha sent a young prophet to Jehu, a bold, rough general of the Israelite army. The prophet anointed him king over Israel and commanded him to destroy all the males of Ahab's family.

Jehu wasted no time. Followed by some soldiers, he drove furiously toward Jezreel, where Ahab's son, King Jehoram, was staying. A watchman in the tower of the palace spied his chariot in the distance and told the king. Jehoram sent a horseman to ask if the riders were coming in peace. The messenger, however, joined up with Jehu's soldiers. The king sent a second messenger. But he did not return either. At last the watchman shouted to Jehoram, "The driving is like the driving of Jehu, for he drives furiously."

When the king heard that it was Jehu, he got into his chariot and rode out to meet him. King Ahaziah of Judah, who was visiting his uncle Jehoram,

Jehu drew a bow   *Throw her down*

followed in his own chariot. They met Jehu on Naboth's land. "Is it peace, Jehu?" King Jehoram asked. "What peace, so long as the wickedness of your mother, Jezebel, is so great?" replied Jehu. Alarmed by these words, Jehoram shouted, "Treachery, O Ahaziah!" And, wheeling his chariot around, he rode off. But Jehu quickly drew his bow and shot an arrow straight through Jehoram's back. The king slumped down dead. Jehu ordered his captain to throw out Jehoram's body on the ground so that the dogs could lick up his blood where they had licked Naboth's, even as the Lord had said. Meanwhile, Ahaziah had fled. But Jehu killed him also, because he, too, was of Ahab's family.

    Jezebel heard of her son Jehoram's death and realized that her own life was in danger. She painted her eyes and fixed her hair and sat at a window above the palace gate. Just as Jehu was about to ride through the gate, Jezebel leaned out and called down to him. Jehu looked up and shouted, "Who is on my side?" A few servants looked out. "Throw her down!" Jehu ordered. The men pushed Jezebel out of the window onto the pavement below, and she was killed instantly. Then Jehu rode over her body with his chariot. A little later, when he sent men to bury her, they found that the wild dogs had eaten her, even as the Lord had said.

    Jezebel and the kings of Israel and Judah were now dead. But Jehu went on through the land like a whirlwind and destroyed every male in Ahab's family. Thus he fulfilled God's judgment upon the wickedness of Ahab. (II Kings 9-10)

You shall have a son *Carry him to his mother*

A BOY MADE ALIVE

Followed by his servant, Gehazi, the prophet Elisha wearily climbed the outside stairs to the little room on the flat roof of the house. He went in and lay down on the bed. It was so pleasant to be able to stop and rest here whenever he passed through Shunem, he thought. How could he repay the mistress of the house for her kindness in having this room built especially for him? "She has no child, and her husband is old," suggested Gehazi. "Call her," said Elisha. Gehazi obeyed, and the woman soon appeared in the doorway. "Next year at this time you will have a son," the prophet told her. A son! "No, my lord," she replied in amazement, "do not lie to me." But, just as Elisha promised, the following year a baby boy was born to her.

One hot, summer morning years later, the little boy went out to the fields where his father was busy with the reapers. He loved to watch them cut the golden grain and tie it into bundles. But suddenly he cried out, "My head, my head!" The busy father hardly stopped from his work. "Carry him back to his mother," he ordered one of the reapers. The servant carried the sick boy back to the house and gave him to his mother. She held him on her lap all morning. But at noon he died.

The broken-hearted woman now had but one thought. She must find Elisha. He was the one who, by the power of God, had given her the child.

She caught him by the feet

She took up her son and went out

He was now the only one who could help. She carried the limp, little body up to the prophet's room and laid it on his bed. Then, without telling her husband why, she saddled a donkey and rode off as fast as she could.

As she neared Mt. Carmel, Elisha saw her coming. He sent Gehazi to meet her and ask if anything was wrong. Gehazi went, but the woman would tell him nothing. She wished to speak to the prophet himself. As soon as she arrived, she threw herself down before Elisha and grasped his feet. Gehazi tried to push her away, but Elisha stopped him. He could see that she was greatly troubled. "Did I ask my lord for a son?" she said. Elisha guessed what was wrong. Turning to Gehazi, he ordered, "Go, lay my staff on the face of the child."

Gehazi went at once. But the mother would not leave until Elisha went with her. On the way back they met Gehazi, who said, "The child did not awake." Elisha hurried on. When he reached the house, he went up to his room and shut the door. He prayed earnestly to the Lord. Then he lay upon the child, and the cold body began to get warm. Elisha got up and walked around a bit and then lay on him again. Suddenly the child sneezed seven times and opened his eyes. He was alive again! Elisha sent for the mother. She came in and fell at his feet in thanksgiving. Then she took her precious son and left the room. (II Kings 4:8-37)

The wild asses quench their thirst   *As for the stork . . .*

GOD'S CARE OVER ALL HIS CREATION

No one can see God. Yet the heavens and the earth show forth His power, His wisdom, and His goodness. For God created all things, and He upholds them day by day. Therefore, the Psalmist sings: "Bless the Lord, O my soul. O Lord my God, Thou art very great."

Then the Psalmist tells of God's wonderful works. The Lord stretches out the heavens like a curtain, he says. The clouds and the winds obey His voice. When God first created the earth, He covered it with water as with a robe. But at His command, the waters fled and the dry land appeared. He then set boundaries for the oceans and seas so that they would not cover the earth again. The Lord causes the rain to fall upon the mountains, continues the Psalmist. It runs off the slopes into brooks and streams, so that the wild donkeys and all other animals may come to them and drink. He causes grass to grow for the animals, fruit and vegetables for man, and the cedars of Lebanon for the birds to nest in. God has created many different kinds of animals. Yet He supplies the special needs of them all. He gives to the long-legged storks the lofty fir trees for their house. The wild goats have the high mountains to play in. And the timid conies a sort of mountain rabbit can hide among the rocks.

God also governs the sun and the moon for the sake of men and animals.

The young lions roar

Man goes forth to his work

He makes darkness, when the wild beasts creep forth in search of food and the young lions roar for meat. But then He causes the sun to come up again. The animals steal back to their dens, and man goes forth to his work." O Lord," exclaims the Psalmist, "how manifold are Thy works! In wisdom hast Thou made them all. The earth is full of Thy riches." The earth, yes, but also the great and wide sea, where tiny fish dart about and smiling porpoises play.

All of these creatures, says the Psalmist, depend upon God for their food, and, in fact, for their very life. When He opens His hand, they gather their food and are filled. But when He turns His face away, they go hungry. When He takes away their breath, they die and return to the dust. But when He sends forth His Holy Spirit, new life is created to take the place of that which died.

When the Psalmist considers the wisdom and power of God in His creation, and when he sees God's goodness in His daily care of all living things, he breaks forth into praise, saying: "I will sing unto the Lord as long as I live. I will sing praise to my God while I have my being." Many, however, refuse to see God's hand in nature. Yet the Lord who causes the earth to tremble and the mountains to smoke has power over these sinners, too. The Psalmist rejoices that they shall not overcome the Lord's chosen people, but that God Himself will be victorious over them. (Psalm 104)

 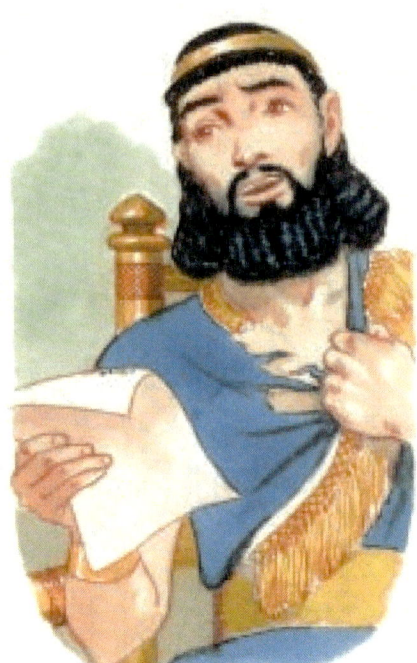

He would heal him of his leprosy   *See how he seeks a quarrel*

NAAMAN THE LEPER

The little Israelite slave-girl felt sorry for her master, Naaman. He was such an important man — general of the whole Syrian army. Yet his skin was rotting away with leprosy. Then she thought of the great prophet, Elisha. Surely he could help Naaman. "Would God that my lord were with the prophet that is in Samaria," she said to her mistress one day, "for he would heal him of his leprosy!"

Someone ran to tell Naaman at once. Naaman, in turn, went to the king and told him what his little slave had said. Eager to help his mighty general, the Syrian king wrote a letter to the king of Israel. He told Naaman to take it to him. Naaman also decided to take along silver, gold, and costly clothes to pay for his healing.

Naaman made the trip at once from Damascus to Samaria, in Israel. He bowed before King Jehoram, and gave him the letter. Jehoram opened it and read, "I have sent Naaman, my servant, to you that you may heal him of his leprosy." The king tore his clothes in dismay. How could he, a mere man, heal someone of leprosy? Was the king of Syria just trying to pick a quarrel? Elisha, however, heard of Naaman's arrival. He sent word to the king, saying, "Let him come now to me, and he shall know that there is a prophet in Israel." Jehoram had not thought of asking God's help! But now he sent Naaman to God's prophet, Elisha.

Naaman stood at the door of the house

His flesh was like the flesh of a child

The Syrian general's splendid chariot clattered up to the door of Elisha's simple house. His long train of horsemen and servants pulled up behind him. Then Naaman sat there, proudly waiting for this prophet to come out and heal him. But Elisha only sent out his servant to tell him, "Go and wash in the Jordan seven times and you will be clean."

Naaman was furious. The prophet did not even pay him the honor of coming out to see him. Nor did he call on his God and wave his hand over the leprous spots. What good would it do, he thought scornfully, to wash in the dirty Jordan? Were not the rivers of Damascus better than all the waters of Israel? He rode off in a rage.

But some of his servants pleaded with him, saying, "My father, if the prophet had told you to do some great thing, would you not have done it? How much more, then, when he says to you, 'Wash and be clean?'" Naaman thought a moment. He did not see how washing in Israel's river would do any good. But perhaps it was worth trying. So he and his servants turned and rode toward the Jordan River. When they arrived, Naaman got out of his chariot and went down into the river. Half doubting, half hoping, he dipped himself under the water once, twice, six times. Then once more, and to his amazement his skin had become as fresh as a little child's. He had, at last, humbled himself to do it God's way. And he had been healed! (II Kings 5:1-14)

A great multitude is coming   *O Lord God of our fathers*

THE LORD'S BATTLE

    Messengers hurried into the palace at Jerusalem and reported to Jehoshaphat, king of Judah, that a great army from Moab, Ammon and Edom was coming against them from beyond the Dead Sea. Jehoshaphat became frightened and prayed for God's help.

    He commanded all the people of his kingdom to fast. By not eating anything, they could show their sorrow for their sins and be better able to pray. From all the cities of Judah, people flocked to Jerusalem and gathered before the Temple to seek the Lord's help in this time of great need. Women and children came, as well as men. Then King Jehoshaphat stood where everyone could see and hear him. He lifted his hands to Heaven and began to pray: "O Lord God of our fathers, art Thou not God in Heaven? And dost Thou not rule over all the kingdoms of the heathen?" The king recalled that the Lord was their God, and that He had driven the heathen out of Canaan to give the land to them. They had built this Temple for Him in Jerusalem so that whenever any trouble came upon them — whether war, plague, or famine they could come and pray to Him as a nation, and He would hear and help. And now they were being attacked by the Moabites, Ammonites, and Edomites, and without good reason. Therefore he pleaded, "O our God, wilt Thou not judge them? For we have no power against this great company. But our eyes are upon Thee."

Believe in the Lord your God

People came to take away the spoil

When Jehoshaphat finished praying, the Holy Spirit came upon one of the Levites, and he replied, "Thus says the Lord, 'Fear not, for the battle is not yours, but God's. Tomorrow go down against them. But you will not need to fight. Stand still, and see the salvation of the Lord.'" When they heard these comforting words, the king and all the people bowed down and worshipped the Lord in thanksgiving.

Early the next morning, the army of Judah marched forth to meet the invaders. Jehoshaphat encouraged them, saying, "Believe in the Lord your God, and believe His prophets." He also commanded the choir of Levites to go before the army, dressed in their Temple robes and singing praises to God. Meanwhile, the Lord caused the different tribes of the enemy to start fighting each other. By the time the army of Judah reached the battlefield, there was not a single soldier left to fight against them. Only dead bodies covered the field.

The battle, indeed, had been the Lord's. All that was left for Jehoshaphat's army to do was to carry away the riches. There was so much of it that it took them three days to strip the dead soldiers of all the precious jewels and other valuables. Then, led by their king, they marched triumphantly back to Jerusalem to the sound of trumpets and harps. There they gave thanks to God.

When the nearby countries heard how the Lord had fought for His people, they became afraid and did not trouble Judah for a long time.
(II Chronicles 20:1-30)

They carried away great riches

He put away the hateful idols

A GOOD BEGINNING, BUT A SAD ENDING

A million Ethiopians had swept into the land of Judah. As godly King Asa and his army faced the enemy, he prayed, "Help us, O Lord our God; for we rest on Thee, and in Thy name we go against this multitude." The Lord heard his prayer and overthrew the Ethiopians. Asa's soldiers chased after the fleeing army and destroyed or scattered them all. Then they headed back to Jerusalem in triumph, loaded with riches and leading droves of captured cattle, sheep, and camels.

On the way back, they were met by a prophet, who said, "The Lord is with you while you are with Him. But if you forsake Him, He will forsake you." The prophet went on to explain that wars and troubles had come upon the people of God in the past because they had forsaken Him and had worshipped idols. But whenever they turned to the Lord again, He helped them.

Encouraged by these words, King Asa continued the work he had started of restoring the worship of the Lord. First, he destroyed all the heathen idols and altars that he could find. Then he fixed up the brass altar of burnt-offerings which stood before the Temple. And he held a great feast at Jerusalem to which he invited the people from his own kingdom of Judah, as well as the godly people from the tribes of the kingdom of Israel. At this feast the people solemnly

All Judah rejoiced at the oath

You have relied on Syria

promised to serve the Lord with all their heart and soul. They were so happy to be worshipping the Lord again that they shouted and blew their trumpets for joy. And God gave them rest from war.

But, sad to say, Asa did not always remain this faithful to the Lord. Some years later, the king of Israel, to the north, invaded Judah. This time, Asa did not pray to God for help, as he had done when the Ethiopians had attacked him. Instead, he sent treasures of silver and gold — taken from his palace and even the Temple — to Ben-hadad, king of heathen Syria, asking him, in return, to attack Israel. Ben-hadad agreed. When the king of Israel heard that Ben-hadad's army was invading his land from the north, he stopped troubling Judah in the south and hurried away to protect his own cities. Asa's plan had worked. But God sent another prophet to him, saying, "You have relied on the king of Syria, and not on the Lord your God. Therefore, from now on you shall have wars." Earlier in his reign, Asa probably would have repented of his sin. But now he became angry with the prophet and threw him in prison.

Two years before he died, Asa was troubled by a very serious disease in his feet. Again, he sought only the help of men — his doctors, rather than also praying to the Lord for healing. As long as Asa put his trust in God, he was happy and healthy. When he put his trust in men, he became unhappy and died. (II Chronicles 14)

The king's son shall reign *They put the crown upon him*

A LITTLE BOY BECOMES KING

King Ahaziah was dead. His wicked mother, Athaliah, wanted to be queen in his place, but she could not take over the throne as long as Ahaziah's sons were alive. These princes were her own grandchildren. But that made no difference to her. She gave her servants the cruel command to murder them all. Then she declared herself queen of Judah.

However, by God's working, one of the princes, a baby named Joash, escaped being killed. His aunt, the wife of the high priest, was given the opportunity to save him, and for six years she and her husband hid him in the Temple. Neither Athaliah nor any of the people knew that he was alive. During those six long years, the queen, who was as wicked as her parents Ahab and Jezebel had been, ruled undisturbed in Jerusalem.

At last, the high priest, Jehoiada, decided it was time to crown his little nephew Joash. The throne rightfully belonged to him, and not to Athaliah at all. For only David's family was supposed to rule over Judah, and Athaliah was not of David's family. Jehoiada secretly called together five army captains and explained his plans to them. These captains then went to all the cities of Judah and told the Levites and the elders to go at once to Jerusalem. As soon as they were gathered in the Temple, Jehoiada brought out the little prince and said, "Behold, the king's son shall reign, as the Lord has said of the sons of David."

Treason! Treason!   *Set the king upon the throne*

How surprised and thankful the Levites and elders were to see that there was one son of Ahaziah left! They remembered that God had promised King David that his sons and sons' sons would rule forever (II Sam. 7.16). In fact, their great Messiah (Jesus Christ) was to be born from David's family and was to have David's throne. But when Queen Athaliah had seemingly wiped out all of David's family, they thought that God had broken His promise. Now they knew that He had not! And they all agreed to help Jehoiada crown Joash king.

    Jehoiada passed out the spears and shields which were kept in the Temple. He stationed the soldiers and elders at all the gates of the Temple and around the courts. The Levites guarded the prince inside the Temple. When everything was ready, Jehoiada brought out Joash and stood him on a platform in the sight of all. As he placed the crown on the seven-year-old prince and anointed him, the people all clapped their hands and shouted, "Long live the king." Trumpets blared forth and the people sang for joy.

    Queen Athaliah heard the rejoicing from her palace, right next to the Temple. She rushed over to find out what was going on. When she saw the Temple court filled with people cheering the new king, she tore her clothes and cried out, "Treason! Treason!" But at Jehoiada's command, the soldiers seized her. They took her outside the Temple grounds and killed her. Then they led little Joash into the palace and set him on the royal throne. (II Chronicles 22:1- 23: 21; II Kings 11)

And they broke down the altars   *Shaphan read it before the king*

GOOD KING JOSIAH

God's judgment fell upon the ten tribes of the northern kingdom of Israel. These tribes had turned away from the Lord and had worshipped all kinds of heathen idols. No matter how many prophets God had sent to turn their hearts back to Him, they would not listen. So He caused the Assyrians to attack Israel and carry most of the people away as captives.

The people in the southern kingdom of Judah were not much better. They, too, worshipped false gods of wood, stone, and brass. But God did not punish Judah for a while longer. Instead, He gave them a few more good kings to witness to them of His goodness. One of these was Josiah, who became king when he was only eight years old. Both his father and grandfather had been extremely wicked rulers. But Josiah served the Lord faithfully, as King David had done.

When Josiah was only twenty, he began to rid the land of idol worship. He broke down the heathen altars and cut down the wooden images. Some idols he smashed to tiny pieces and scattered their dust upon the graves of those who had worshipped them. And he burned the bones of the heathen priests upon their altars.

When he was twenty-six years old, he began to repair the Temple in Jerusalem, for in many places the stones were crumbling and the timbers had rotted away. He ordered the high priest, to count the money that the people had

Thus says the Lord

He read all the words of the book

brought to the Temple and use it to pay the carpenters and builders. While the high priest was emptying the money chests, he found nearby a book that no one knew was there. It was the book of God's Law, written by Moses, which was supposed to be read to the people every seven years. This had not been done for a long, long time.

The high priest gave the book to Shaphan, the scribe. Shaphan took it to the palace and read it to King Josiah. The good king tore his clothes in grief when he heard all of Gods commandments and the punishments which God promised to send if they were not obeyed. Josiah sent messengers to a prophetess to find out what would happen to Judah because they had forgotten this Law. She told them, "Thus says the Lord, 'Because they have forsaken me, and have burned incense to other gods, My anger shall be poured out upon this place, and shall not be quenched.'" But as for Josiah, she went on, since he had humbled himself when he heard the Law, he would die in peace before all this evil came upon Judah.

When the messengers reported this to Josiah, he commanded the people to gather before the Temple. Then he stood up and read aloud all the book of God's Law. He himself promised to obey all the commandments written in it and made the people promise, too. So they served the Lord outwardly, at least as long as Josiah ruled. But later, God punished them for their disobedience, even as He had punished Israel. (II Chronicles 34; II Kings 22)

Cyrus brought forth the vessels   *The whole congregation together*

THE DECREE OF CYRUS

To punish the kingdom of Judah for its stubborn disobedience, the Lord allowed King Nebuchadnezzar to destroy Jerusalem completely in 586 B.C. and carry most of the people far away to Babylon as captives. But God also prophesied by Jeremiah that after Babylon itself was conquered, the people of Judah, called the Jews, would be permitted to return home again (Jer. 29:10). And being Lord over heathen nations, too, God worked in the heart of King Cyrus of Persia to make this possible after he defeated Babylon.

In the first year of his reign (536 B.C.), Cyrus sent a decree throughout his land which read: "The Lord God of Heaven has given me all the kingdoms of the earth; and He has charged me to build Him a house at Jerusalem." Cyrus then urged the Jews living in Babylonia to go back to Jerusalem and rebuild the Temple. Any who did not wish to return were to help the others by giving them gold, silver, animals, or other goods. Cyrus himself gave them all the gold and silver dishes which belonged to the Temple.

About 50,000 men, women, and children answered Cyrus' call and started back to Judah under Zerubbabel. Most of them walked all the way, for their donkeys and camels were loaded down with household goods. It probably took about four months for them to travel the 800 miles to Judah. But they sang and were happy, for they were going home.

After they arrived and had gotten somewhat settled in the cities of their

The people shouted

We ourselves will build

fathers, they assembled at Jerusalem. The city was in a sorry state, with its walls and houses in ruins and the Temple a heap of rubbish. First, they cleared a place in the Temple court and rebuilt the altar of burnt-offerings. After that they offered the sacrifices which the Law of Moses demanded, and also began again to keep the special feasts.

But still the Temple lay in ruins. So with money which Cyrus had given them, they sent for cedar wood from Lebanon and hired carpenters and stone cutters. The foundation was soon laid, and the people celebrated. The priests blew their trumpets. The Levites sang praises to God. And most of the people shouted for joy. But those who were old enough to remember the glory of Solomon's Temple wept when they saw how much simpler this new one would be.

When the people of Samaria, to the north, heard that the Jews were starting to rebuild the Temple, they came and said, "Let us build with you, for we seek your God." The Samaritans claimed to worship the Lord. But God was displeased with their worship, for it was so full of evil heathen ideas. Zerubbabel "said, We ourselves will build to the Lord, as King Cyrus has commanded us." The Samaritans then became angry and did all they could to hinder the work. They even paid men to speak evil of the Jews before King Cyrus. They caused so much trouble that the Jews soon became discouraged and stopped work altogether. (Ezra 1:1-3:5)

Why is your face sad?

Viewed the walls of Jerusalem

THE WALLS OF JERUSALEM

Nehemiah handed a goblet of wine to the Persian king, Artaxerxes. As the king took it from his Jewish cupbearer, he studied him carefully. "Why are you sad?" the king asked. Nehemiah was afraid. He hardly dared tell him the disturbing news he had received from Jerusalem. Yet he replied, "Why should I not be sad when the city of my fathers lies waste, and its gates have been destroyed by fire?" "What do you ask?" the king said. For weeks Nehemiah had prayed earnestly that God would give him mercy in the sight of the king. Now he silently prayed once more. Then he answered, "That you would send me to Judah so that I may build the city again." The lord answered Nehemiah's prayers. The king gave him permission to go, and he also gave him a guard of horsemen and letters to all the governors through whose provinces he had to travel.

When Nehemiah first arrived in Jerusalem, he did not tell the rulers why he had come. After three days, he went out secretly one night to look at the walls of Jerusalem. In the 100 years since the Jews' return, the Temple and some of the houses had been rebuilt. But as Nehemiah rode around the walls, he saw that they were still completely in ruins. In some places, his horse could not even get past the heaps of stones. In such a state, the city was wide open to the attacks of an enemy.

What are these feeble Jews doing? *Each one had his sword*

Then Nehemiah went to the rulers and explained how God had moved the Persian king to send him. "Come, and let us build up the wall of Jerusalem," he said. The rulers quickly agreed. Nehemiah assigned a section of the wall to each household, and everyone started working hard.

The Jews' enemies, the Samaritans, at first made fun of them. "What are these feeble Jews doing?" sneered one. Another said mockingly, "If a fox goes up, he shall break down their stone wall." Nehemiah only prayed for God's help, and the people worked even harder.

When the Samaritans saw that mocking words could not discourage the Jews, they planned an attack. But Nehemiah heard of it. He stopped the work and put fully armed men outside the walls. As soon as the greatest danger was past, he sent the people back to work again. But they were still ready for an attack. Everyone who had to go outside the city to haul stones took a spear with him. Each builder worked with his sword strapped to his side. Half of Nehemiah's own servants worked along with the people of Judah, while the other half held their weapons. Nehemiah had a trumpeter at his side at all times to sound the alarm in case of an attack. And no one was allowed to leave the city at night. From daybreak until dark they kept at it, and God blessed their work. To the disappointment of their enemies, they finished the wall in only fifty-two days! (Nehemiah 1-6)

Mordecai did not bow

Do with them as it seems good

HAMAN'S DECREE

Haman was the most important man in all Persia except for the king. Whenever he proudly rode through the palace gate, everyone except Mordecai the Jew bowed low before him, as the king had commanded. When Haman was told that Mordecai refused to bow down, he was furious. Not only would he put Mordecai to death, he decided; he would also destroy all the other Jews throughout the whole kingdom of Persia, from India to Ethiopia.

Haman went to King Ahasuerus. He told him that there was a certain people scattered throughout his kingdom which did not obey his laws. He offered the king 10,000 talents of silver to have them destroyed. Without thinking twice about it, the cruel king gave his signet ring to his favorite nobleman, saying, "You may keep the silver. The people are yours to do with them as you wish." At once Haman wrote out a decree that in eleven months all the Jews — both young and old, little children and women — were to be destroyed on one day and their goods seized. He signed the king's name and sealed it with the king's ring. Messengers on horse back then sped out of the capital in every direction to deliver the decree to the governors of the 127 provinces.

What weeping and wailing there was among the Jews as the news of this dreadful decree spread! Many of them fasted and put on sackcloth and ashes as a sign of their great grief. Mordecai, too, put on sackcloth and ashes and

Mordecai cried with a bitter cry

If I die, I die

went through the city weeping loudly. He came as far as the palace gate, but he could not enter the palace dressed in sackcloth.

Beautiful Queen Esther — Mordecai's cousin, whom he had brought up as his own daughter — heard of his strange behavior. Since she knew nothing of the decree, she sent one of her servants to Mordecai to find out what was wrong. Mordecai gave him a copy of the decree to show to Esther, and urged her to go to King Ahasuerus and plead for her own life and the lives of her people. For the king did not know that she was a Jewess.

Esther sent back word reminding her cousin that anyone who appeared before the king without being called would be put to death, unless the king held out his golden scepter to him. And it had been a month since the king had called for her. Mordecai sent back this message: "Do not think that you will escape in the king's house. If you are silent at this time, then help will come to the Jews from another place; and you and your father's family will be destroyed. And who knows whether you have come to the kingdom for such a time as this."

Esther saw that she had to risk her life to help God's chosen people. She commanded Mordecai and all the Jews of the city to fast three days for her. She and her maids would do the same. "I will go in to the king, which is not according to the law," she said bravely. "And if I die, I die." (Esther 3-4)

The king held out the golden scepter *Let a gallows be made*

THE JEWS ARE SAVED

For three days Queen Esther and all the Jews in the Persian capital fasted. On the third day she put on her splendid royal robes. Fearfully, she came and stood at the entrance of the throne room. If the king did not hold out his golden scepter to her, she would be put to death. At last the king looked up and saw Esther standing there. How beautiful she was! He held out his scepter. With a thankful heart, Esther drew near and touched it. 'What do you wish, Queen Esther?" he asked kindly. "If it seem good to the king," she replied, "let the king and Haman come this day to a banquet that I have prepared for him." The king called for Haman, and together they went to the banquet.

At the end of the meal, the king again asked Esther what she wished. For he knew that she had not risked her life just to ask him to dinner. But Esther was not yet ready to tell him. She only asked the king to return the next day with Haman for another feast.

Haman left the banquet feeling very pleased and proud. He, alone, had been invited to feast with the king and queen! And now he had been invited a second time. What an honor! But when he rode out of the gate and saw that Mordecai still did not bow down, he was filled with anger. At home, he complained that his many great honors meant nothing as long as Mordecai was alive. His friends told him to build a high gallows and get permission to hang

The enemy is this wicked Haman

Haman had fallen upon the couch

Mordecai on it. Haman liked the idea and had the gallows built.

The next day Haman and the king again went to Esther's banquet. And again at the end of the meal the king asked her what she wished. This time the queen said: "If I have found favor in your sight, O King, and if it please the king, let my life and the life of my people be given at my desire. For we are sold, I and my people, to be destroyed, to be killed, and to die." "Who is he who dares to do so?" the king asked in anger. "The enemy," replied Esther, "is this wicked Haman!"

The king could hardly control his rage. He got up and stalked out to the garden. Haman was terrified. He flung himself upon Esther's couch and begged for mercy. Just then the king returned. Seeing Haman on the couch, he thought that Haman was now trying to force the queen. He became even more furious and had Haman taken away and hanged on the very gallows he had built for Mordecai.

As for the Jews, Haman's decree could not be changed. But on the day that they were supposed to die, they were allowed to defend themselves, and they killed 75,000 of their enemies. So God saved His people from being completely wiped out by means of Esther, whom He had, indeed, raised up as queen "for such a time as this." (Esther 5-7)

He makes me lie down in green pastures   *He leads me beside the still waters*

THE SHEPHERD'S CARE

In the burning heat of the day and the chill of the night, the boy David spent many a year on the hills around Bethlehem, looking after his father's sheep. He loved those sheep and took care of all their needs. Years later, he thought of how much his care over his sheep was like God's care over him. Just like a shepherd, the almighty, loving God looks after His people — those who truly love and serve Him — giving them everything that is good for them and protecting them from all evil. So David wrote the Twenty-Third Psalm, which he began with the words, "The Lord is my Shepherd, I shall not want."

David recalled how hard it used to be during the long dry seasons to provide food and water enough for his flock. Yet, by searching, he always managed to find a green slope where there was enough tender grass for them to eat and a soft, cool spot where they could lie down and rest. Even harder to find was a brook or spring. But once a day he led his thirsty, bleating sheep to where they could lap up water to their fill. Thus, still thinking of how much God, like a shepherd, supplied his needs, David went on to sing, "He makes me lie down in green pastures. He leads me beside the still waters."

The David remembered how he used to protect his sheep from the many dangers which could harm them. With his long staff he had kept the straying ones from going too far from the flock or from falling off a rocky cliff. With

Thy rod and Thy staff they comfort me

The valley of the shadow of death

his short rod, or club, he had killed any lion or bear that tried to seize and eat one of his lambs. He had especially been on his guard when he led his sheep through narrow, dark passes. For lions or wolves could spring out from behind the rocks and throw the whole flock into a panic. Recalling how his sheep trusted that he would protect them, David overcame his fear of danger because the Lord was his Shepherd. "Yea, though I walk through the valley of the shadow of death," he said, "I will fear no evil, for Thou art with me. Thy rod and Thy staff they comfort me."

Even when his enemies pressed about him like wolves, the Lord richly supplied all his needs. He gave David not only those things which were absolutely necessary for life, but much, much more. Just as water spills out over the edge of a cup that is too full, so God's blessings overflowed in his life. Thus he wrote, "Thou preparest a table before me in the presence of my enemies. Thou anointest my head with oil; my cup runs over."

As one of God's sheep, David had known only the mercy and love of his Shepherd. And he trusted that God would always treat him in the same, loving way. "Surely," he confessed, "goodness and mercy shall follow me all the days of my life. And I will dwell in the house of the Lord forever." (Psalm 23)

The woman was very beautiful

Uriah the Hittite died also

DAVID PRAYS FOR MERCY

David was the best king Israel ever had. Not only was he a fearless fighter and a wise ruler, but most important, he served the Lord with all his heart. The Bible tells us that "David did that which was right in the eyes of the Lord, and turned not aside from anything that He commanded him all the days of his life..." (I Kings 15:5). But, sad to say, the Bible then adds, "except in the matter of Uriah the Hittite." For David fell deep into sin.

King David desired a beautiful woman named Bathsheba for his wife. When he learned that she was already married to one of his soldiers, Uriah the Hittite, he still wanted her and even committed adultery with her. Then, in order to get rid of her husband, David ordered his general to put him in the hottest part of the battle where he knew he would be killed. Thus David became a murderer as well as an adulterer. With Uriah out of the way, David then married Bathsheba, and for many months he did not fully repent of his wrong.

At last, God sent His prophet Nathan to David. David's sins had been very great. But when Nathan pointed them out to him, David was deeply sorry for them. Soon afterwards, he wrote a beautiful psalm (Psalm 51), in which he prayed to the Lord to forgive him for the evil which he had done. "Have mercy upon me, O God," he began, "according to Thy loving kindness. According to the multitude of Thy tender mercies blot out my transgressions. Wash me thoroughly from my iniquity,

The Lord sent Nathan to David *Have Mercy upon me, O God*

and cleanse me from my sin. For I acknowledge my transgressions, and my sin is ever before me."

Then he confessed, "Against Thee, Thee only, have I sinned and done this evil in Thy sight." David knew that he had wronged both Bathsheba and her husband. But it was God whose commandments he had broken. God had created him, and therefore, could demand David's obedience to His holy Law. Yet David had rebelled against his Creator's commands. God had also raised him up from a simple shepherd boy to be king over all Israel. Yet David had repaid His love by sinning against Him.

David realized that simply to sacrifice a lamb or a bull on the altar would not win God's pardon if his heart was not right. "The sacrifices of God," he said, "are a broken spirit and a contrite heart." He knew, that unless God also renewed his heart, he would fall right back again into the same sins. So he prayed: "Create in me a clean heart, O God, and renew a right spirit within me. Cast me not away from Thy presence, and take not Thy Holy Spirit from me.

If the Lord would forgive his sins and renew his heart, David promised that he would show his thankfulness by telling others of God's mercy. "Then will I teach transgressors Thy ways," he promised, "and sinners shall be converted to Thee. Deliver me from blood guiltiness, O God, Thou God of my salvation. And my tongue shall sing aloud of Thy righteousness." (Psalm 51)

He was numbered with the transgressors *All we like sheep have gone astray*

THE SUFFERING SERVANT

Why did the Lord Jesus have to die on the cross? Was He, like the two robbers who were crucified with Him, being punished for His own sins? The prophet Isaiah answered this question about 700 years before Jesus was even born. Yet the Holy Spirit showed him so clearly what would happen — and why — that he wrote about it as though it had already taken place.

"We esteemed Him stricken, smitten by God, and afflicted," wrote Isaiah. Those who saw Jesus hanging on the cross were sure that God was punishing Him for some evil which He had done. But that could never be. For, said Isaiah, "He had done no violence, neither was any deceit in His mouth." Jesus could never have been punished for His own sins because He never committed any.

Why, then, was He crucified? If He was not to blame for any crime, was it just a terrible mistake that He was put to death? The wonderful reason, said Isaiah, is that "He was wounded for our transgressions and He was bruised for our iniquities." Jesus had not sinned; we had. "All we like sheep have gone astray," continued the prophet. "We have turned everyone to his own way." Just as sheep wander off from their shepherd, so we turn away from God and follow our own sinful desires. Therefore, we are the ones who should be punished. But Isaiah said that "the Lord has laid on Him (that is, on Jesus) the iniquity of us all." Jesus was a substitute. He took the place of all those who trust Him to be

For many bore false witness against Him   *As a lamb to the slaughter*

their Saviour. He suffered God's holy anger against sin so that those who believe in Him may go to Heaven rather than be punished for their sins in Hell.

Jesus' greatest agony was on the cross. But He also suffered for His people's sins during His whole life. He was, as Isaiah wrote, "despised and rejected of men, a man of sorrows, and acquainted with grief." He was born in a stable. Wicked King Herod tried to kill Him when He was only a small child. The Pharisees hated Him. His own disciples ran away from Him in Gethsemane. Men told lies about Him before the High Priest and before Pilate. He was unjustly condemned to death. And the Roman soldiers slapped Him and spit in His face. Yet in all of this suffering, Isaiah said, "He opened not His mouth. He was brought as a lamb to the slaughter. And as a sheep before its shearers is dumb, so He opened not His mouth."

Men hated and crucified Him. But God said through Isaiah, "Behold, my Servant (meaning Jesus) . . . shall be lifted up and praised and be very high." The Apostle Paul says that it was just because Jesus — who was God's Son — became a man and died on the cross that His Father "also highly exalted Him and gave to Him a name which is above every other name — so that at the name of Jesus every knee should bow . . . and every tongue should confess that Jesus Christ is Lord, to the glory of God the Father."
(Philippians 2:9-11; Isaiah 52:13-53:12)

And Baruch wrote   *Then Baruch read in the book*

A SCROLL IS BURNED

"Take a scroll," God told His prophet Jeremiah, "and write in it all the words that I have spoken to you against Israel and against Judah. It may be that the house of Judah will hear all the evil which I plan to do to them; that they may return every man from his evil way, that I may forgive their sin." For twenty-three years, God had been warning the people of Judah through Jeremiah's preaching that unless they stopped worshipping idols, He would send an enemy from the north to destroy them. But they had not listened. Now He was going to give them one more chance, by putting these warnings in writing.

Jeremiah sent for Baruch, who wrote down on a scroll everything that Jeremiah dictated to him. Then Jeremiah commanded him to take the scroll into the Temple and read it before all the people. So, the next fast-day, when the Temple was crowded with worshippers from all over Judah, Baruch went and stood in the upper court. He unrolled the scroll and solemnly read aloud that God was going to send the king of Babylon to destroy them unless they turned back to Him.

One young man became so alarmed at these words that he hurried to the king's palace and burst into the room where his father and some other noblemen were gathered. He told them excitedly about the scroll which Baruch had just read. The nobles immediately sent for Baruch and had him read the scroll to them.

We will surely tell the king   *Cast it into the fire*

When he had finished, they looked at each other in terror. "We will surely tell the king all these words," they said. They were afraid, however, that King Jehoiakim might become angry and try to kill Jeremiah and Baruch. So they told Baruch that he and Jeremiah must hide at once.

    It was a chilly, winter's day, and the king was sitting before a small fire when his nobles entered the room. The nobles bowed and began telling the king all about the scroll. He, too, wanted to hear it. So a young man brought it and began reading. But unlike his nobles, Jehoiakim was not frightened by God's warnings. Instead, after a portion of the scroll had been read, he cut that piece out with his penknife and carelessly tossed it into the fire. His nobles tried to stop him. But he kept right on cutting out the parts as they were read and throwing them into the fire, until the whole scroll was burned up. Jehoiakim foolishly thought that by burning the scroll, he could escape the punishments that were written in it. But God had said that he could escape them only by turning from his evil ways.

    Soon afterwards, God commanded Jeremiah — who was safely hidden from the king's anger — to write the same warnings down on another scroll. All the evil which He had promised to send, God said, would still come upon Judah. Furthermore, wicked Jehoiakim's dead body would not be buried in honor, but would be thrown out to the heat of the daytime and the frost of night.
(Jeremiah 36)

 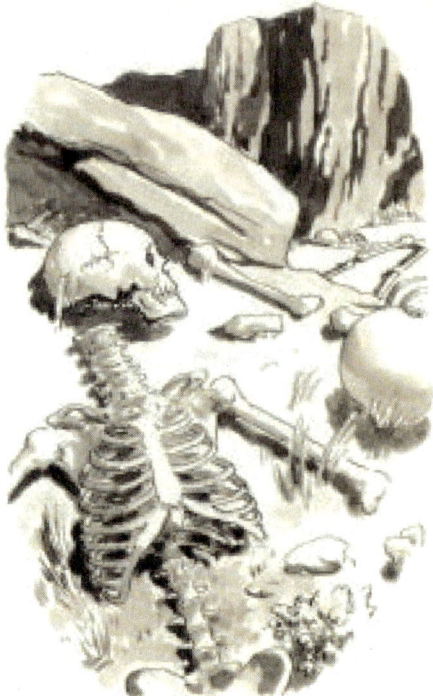

Behold, there were very many   *The bones came together, bone to bone*

DRY BONES

One day the great prophet Ezekiel had a strange vision. In it, he was carried away by God and set down in a broad valley. He looked around. Scattered all over the ground lay the bones of men. God told him to walk around and look at them. Ezekiel did so and saw that there were very, very many of them and that they were as dry as dust from lying in the blazing, hot sun so long.

Then God asked him, "Son of man, can these bones live?" It certainly did not seem as though such dried out bones could ever have life again. But knowing that with God all things are possible, Ezekiel replied, "O Lord God, Thou knowest." God then told him to speak to the bones, saying, "O you dry bones, hear the word of the Lord: 'I will lay sinews upon you and will bring up flesh upon you, and cover you with skin, and put breath in you, and you shall live. And you shall know that I am the Lord.'"

It must have taken a strong faith for Ezekiel to tell those scattered, dry bones that God would give life to them. But he did as the Lord commanded him. And even before he finished speaking, he heard a loud, rumbling noise. Then he saw the bones moving about. A foot bone joined itself to a leg bone. The leg bone joined to a thigh bone, and the thigh bone to a hip bone. Complete skeletons came together before his very eyes. As he continued watching, flesh and skin gradually came up over the skeletons. Now, instead of bones, human

There was no breath in them   *They lived, and stood up upon their feet*

bodies lay on the ground. But still there was no life in them.

   Then God commanded Ezekiel to say, "Come from the four winds, O breath, and breathe upon these slain, that they may live." Once more Ezekiel obeyed. And just as God had breathed into the first man, Adam, making him a living soul, so He now breathed into these lifeless bodies. As Ezekiel watched, the bodies stood up on their feet. The valley which had been strewn with dry bones was now filled with living people!

   God then explained to Ezekiel the meaning of the miracle. "Son of man," He said, "these bones are the whole house of Israel." Both the people of Israel and those of Judah had been carried away captive. They had lived so long in a faraway land that they had lost all hope of ever seeing their homeland again or of ever again worshipping the Lord in His Temple. They had become not just like dead men, but even worse, like dry bones in a grave. So God now showed this vision to Ezekiel to comfort them. Just as He had given life to the dead, dry bones, so He would give life and hope to His people and would carry them back home. "O my people," He said, "I will put My Spirit in you, and you shall live. And I will place you in your own land. And you shall know that I, the Lord, have spoken it and done it." (Ezekiel 37:1-14)

All the people . . . fell down and worshipped   *But if you do not worship*

THE FIERY FURNACE

From every province of Babylonia, King Nebuchadnezzar had assembled his most important officials for the dedication of his new golden statue. When they were all gathered around the base of the tremendous image, a herald stepped forward. He announced that when the musical instruments started to play, everyone had to fall down and worship the image. Anyone who did not do so would be thrown into a furnace of fire.

Then the music began, and everyone fell to the ground, except three Jews — Shadrach, Meshach, and Abednego. They refused to bow down to worship anything or anyone else than the true God. Some Chaldeans who were jealous of these Jews told Nebuchadnezzar that the foreigners whom he had set over the province of Babylon had disobeyed him by refusing to worship the golden image.

The king was furious. He sent at once for the three Jews. When they were brought before him, Nebuchadnezzar asked them if they had purposely refused to bow down. He even offered to give them another chance, in case there had been some mistake. But then he threatened, "If you do not worship, you shall be thrown the same hour into the burning, fiery furnace. And who is that god that shall deliver you out of my hands?"

The three Jews stood calmly before the angry king. "Our God," they replied in faith, "is able to deliver us from the burning fiery furnace. But if He will not,

The flame of the fire slew those men   *Nor was a hair of their head singed*

be it known to you, O King, that we will not worship the image which you have set up.

    Nebuchadnezzar was now wild with rage. "Heat the furnace seven times hotter than usual," he shouted to his servants. "And tie these men and throw them in." Some of his strongest soldiers seized Shadrach, Meshach, and Abednego and tied them up, with their rich robes and turbans still on. When the furnace was ready, the soldiers threw the three Jews down into the fire. But as they did so, roaring flames leaped out and burned the soldiers to death.

    A moment later Nebuchadnezzar sprang out of the chair from where he had been watching. "Did we not throw three men, tied, into the fire?" he asked his advisers. "True, O King," they replied. "Lo, I see four men loose, walking unharmed in the midst of the fire," Nebuchadnezzar said in amazement. "And the fourth is like the Son of God." Then the king called to them, and Shadrach, Meshach, and Abednego came out of the fire. Nebuchadnezzar and his advisers crowded around them. They could hardly believe their eyes! The men were not harmed in the least. Not a single hair of their heads was singed. Nor did their clothes even smell of fire. The king cried out, "Blessed be the God of Shadrach, Meshach, and Abednego, who has sent His Angel and delivered His servants that trusted in Him." The king then made a decree that anyone who said anything against the God of Shadrach, Meshach, and Abednego would be cut in pieces. And he promoted the three men to even higher positions. (Daniel 3)

These men assembled, found Daniel praying   *That Daniel . . . makes petition 3 times a day*

THE DEN OF LIONS

"Be it known that whoever makes a request of any god or man except the king for thirty days will be thrown into the den of lions." So read the decree of King Darius the Mede. This law, however, was not his idea, but had been urged upon him by his governors and advisers. For they were bitterly jealous of a Jew called Daniel and wanted to get rid of him. Not only had he, a foreigner, been one of the three presidents, but now the king was thinking of promoting him to rule over the entire kingdom. At first, they had watched Daniel closely to see if they could find something wrong with the way he ruled. But Daniel ruled so wisely that at last they admitted, "We shall not find any occasion against this Daniel, except concerning the law of his God." Knowing that he prayed regularly, they felt sure that they could trap him with this new decree.

Daniel soon learned of the new law. But, like his friends Shadrach, Meshach, and Abednego, he would not obey any order which would cause him to give to man the honor which belonged to God alone. So three times a day, just as he had always done, he knelt before his open window and prayed to the Lord. As soon as his enemies spied him praying, they hurried to the king and told him that Daniel had disobeyed his decree.

Too late, Darius realized that he had been tricked. All day long he tried to think of some way to save his faithful servant. But at sunset his officials

Your God . . . He will deliver you

My God has sent his angel

reminded him, "Know, O King, that it is a law of the Medes and Persians that no statute which the king makes may be changed." Sadly, he had Daniel brought before him. "Your God, whom you serve continually," said the king, "He will deliver you." Then he unwillingly gave the order for Daniel to be thrown into the den filled with hungry, roaring lions. A stone was rolled over the mouth, and both the king and his noblemen sealed it with their rings.

With a heavy heart, King Darius returned to his palace. He ate nothing that night, nor did he call for the usual music and dancing. When he went to bed, he could not sleep, but worried all night about Daniel. As soon as it was light, he hurried to the den and anxiously called out. To his great amazement, Daniel's voice answered, "O King, live forever. My God has sent His angel and has shut the lions' mouths, and they have not hurt me." The king was overjoyed. He ordered Daniel lifted out of the den at once. After a whole night among fierce lions, Daniel now stood before the king without even a scratch. His God, whom he had faithfully served in spite of the decree, had saved him!

As for Daniel's enemies, the king commanded that they, with their wives and children, be thrown into the same den. This time, no angel shut the lions' mouths, and they were torn to pieces almost before they reached the bottom. (Daniel 6)

Arise, call upon your God   *Where do you come from?*

JONAH FLEES

"Arise," God told His prophet Jonah, "go to Nineveh, that great city, and cry against it, for their wickedness has come up before me. But Jonah did not want to go. He was afraid that if the Ninevites repented at his preaching, God might forgive them. And Jonah did not feel that God should forgive a heathen city.

So Jonah did not obey the Lord. Instead of traveling east, he traveled west. He went to the busy seaport of Joppa, where he found a ship bound for faraway Tarshish. He paid his fare and boarded the ship. Then he went below deck and fell fast asleep.

Jonah had thought that he could flee from his duty. But God would not let him run away. Shortly after the ship set sail, He caused a great storm to come up upon the sea. The wind howled and the waves battered the ship until it almost broke in two. The frightened sailors threw their cargo overboard to lighten the ship. Then they knelt down and prayed to their gods. The captain even went below deck to waken Jonah and tell him to pray. But still the storm raged. At last, the sailors cast lots to see whose fault it was that such a fierce storm had come upon them. And God caused the lot to fall upon Jonah.

The sailors turned to Jonah and asked, "Who are you and where do you

Cast him forth into the sea   *The weeds were wrapped about my head*

come from?" "I am a Hebrew," he replied, "and I fear the Lord." When he admitted to them that he was fleeing from the presence of his God, they became even more afraid. "What shall we do to you," they asked, "that the sea may be calm for us?" "Take me up and throw me out into the sea," he answered. "For I know that for my sake this great storm is upon you." As frightened as the sailors were, they did not want to throw Jonah overboard. Seizing the oars again, they rowed toward land with all their strength. But they could make no headway. Now they had no other choice but to throw Jonah out. After praying to God not to blame them for Jonah's death, they lifted him over the side and dropped him into the raging sea. At once, the wind died down and the sea became calm again.

    Jonah sank down, down into the deep. The waves rolled over him. Seaweed wrapped around his head. But before Jonah could drown, God sent a huge fish which swallowed him whole. For three days God kept His disobedient servant alive inside the fish's stomach in a miraculous way. Locked in the prison of the fish's belly, Jonah called out to God for mercy. The Lord heard Jonah's prayer. On the third day He caused the great fish to vomit Jonah up on the beach. The prophet had learned his lesson. As he stood up on the sand in the bright sunlight, he was now ready to obey the Lord. (Jonah 1, 2)

Yet 40 days, Ninevah shall be overthrown   *The king . . . covered himself with sackcloth*

JONAH'S LESSON

A second time God said to Jonah, "Arise, go to Nineveh, that great city, and preach to it the preaching that I tell you." This time Jonah obeyed. After traveling northeast some 500 miles, he reached the edge of Nineveh. Then he started walking through the wicked city. At busy street corners and crowded marketplaces he stood and cried out, "Yet forty days, and Nineveh shall be overthrown."

The Ninevites stopped to listen to this stranger. They did not laugh at his warning of judgment as the people in the days of Noah had done, but they believed his message. When news of Jonah's preaching reached the king, he took off his royal robes and put on sackcloth. Then he sent out a decree that every man and beast should wear sackcloth, too, and also fast. Finally, he commanded his subjects to pray earnestly to God and to turn from their evil ways. "Who can tell," he said, "if God will turn away from His fierce anger, so that we do not perish?" And when heathen Nineveh repented as Israel had seldom done, God, in His great mercy, did not destroy it.

Instead of being happy that the Ninevites were saved because of his preaching, Jonah became angry, very angry. He reminded the Lord that it was just because he was afraid that Nineveh might be spared that he had tried to flee in the first place. He was so displeased that he even begged God to let him die.

A shade over his head *It is better for me to die than to live*

But the Lord did not let His hard-hearted prophet die. Instead, He taught him a lesson.

Jonah went out on the east side of Nineveh to wait and see what would happen to the city. To protect himself from the burning rays of the sun, he made a rough, little hut to sit under. God caused a fast-growing gourd, or vine, to spring up in one day beside Jonah's hut and cover it with delightful, leafy shade. But the next morning the Lord sent a worm which chewed through the stem of the plant. In no time, the vine withered and died. Without the protection of the vine, Jonah fainted from the blazing sun and from the hot east wind which God then sent. He again asked the Lord to let him die. God replied, "Do you do well to be angry for the gourd?" When Jonah replied that he did, God showed him how selfish he was. He reminded Jonah that he had neither planted the vine nor cared for it. It had grown up in a night and had died in a night. Yet Jonah felt sorry that it had died because it had given him such refreshing shade. If he felt so sorry for a mere vine, said God, should not He, the Lord, feel sorry for Nineveh? It had, indeed, been a wicked city, but it had repented. And besides the many cattle in it, there were 120,000 young children — those who could not tell their right hand from their left — who had not sinned like their parents. Were not, therefore, the thousands of repentant heathen and their children more to be pitied than a short-lived vine? (Jonah 3-4)

Think upon your ways   *Who has commanded you to build?*

THE SECOND TEMPLE IS FINISHED

In response to the decree of Cyrus, King of Persia, 50,000 Jews left Babylonia and returned to Judah to rebuild the Temple. The foundation was soon laid, but then little more was done on it for the next sixteen years. The kings who came after Cyrus did not support the work as he had done. The Jews had their own houses to build. And they were poor because for years their harvests were not good.

At last, God sent the prophet Haggai to stir up the people to start work again. They had said that it was not yet time to build the Temple. But Haggai rebuked them sharply, asking, "Is it time for you to live in your finished houses, and shall this House lie waste? Now, therefore, thus says the Lord of hosts: 'Think upon your ways. You have sown much, and bring in little. You eat, but you do not have enough. You clothe yourselves, but no one is warm. And he that earns wages earns wages to put them into a bag full of holes.'" They had thought that they were too poor to build the Temple. But Haggai explained that they were poor just because they had not built the Temple. Instead of seeking first the glory of God, they had spent all their energies to provide for their own comfort. And God had not blessed the work of their hands. In fact, he had caused the heavens to withhold the dew and the earth to withhold its fruit. So Haggai urged them: "Go up to the mountain and bring wood and build the Temple."

There was found . . . a roll   *The Lord will fill this house*

The people were pricked in their hearts by these words and started building again with renewed faith. But then Tatnai, the governor over the western part of Persia, came and asked, "Who has commanded you to build this House?" The Jews explained that King Cyrus himself had ordered them to rebuild the Temple which Nebuchadnezzar had destroyed.

Tatnai sent a letter to Darius, who was then king of Persia, asking if this was so. Darius searched among the records and did indeed find the scroll on which Cyrus' decree was written. He sent back word to Tatnai that no one was to hinder the work of the Temple. Furthermore, the king ordered him to pay all the expenses for it from the royal treasury and to supply the Jews with all they needed for the daily sacrifices. Thus, when the Jews sought God's glory by starting work again on the Temple, they found that He Himself provided all the materials they needed in a most unexpected way. With hard work, they finished the Temple in four years. Although it could not compare in outward glory with Solomon's Temple, Haggai comforted the people, saying, "The Lord will fill this House with glory. And in this place will He give peace." He was, of course, referring to the time about 500 years later when the Lord of Glory and the Prince of Peace, Jesus Christ, would preach and teach in that very Temple. (Haggai; Ezra 5-6)

It was his lot to burn incense *He was not able to speak*

JOHN THE BAPTIST IS BORN

In the hill country of Judea, south of Jerusalem, there lived an old priest named Zacharias with his wife Elizabeth. They both loved the Lord God and tried to keep His commandments. But they were sad, for they had no children and could never hope to have any because Elizabeth was now too old.

Because there were so many priests in Israel, each one had to serve in the Temple at Jerusalem only twice a year, for a week at a time. One day, while Zacharias was taking his turn, he got a chance to do something very special. He was chosen to go into the Holy Place to burn incense and to pray to the Lord.

So while the people stood outside praying, Zacharias carried the incense into the Holy Place and laid it upon the altar. Suddenly an angel of the Lord appeared before him. At the sight of this heavenly messenger, the old priest trembled with fear. But the angel said unto him, "Fear not, Zacharias, because your prayer has been heard, your wife Elizabeth shall bear a son to you, and you shall call his name John." Then the angel went on to tell what John's work would be. With the same spirit and fearlessness of Elijah, he would turn many of the Israelites back to God. And in so doing, he would make the people ready for the coming Messiah.

What a wonderful message! Not only did the angel promise Zacharias a son to cheer his old age; he also said that this child would prepare the way for

None of your kindred is called John   *He wrote, John is his name*

the Saviour. But how could such an old couple still have a son? It was unbelievable! Even this faithful old priest doubted God's promise and asked the angel for a sign.

The angel replied that he was Gabriel, sent by God to bring this good news. "And behold," he said, "you shall be dumb and not able to speak until the day in which these things shall take place, because you did not believe my words."

When his week was over, Zacharias returned home. And according to the promise of God, his aged wife bore a son before a year had passed. How amazed everyone was!

When it was time to give the baby a name, friends and relatives came to celebrate the happy event. The guests wanted to call the baby Zacharias, after his father. But Elizabeth said that he should be called John. This the friends could not understand! There was no one in Zacharias' family named John! So they made signs to the deaf and dumb father to find out what he wished the child to be called. Asking for a tablet, Zacharias wrote, in obedience to the angel's command, "John is his name."

At that moment his punishment was lifted and he could speak again. Filled with the Holy Spirit, Zacharias praised God for His wonderful works.
(Luke 1:5-25; 57-80)

You shall go before the Lord Repent!   *The kingdom of Heaven is near*

THE VOICE IN THE WILDERNESS

When John the Baptist was born, his father Zacharias foretold that he would "go before the face of the Lord to prepare his way" (Luke 1:76) that is, as a messenger is sent before a king to tell of his coming, so John would make the hearts of the Jews ready for their coming King, Jesus Christ.

When both he and Jesus were about thirty years old, John began this work near the Jordan River (see map). He dressed in a rough coat of camel's hair, with a leather belt around his waist. And all that he ate were locusts and wild honey. John did not have the fine food and clothing of one who lived in a king's palace. But Jesus later said of him, "There has not ever risen among those born of women any greater than John the Baptist" (Matt. 11:11).

John was a fearless preacher. He called upon all to repent of their sins and to be baptized. He warned not only the publicans and soldiers, but also the leaders of the Jews — the Pharisees and Saducees. Just because they were children of Abraham, he said, they would not necessarily be saved. They had to confess their own sins and then show by changed lives that they were truly sorry for them.

Before Jesus began His preaching, He also came to John to be baptized. But John said, "I have need to be baptized by Thee, and comest Thou to me?" Of all men, Jesus alone did not need to be baptized. Yet Jesus had John baptize Him

The Spirit coming down like a dove

Who are you?

in order that He might fulfill all of the Law's demands. Although He was God, He had also become true Man. And as Man, He had to obey the Law, just like his fellow men.

As soon as John had finished baptizing Jesus, he saw the heavens open up and the Holy Spirit come down in the form of a dove and rest upon Him. This was the sign God had promised before to John whereby he could recognize the Saviour! Then the voice of God the Father resounded from heaven, saying, "This is My beloved Son, in which I am well pleased." With these two signs, John was now sure that Jesus was the Messiah, whose coming he was to proclaim.

From Jerusalem, Judea, and the area around the Jordan River, the people flocked to hear John and to be baptized. They were coming in such great numbers that the leaders in Jerusalem were getting worried. Could this man, perhaps, be the Christ? They sent some priests and Levites to ask him, "Who are you?" John answered, "I am not the Christ." Neither, said he, was he Elijah nor the prophet about whom Moses had spoken. "Well, who are you then?" they then asked. John replied, "I am a voice crying in the wilderness, 'Make straight the way of the Lord' (Isaiah 40:3). For there is One standing among you whom you do not know. He is the One whose sandal I am not worthy to untie."
(John 1:19-34; Matthew 3; Mark 1; Luke 3)

Fear not, Mary   *Behold the maid-servant of the Lord*

GABRIEL'S MESSAGE TO MARY

The angel Gabriel was the one whom God had sent into the Temple to tell Zacharias that he would have a son. Now he had an even more wonderful message to deliver in the distant town of Nazareth (see map). There, in a simple home, lived a young woman called Mary, who was soon to be married to a carpenter named Joseph.

As Gabriel entered her house, he said, "Hail, favored one! The Lord is with you." Mary was amazed, not so much because an angel appeared unto her, but because of what he said. What did he mean when he called her "favored one"?

Gabriel went on to explain: "Fear not, Mary, for you have found favor with God. And behold! you shall conceive in your womb and bring forth a Son, and you shall call His name Jesus. He shall be great, and He shall he called the Son of the Highest. And the Lord God shall give Him the throne of David His father; and of His kingdom there shall never be an end."

Not with the unbelief that Zacharias had shown, but in wonder and awe, Mary asked, "How can this be when I am not even married?" Then Gabriel told Mary one of the greatest mysteries of all time: "The Holy Spirit shall come upon you," he replied, "and shall overshadow you: wherefore also the Holy Thing born of you shall be called the Son of God." Thus, before Mary was married, she

Mary went into the hill-country   *Blessed are you among women*

would have a son. But in a way we can never understand, the Holy Spirit, not Joseph, was to be the cause of his birth.

Gabriel then gave Mary a sign to show her that God can indeed do things that seem impossible to men. Her cousin Elizabeth, who had never been able to have any children, was soon to have a son.

The angel's message was almost unbelievable! Could God really have chosen someone as lowly as she to be the mother of the Messiah? Not understanding why or how it could all happen to her, Mary nevertheless believed that it would. In faith and obedience to God, she answered humbly, "Behold the maidservant of the Lord! Let it be to me according to your word."

In the days that followed, Mary thought again and again about the angel's message. But there was no one in Nazareth with whom she could share her secret at this time, not even Joseph. No one except Elizabeth — in whom God had also worked a miracle — would believe her. So she got a few things together and hurried south to where her cousin lived. Just as she was entering the house, the Holy Spirit told Elizabeth that Mary would be the mother of the Christ. Elizabeth then exclaimed to her, "Blessed are you among women. And how is it that the mother of my Lord should come to me?"

So God had already told Elizabeth the wondrous news, thought Mary. Now she was more sure than ever that all that the angel had said would really come true. (Luke 1:26-56)

There was no room in the inn   *She laid Him in a Manger*

JESUS IS BORN

Mary stayed with Elizabeth three months before returning to Nazareth. Soon after she was back home, Joseph realized that she was going to have a baby. Knowing that this baby was not his, he decided that it would be best not to marry her. But then God sent an angel to him in a dream to tell him not to be afraid to marry Mary. For this baby would not be an ordinary one, but would be the Son of God. After hearing such amazing news, Joseph obediently took Mary for his wife.

Then something happened that upset their peaceful lives. Emperor Augustus at Rome ordered that all the people in his empire be counted. In Syria and Palestine, that meant that everyone who was not already living in the town of his forefathers had to go there to be counted, or enrolled. Since David was the forefather of both Mary and Joseph, they had to go to his city, which was Bethlehem. Ordinarily Mary would not have chosen to make such a long and tiring trip just before her Baby was to be born. But God was using this heathen king to bring her to Bethlehem. For it was in that city that the prophet Micah had said that the Christ child must be born.

When Mary and Joseph at last arrived in Bethlehem, they found the town already crowded with many others who had also come to be enrolled. The inn was full, and the only place they could find in which to stay was a stable. But at least they had a roof over their heads and soft hay for a bed. And so it

I bring you good tidings *They came and found the babe*

happened that while they were there Jesus was born. Having no crib in which to put her Baby, Mary laid Him in the feedbox of a donkey or cow.

Thus the Creator of heaven and earth was born in a stable! His Father was God Almighty, but His mother was only a poor, unknown young woman. As He lay asleep in the manger, He looked no different from any other baby. No one would have guessed that He was the Son of God. But God made His birth known in a wondrous way.

In that still, dark night, some shepherds were keeping watch over their sheep in the pastures just outside Bethlehem. Suddenly an angel as bright and shining as the sun stood by them, and they were greatly frightened. But the angel told them not to be afraid, for he was bringing them good news: the Saviour had just been born in Bethlehem. They would find Him wrapped in tight clothes and lying in a manger.

As soon as the angel had finished speaking, the sky was filled with thousands of angels, singing "Glory to God in the highest." Then, when their song was over, they disappeared, and it was dark and quiet once more.

At once the shepherds hurried to Bethlehem and found the baby lying in a manger, just as the angel had said. Filled with joy at seeing the promised Christ child, they went out and told everyone they met what they had seen and heard that night. (Luke 2:1-20)

Wise men came from the east *Herod called the wise men aside*

WISE MEN FROM THE EAST

Some time after the Lord Jesus had been born in Bethlehem, perhaps a year or more, some men came riding through the streets of Jerusalem on camels. Their clothes were very dusty, for they had come a long, long way. They were wise men from the east who studied the stars. God had showed them by means of a bright, new star in the sky that a king of the Jews had been born. These wise men were not Israelites. They were heathen Gentiles. Yet they had believed the sign that Israel's God had given them and had made the long trip across the great desert to Jerusalem. There, in the chief city of the Jews, they hoped to find the new king.

"Where is He who has been born King of the Jews?" they asked those they met in the streets. "We have seen his star in the east, and have come to worship Him."

When news of these strangers reached King Herod, he became very troubled. He called together the chief priests and scribes and asked them where their King — the Christ or the Messiah — was supposed to be born. "In Bethlehem of Judea," they answered, "for the prophet Micah has said that out of Bethlehem shall come a Governor who will shepherd God's people Israel."

Herod then secretly called the wise men to him. "Exactly what time did you first see this star?" he asked them. When they told him, he said: "Go to

The star went before them

They presented gifts to Him

Behtlehem. Find this young child. Then come back and tell me all about him so that I may go worship him, too." Of course, Herod did not really want to worship the child. He only wanted to know where he was so that he could kill him. Then he would not have to worry that the child would gorw up to be king instead of Herod or his family.

The wise men, believing what God had told the prophet Micah, started right out for Bethlehem. The star which they had seen in the east went before them to show them where to find the Lord Jesus.

But how unbelieving the Jews at Jerusalem were! They were supposed to be God's people. They had been waiting for the Messiah who had been promised by God through the prophets. They even knew where He would be born. Yet they did not take the trouble to go the five miles to Behtlehem to see if He had really come.

When the wise men arrived in Behtlehem, the city of King David, they found the new king, Jesus, and His mother Mary in a simple little house. Falling down and worshipping Him, they opened their treasures and gave Him rich gifts: gold, frankincense, and myrrh.

That night God sent them a dream. He told them that they should not go beck to tell Herod where the child was. Once more these Gentiles believed God and returned to their own country by another way. (Matthew 2:1-12)

An Angel appears to Joseph

Then Herod was very angry

THE FLIGHT INTO EGYPT

In a dream, God had told the wise men not to go back to Herod. But even though they left Israel without telling Herod where the young king was, Jesus would not he safe for long. For the cruel king would not rest until he had found the child and killed him.

God the Father, however, was watching over His Son and protecting Him. He would not allow Jesus to be killed before He had done the work which He had been sent to do. So God sent an angel in a dream to Joseph, Mary's husband, saying: "Arise, take the young child and His mother, and flee into Egypt and stay there until I shall tell you: for Herod will look for the little child in order to kill Him.

The Bible does not tell us much about Joseph. But time and again it says that Joseph arose and did what God commanded. Here, too, the Bible tells us that Joseph got up in the middle of the night, took Jesus and His mother, and started right out for Egypt. It must have been a long and tiresome trip, taking several days. But in Egypt Jesus would he safe from Herod.

King Herod, meanwhile, waited in vain for the wise men to come back to him. When he realized that they had gone away without telling him where the

He put to death all the boys

Joseph came and lived in Nazareth

new king was, to be found, Herod became furious. But he was still determined to get rid of the young child. He sent his soldiers to Bethlehem to kill every baby boy up to two years of age. In that way, figuring the age of the child from when the wise men had first seen the star, he felt sure that the new king would be killed, too. What a dreadful day that was for the mothers of Behtlehem! And in spite of all the crying and weeping he had caused, Herod had failed in his plan. For the very One whom he had wanted to kill was safely on the way to Egypt. There He stayed until Herod's death, perhaps a year or so.

    When Herod died, an angel again appeared to Joseph in a dream and said: "Arise and take the little child and His mother, and go into the land of Israel: for they have died who were seeking the life of the little child." Once more Joseph obeyed. He took little Jesus and Mary and went back to Israel. Perhaps he was planning to live in Judea again. But when he heard that Herod's son Archelaus was now king over Judea, he was afraid to go there. Archelaus was as cruel as his father had been, and Joseph did not feel that Jesus would be safe in that part of the country. Besides, God warned him in another dream that he should not live in Judea. So Joseph took his little family and went back to Galilee. There they settled in the town of Nazareth, where Joseph and Mary had lived so peacefully before Jesus was born. (Matthew 2:13-23)

They sought Him among friends *They returned to Jerusalem*

IN HIS FATHER'S HOUSE

Jesus grew up to be a fine young boy. Not only did He grow bigger and taller each year, His mind also grew as He learned more and more about the world around Him. He was especially interested in learning all He could about God, His Father. He listened carefully as He was taught from the Law of Moses and the prophets.

But how was it that Jesus had to learn these things? Since He was God, did He not already know everything? As God, of course, Jesus knew all things. But as a human, He had to grow and learn, just as all children do. You see, Jesus was both God and man.

There is so much that we would like to know about Jesus when He was young. But the Bible tells us of only one event that took place during His childhood.

Every spring Mary and Joseph used to go from their home in Nazareth to Jerusalem for the Passover Feast. When Jesus was twelve years old, He was allowed to go with them for the first time. How happy and excited He must have been to be able to see the holy city and to go into God's Temple!

When the Feast was over and it was time to go back home, Mary and Joseph started out with the large group of friends and relatives with whom they had come. They did not see Jesus anywhere around. But they were not worried, for they thought He was probably walking along with some of His friends. However, when they all stopped for the night, His parents began looking for Him. They asked one

And all hearing Him were astonished

She kept all these sayings in her heart

family after another, but no one had seen Jesus all day! He must still be in Jerusalem.

So early the next morning, Mary and Joseph started back, wondering if they would ever be able to find Him in that great, crowded city. When they arrived, they began searching in the streets and marketplaces. But nowhere could they find Him.

At last they thought of the Temple. Hurrying up the marble steps and across the courts, they soon came upon a group of people sitting and talking with the teachers of the Law. And there among them was Jesus! He had been listening to these learned doctors explain many things from the Old Testament. He Himself had also been asking such hard questions and giving such wise answers that everyone was amazed. How could a boy so young have such a clear understanding of the things of God?

Mary came up to Him and gently scolded Him, "Son, why did you do this to us? Your father and I have been so worried, looking for you." Jesus answered her: "Why is it that you were seeking Me? Do you not know that I must be about My Father's business?" Jesus' mother had to begin to realize that although He was her Son, He was, first of all, God's Son. She could never stand between Him and the work He came to do for His heavenly Father.

His parents did not understand what He meant. But many times after that Mary thought about what had happened that day, and kept all these sayings in her heart. (Luke 2:40-52)

Command these stones to become bread   *He set Him on the edge of the Temple*

THE TEMPTATIONS OF JESUS

The Lord Jesus was the only man on earth who never sinned. Yet Satan tried many times to tempt Him to do so. Once, when Jesus was about thirty years old, the Holy Spirit led Him into a lonely, desert place. For forty days Jesus ate no food and drank no water. He was probably praying to His heavenly Father and getting ready for His great work of preaching and healing.

When the forty days were over, Jesus was very hungry. Then Satan, the Tempter, came to Him, saying, "If you are the Son of God, command that these stones become bread." As the Son of God, Jesus knew that He could easily change the stones into the bread He wanted so much. But He also knew that He had to obey His heavenly Father. And at this time God did not want His temptation to be made easier by the use of His heavenly power. So Jesus answered the Devil with Scripture: "Not by bread alone shall man live, but by every word coming out of the mouth of God." Jesus trusted that God would keep Him alive by His word of special power, even without ordinary bread. He who had sent manna to the Israelites in the wilderness would surely take care of His own Son's needs.

Then the Devil took Jesus to Jerusalem and set Him high up on the Temple. Again he began: "If you are the Son of God, throw yourself down. It is wirtten that God will send His angels to keep you from getting hurt!" But

He shows Him all the kingdoms

The angels came and ministered unto Him

Jesus would not do this either. God would take care of Him as long as He was doing what He had been sent to do. But Jesus could not do a stunt like that and still expect the Father to protect Him! He again answered from Scripture: "It is written that you must not put God to a test."

Failing this, the Devil tried once more to tempt Jesus to sin. He took Him to a very high mountain and showed Him the glory of all the kingdoms of the world. Then he said, "All these things I will give to you if you will fall down and worship me." Jesus knew that since He was the Messiah all these kingdoms of the world would some day be His. Every knee would bow and every tongue would confess that He was Lord. But first He had to be obedient to God the Father — not Satan — and go to the cross. (Phil. 2:8-11) Jesus answered: "Go away, Satan: for it is written. 'You shall worship the Lord your God, and Him alone you shall serve.'"

Jesus had won. The Devil left Him "for a season." Then God the Father, knowing that His Son was weak and tired, sent His angels to strengthen Him. Thus Jesus was refreshed by the word of God to the Angels and not by His turning stones into bread.

No, Jesus never sinned. But because He went through all kinds of temptations Himself, He can understand from experience our many temptations and can help us to overcome them. (Matthew 4:1-11; Luke 4)

They brought all the sick to Him

He sat down and taught them

THE KINGDOM OF HEAVEN

About a year after Satan had tempted Christ in the wilderness, Jesus was preaching in Galilee, saying, "Repent! for the kingdom of Heaven has come near." Going into their synagogues, He taught and preached the Gospel of His kingdom. He also healed all who were sick or under the power of evil spirits. As news of Jesus spread, people came to Him from all over Galilee, Syria, Judea, and from beyond the Jordan River.

One spring morning Jesus sat down on the side of a mountain near Capernaum (see map). As the crowds gathered around, He preached His well known "Sermon on the Mount."

"Blessed are the poor in spirit," He began, "for theirs is the king' dom of Heaven." The One whom the wise men had worshipped as King of the Jews was now explaining what His kingdom was like. It is not a kingdom of this earth, but a kingdom of Heaven. Its members are not the strong and the proud, but rather the "poor in spirit:" that is, those who know that they are sinful in God's sight and who trust in God's goodness and mercy.

"Blessed are you," Jesus went on, "when men shall persecute you on account of Me. Rejoice, and be glad, for great is your reward in Heaven. For they persecuted the prophets of old in the same way."

How different Jesus' teaching was from that of the scribes and Pharisees! Outwardly they kept all the laws of Moses and taught the people to do so, too.

Do not make a show of doing good *They love to pray on corners*

Yet inwardly they were evil and proud. Their hearts did not have the love either for God or man that the Law demanded. Jesus told the people: "Unless you are holier than the scribes and Pharisees, you cannot enter into the kingdom of Heaven." They think, for example, that they have obeyed the commandment "You shall not kill" if they do not actually have a man's blood on their hands. But I say to you that anyone who is angry with his brother without a cause has, in his heart, already killed him.

"They have told you, 'Love your neighbor and hate your enemy.' But I say unto you, Love your enemies. Do good to those that hate you. And pray for those who persecute you. For if you love only those who love you, what reward do you have? Even the Gentiles do the same."

Jesus went on warning against the Pharisees: "When you give money to the poor, do not make a big show of it, as do the hypocrites. When they give to the poor they do so only becasue they want people to praise them, not becasue they love God or the poor. And when you pray, do not stand on the busiest street corners to do it, as the hypocrites do, so that all men may see them. Truly I say unto you, such people have already received their reward — from men. When you give to the poor or pray, do it in secret where no one can see you except your heavenly Father. And your Father, who sees in secret, will reward you." (Matthew 4:1-6:18)

Where moth and rust spoil *Where thieves break through and steal*

TREASURES IN HEAVEN

The people listened carefully to Jesus as He preached to them on the mountainside. Never had they heard anyone speak as He did!

Continuing His sermon, Jesus began to explain how much more important the things of His kingdom are than anything else on this earth. He said: "Do not store up for yourselves treasures on the earth, where moth and rust spoil, and where thieves break through and steal: but store up treasures for yourselves in Heaven, where neither moth nor rust spoil, and where thieves do not break through nor steal. For where your treasure is, there your heart will be also."

By this, the Lord Jesus meant that they should not love their riches above all else. First of all, He warned, these riches can so easily be taken from them. The moths can eat into their beautiful woolens and silks. And thieves can break into their houses and steal their gold and silver. Then they will have lost what is dearest to their hearts.

But more important, such riches will lead them away from God. If their riches are the most important things in their lives, they will have little interest in God. If their treasures are on earth, their hearts will be there, too, far from God. And gold and silver, rather than God, will be their lord. For no one is able to serve two lords. But if God and His kingdom are the most important things to them that

Look at the birds of the sky   *Look at the lilies of the field*

is, their treasures then their hearts will be with God in Heaven.

But then there are others who do not seek great wealth. They want just enough food to eat and clothes to wear. Yet if they worry too much about their needs, they are little better than those who want great riches. To them Jesus said: "Do not be anxious as to your life, what you should eat and what you should drink: nor for your body, what you should put on. If God created your body and gave you life, will He not also give you the food which that body needs? Your heavenly Father feeds the birds of the heaven, who neither plant nor reap nor gather into barns. Will He not therefore also feed you, who are worth so much more to Him than the birds? You are worried about clothes to wear. The lilies of the field do not work nor spin. Yet I say to you that not even Solomon in all his glory was clothed like one of these. If God so clothes the flowers of the field which today are and tomorrow are gone, will He not take even better care of you, O you of little faith?"

In saying this Jesus did not mean that His hearers should stop planting and reaping, building and weaving. They still had to work in order to feed and clothe themselves. But He did not want them to worry about the things they needed. "For," said Jesus, "your heavenly Father knows that you have need of all these things. Seek first the kingdom of God and His righteousness, and all these things shall be added unto you." (Matthew 6:19-34)

Behold! The Lamb of God! *We have found the Messiah*

JESUS CHOOSES HIS DISCIPLES

    John the Baptist had been sent by God to tell the people of Israel that the long-awaited Christ was coming. He warned them that they should repent of their sins, for this Messiah was coming to judge them. Just as unfruitful trees are cut down and burned, he said, so everyone who did not bring forth good fruit would be thrown into the fire of hell.

    John understood that the coming Christ would be more than a Judge. In the Old Testament days the priests offered up lambs for the sins of the people. But those lambs did not themselves take away sin. They only pointed forward to Jesus, the true Lamb of God, who would take away sin by offering Himself on the cross. Therefore, one day when John saw Jesus, he said to two of his own disciples who were standing with him, "Behold! The Lamb of God."

    These two disciples were Andrew and the John who wrote the Gospel of John. That very day, Andrew went to get his own brother Simon, and said to him, "We have found the Messiah." Simon went with him to meet Jesus. The Lord looked at this big, rough fisherman. He looked deep into his soul and saw his strength, but He also saw his weaknesses. That day Jesus changed Simon's name to "Peter," which means "Rock." Although Simon would prove many times to be as unsteady as sand, Christ, through His grace and power, would change him into Peter, a firm rock.

Nathanael said to him   *Rabbi, Thou art the Son of God!*

    The Lord gradually gathered other disciples. He did not choose them from among the leaders at Jerusalem. They were too proud to believe in this Carpenter from Nazareth. Rather, Jesus chose His followers from men such as fishermen and even tax collectors.

    Andrew had brought Simon Peter to the Lord. His friend John went and got his brother, James. Philip, whom Jesus Himself had called, went and told his friend Nathanael (or Bartholomew). At first, when Nathanael heard that Jesus was from Nazareth, he did not believe, but asked, "Can any good thing come out of Nazareth?" He knew from the prophet Micah that the Messiah was to come from Bethlehem, not Nazareth. But Nathanael went to see Jesus anyway. And when the Lord told Nathanael things about himself that only God could know, Nathanael confessed, "Rabbi, Thou art the Son of God!"

    To these six, Jesus also added six more, until finally He had twelve disciples who followed Him everywhere. Then, as He began to teach and preach, many others who had been disciples of John the Baptist left their master and began to follow the Lord. But, unlike the chief priests and elders, John did not become jealous of Jesus. God had sent him to point the way to the Christ. If men had been able to find the Lord through his preaching, then John knew that he had done his work well. He was but the morning star. When the Sun, Jesus Christ, began to come up in all His glory, then the morning star would slowly fade away. (John 1:35-51)

Go in through the narrow gate   *Every good tree brings forth good fruit*

DOERS OF THE WORD

The Lord Jesus had been talking to the crowd for a long time and the people had been listening to His words with great interest. But Jesus wanted more than good listeners. He wanted them to be doers of His words as well as hearers. So he ended this great sermon by giving them three different examples to show the difference between just being hearers of His words and doers of them.

First He said: "Enter in through the narrow gate: for wide is the gate and broad is the way that leads to death, and many are they who enter in through it: For narrow is the gate and narrow is the way that leads unto life, and few are they who find it." The broad way is the way of unbelief and disobedience. Many people are on it because it is such an easy way to go. But it leads to death — that is, to hell. So Jesus told them to choose the narrow way of faith and obedience to God. It will not he an easy way, and only a few people will be travelling on it. But it leads to life eternal.

Next He explained that it is not what they say but what they do that shows what kind of person they are. "Not everyone who says unto Me, Lord, Lord,' shall enter into the kingdom of Heaven: but he who does the will of my Father who is in Heaven. Some people will say that they are prophets; others

The house on the rock did not fall   *The house on the sand fell*

will say that they performed miracles in My name. But I will not judge them by what they say. Rather, by their fruits (their actions) they shall be judged. Men do not gather grapes from bramble bushes nor figs from thistles. Every good tree brings forth good fruit, but a bad tree brings forth bad fruit. In the day of judgment I will say to those who cried 'Lord, Lord,' but who did not do my Father's will: 'I never knew you! Go away from me!'"

Finally, Jesus said: "Everyone therefore who hears these words of Mine and does them is like a wise man who built his house on a rock. Everyone who hears these words of Mine and does not do them is like a foolish man who built his house upon the sand. The rains came, the floods rose, and the winds blew, and beat upon that house. And it fell; and great was the fall of it." In this parable Jesus calls the man wise who builds his life on the rock of obedience to God. This man hears Jesus' words and by God's grace does them. But the man who builds his life on the sands of disobedience Jesus calls a fool.

When the Lord finished speaking, the people were amazed at His teaching. For He did not teach as did their scribes, but as one having authority — as a King. (Matthew 7:13-29)

The fishermen were washing their nets   *They signaled to the partners*

THF GREAT CATCH OF FISH

Not until Jesus was thirty years old did He begin His preaching. But the people soon realized how different His teachings were from those of the scribes and Pharisees. For He spoke as One sent from God. The people, therefore, came in great numbers to hear Him.

Once, on the narrow beach of the Sea of Galilee, so many people were pushing and crowding around the Lord that He could not talk to them quietly. Nearby, some fishermen were busy washing their nets while their two boats were pulled up on the sand. Jesus asked if He could use one of their boats to sit in while He talked to the crowd. Simon and his brother Andrew at once got into their boat with the Lord and pushed off a little way from the shore. From there, Jesus could be seen and heard easily by all.

When He had finished speaking to the people, He told Simon to row out into deep water and let down the nets. Simon answered: "Master, we have worked through the whole night and have taken nothing. Nevertheless, at Thy word I will let down the net." Simon and Andrew had been fishermen all their lives. They knew that daytime was not the best time to catch fish. Besides, they had been fishing all night in this same spot without catching a thing. Yet because they had learned to love and respect the Lord — without fully realizing who He was — they rowed out and dropped the net over the side of the boat.

They filled both the ships   *I am a sinful man, O Lord*

In no time it became so full of fish that some of the strings of the net began to snap under the strain. Simon and Andrew shouted and waved to their partners on the shore to come help them. These men, James and John, the sons of Zebedee, rowed to them as fast as they could and began helping them haul the fish into the boats. They had to work carefully so that the net would not rip any more. When they finally got all the fish into the two boats, they were amazed at the number they had caught. Never had these men seen so many fish from one haul. In fact, the boats were so weighted down that it almost looked as though they would sink.

The fishermen then realized that this was no "lucky catch," but a miracle performed by Jesus. In the presence of such divine power and holiness, Peter felt how sinful he was and how weak his faith. He did not deserve to have Jesus near him. Falling down at the Lord's knees he said, "Depart from me, for I am a sinful man, O Lord."

But Jesus answered him, "Fear not, from now on you shall catch men." These four men had come to believe on the Lord some time before. But they had kept on with their regular daily work. Now Jesus was calling them to work for Him. Instead of catching fish they were to catch men — that is, they were to help bring other people to faith in Jesus.

So after they came to land and took care of their catch, they left their boats, nets, homes, and families and followed the Lord. (Luke 5:1-11)

Whatever He may say, do it   *They filled them up to the brim*

THE WEDDING FEAST AT CANA

Three days after Philip and Nathanael had begun to follow the Lord, Jesus and His disciples arrived in the village of Cana (see map). Mary, the mother of Jesus, was already there, for she had come from her home in nearby Nazareth to attend a wedding feast. Possibly, she was even helping to get things ready for the wedding party. Jesus and His friends were also invited to take part in this happy celebration.

Everyone was having a good time laughing and talking, eating and drinking. Perhaps even more people had come than the bridegroom had planned for. For before the feast was over, when the servants went to get more wine for the guests, they found that it was all gone. What could they do now? Would the bridegroom have to send everyone home early just because there was no more wine?

When Mary heard what had happened, she went to Jesus and said, "They have no wine." Exactly what she expected her Son to do, we do not know. Up to this time, Jesus had not performed any miracles. Yet Mary knew that she had a very unusual Son. Surely He could do something now to help out in this embarrassing situation!

Kindly, but firmly, Jesus let His mother know that she could no longer direct His life. He was now beginning the work which God His Father had sent Him to do. Therefore, His Father, and not Mary, was the One to whom He must

The master of the feast tasted

You have kept the good wine until now

now listen. Mary said no more to Him, but told the servants to do whatever Jesus said.

Six very large stone jars were standing off to one side. They had been full of water so that, as the guests arrived, they could dip out what they needed in order to wash their hands and feet, according to the Jewish custom. Some of this water had also been used to wash the cups and dishes, so that now the jars were far from being full.

Jesus said to the servants, "Fill the waterpots with water." The servants could not see how that would help matters at all, but they obediently filled them right up to the brim. "Now fill your pitchers from the waterpots and carry them to the master of the feast," said Jesus. Again the servants obeyed. And as they did so, they realized to their amazement that the water which they had poured into the jars had miraculously turned into deep red wine.

Neither the master nor the guests had seen where this wine had come from. But after tasting it, the master knew that it was much better than what they had been drinking. Calling the bridegroom to him, he said: "Every man, at first, sets out the good wine. And when they have drunk freely, then he sets out that which is worse. But you have kept the good wine until now."

This was the first miracle which Jesus performed. Those few who saw it had their faith in Him greatly strengthened. For who else besides God could change water into wine! (John 2:1-11)

He came to Jesus by night   *How can these things be?*

A VISIT BY NIGHT

One night, a ruler of the Jews — a Pharisee named Nicodemus came to talk with Jesus. Having seen some of the miracles which Jesus had performed, Nicodemus believed that this young Rabbi from Galilee was not just an ordinary person, but a teacher sent from God. Possibly Nicodemus feared what the other rulers would think if he went to talk with Jesus. So he waited until it was dark so he could go to Him secretly.

Nicodemus wanted to ask Jesus how he could enter the kingdom of God. Was it enough to obey the Law of Moses, as he had always tried to do, or was there something else that was necessary? Knowing what Nicodemus was thinking, the Lord answered his question before he even asked it: "Verily, verily, I say unto you, Except a man be born again, he cannot see the kingdom of God."

Nicodemus did not understand this at all. "How can a man become a baby again when he is already old?" he asked. But Jesus was not talking about that kind of birth. He meant that no one — not even a ruler of Israel — can enter the kingdom of God unless the Holy Spirit gives him a new heart, a heart which can understand and believe the things of God.

Jesus' night visitor wondered how the Holy Spirit worked in people's hearts to cause them to be born again. The Lord explained that just as the Spirit breathes wherever He wants to, so the Spirit works in whomever He wants to. No one can tell the Spirit where to go, or what to do. Furthermore, the Spirit cannot

Moses lifted up the serpent

Are you also of Galilee

be seen. We can see the changes which the Spirit makes in the lives of men, but we cannot see the Spirit Himself.

"How can these things be?" questioned Nicodemus. He still did not understand what the Lord was trying to teach him.

Jesus then went on to tell him even more wonderful things. "Even as Moses lifted up the serpent in the wilderness," He said, so must the Son of man be lifted up." Every Jew remembered how God had punished the complaining Israelites by sending poisonous snakes to bite them. But when they confessed their sin, God told Moses to make a serpent of brass and hold it up on a pole for all to see. Then anyone who was dying from a snake bite could look at that serpent of brass and be healed (Numbers 21:9). In the same way, Jesus said that He would be lifted up on the cross in order to save from eternal death all those who would look to Him, that is, believe on Him. "For God so loved the world that He gave His only begotten Son, that whosoever believes in Him should not perish, but have everlasting life."

If Nicodemus did not understand everything that Jesus said to him that night, he at least began to be a follower of the Lord. For one day after this, he tried to defend the Lord Jesus against the unfair charges of the Pharisees, asking, "Does our Law judge a man, unless it has first heard from him, and knows what he does?" But they made fun of him, saying, "Are you also of Galilee?" (John 3:1-21)

He sent elders of the Jews

They begged Him earnestly

THE ROMAN CENTURION

In the city of Capernaum there was stationed a Roman centurion, that is, an officer who was in charge of one hundred soldiers. As a rule, the Jews hated the Roman soldiers who were placed over them. But they were very fond of this officer, for he was a kind and humble man. He himself had come to love the Jews and had even built a synagogue for them.

One time, a servant of this centurion became very sick. He got worse and worse until his master, who loved him very much, feared that he might die at any moment. It was then that the centurion heard that Jesus had just arrived in Capernaum. As a Gentile, he did not feel worthy to go to the Lord himself for help. So he sent some of the Jewish elders to ask Jesus to come and heal his servant.

The Jews were glad to do this for the centurion. Not only did they ask Jesus to go, but they begged Him to do so, saying: "He deserves to have Thee come, for he loves our nation, and he built a synagogue for us." The Lord replied, "I will come and heal him."

As Jesus was drawing near to the house, the centurion sent other friends with this message: "Lord, do not trouble Thyself, for I am not worthy that Thou shouldest come under my roof. That is why I did not come to Thee myself. But just say the word and my servant shall be healed. For I also am a man placed

And I say, Go! and he goes   *They found the servant in good health*

under authority, having soldiers under me. And I say unto this one, 'Go!' and he goes; and to another, 'Come!' and he comes: and to my servant, 'Do this!' and he does it."

This Roman officer had such great trust in the power of Jesus that he believed that just as he himself gave orders to his own soldiers, so the Lord could command sickness to leave his servant, even without seeing him. Amazed at such faith in a Gentile, Jesus turned to the curious people following Him and said: "I say unto you, not even in Israel have I found such great faith. But I say unto you that many shall come from the east and west and shall sit down with Abraham and Isaac and Jacob in the kingdom of Heaven. But the children of the kingdom shall be cast out into outer darkness: there shall be weeping and gnashing of teeth."

With these words, Jesus greatly praised the centurion for his faith. But at the same time, He gave a warning to the Jews that many people from the east and the west — that is, from heathen lands — would enter the kingdom of Heaven, while many of the children of the kingdom — that is, the Jew — would be cast out.

Jesus then sent the friends back to the centurion with the message, "As you have believed, so it will be done unto you." When they arrived at the house, they found that the servant had been healed in that same hour.
(Luke 7:1-10; Matthew 8)

He was crying and cutting himself

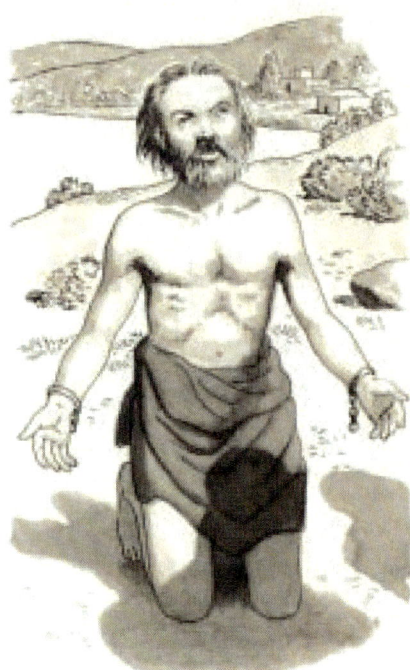
He ran and worshipped Him

PIGS INTO THE SEA

Once, after Jesus and His disciples left Capernaum by boat, they crossed over to the east side of the Sea of Galilee, to the land of the Gadarenes (see map). This was heathen country, yet even here the people had heard about Jesus.

A man who was in the power of demons lived in some tombs outside a city there. He was so wild and fierce that he tore off all the clothes and broke all the chains that men tried to keep on him. Night and day he would cry out and cut himself with sharp stones. No wonder people were afraid to go anywhere near him!

When this wild man saw Jesus getting out of the boat, he ran and fell down before Him. He wanted Jesus to help him so badly. Yet the demons who lived in him made him say things he did not really mean. When Jesus commanded the unclean spirits to come out of him, he answered, "What have I to do with Thee, Jesus, Son of the Most High God?"

Jesus asked the man, "What is your name?" He answered, "My name is Legion, for we are many." Since in the Roman army, a legion was a troop of about 6,000 soldiers, the man meant that a countless number of demons was living in him. However, although the demons were many and powerful, they knew that the Lord Jesus was more powerful than they. They begged Him not to send them out of the country, but to let them go instead into a large herd of swine (or pigs)

The herd rushed down into the sea   *They began to beg Him to go away*

that was feeding on the mountainside.

When Jesus gave them permission to do so, they immediately came out of the man and entered the pigs. Then the whole herd — about 2,000 of them — rushed wildly down the steep slope of the mountain right into the sea and were drowned! The man must have been amazed, and fearful too, to see this terrible power of the demons who just a short while before had been living in him.

The men who had been taking care of the pigs rushed off to tell what had happened. What excitement there was! Those who hurried to the spot found that it was just as the herders had said. And there was the man who had been so wild, now clothed and sitting quietly near Jesus.

But the people were not happy that the poor man had been freed from the demons. They were afraid of Jesus and asked Him to leave their country at once. They cared more for their pigs than they did for the man or for the Saviour who could help them, too.

As Jesus was about to go, the man whom He had healed begged to go with Him. But Jesus had work for him to do right where he was. "Go home to your family and friends," Jesus said to him, "and tell them how much the Lord did for you."

With a thankful heart, the man obeyed Jesus. And all who heard his story were amazed. (Mark 5:1-20; Matthew 8; Luke 8)

And seeing Him he falls at His feet   *She touched His clothes*

JAIRUS' DAUGHTER IS RAISED

After crossing back over the Sea of Galilee, Jesus found a large crowd waiting at Capernaum to welcome Him. Hardly had He gotten out of the ship when a ruler of the synagogue, named Jairus, came and fell down at His feet. "My little daughter is at the point of death," he said to Jesus. "Please come and lay Thy hands upon her so that she may be cured."

At once Jesus set out for Jairus' house. In the crowd that followed Him there was a woman who had a flow of blood for twelve years. She had spent all her money on doctors, but instead of being made better, she was now worse than ever before. This woman had heard of Jesus' miracles and was sure that He could heal her, too. But she did not dare to come right up to Jesus and ask for help. So she thought, "If I just touch His clothes, I shall be made better." She worked her way through the crowd and, coming up behind Him, touched the hem of His robe. Immediately her bleeding stopped and she was healed.

Jesus turned around and asked, "Who touched my clothes?" The disciples thought that that was a strange thing to say since so many people were crowding about Him! But Jesus kept on looking around for the one who had touched Him. Knowing now that she could not stay hidden, the woman came forward, trembling and afraid. She fell down at Jesus' feet and told Him her whole story.

Jesus knew all the time who had touched Him. But He made her come

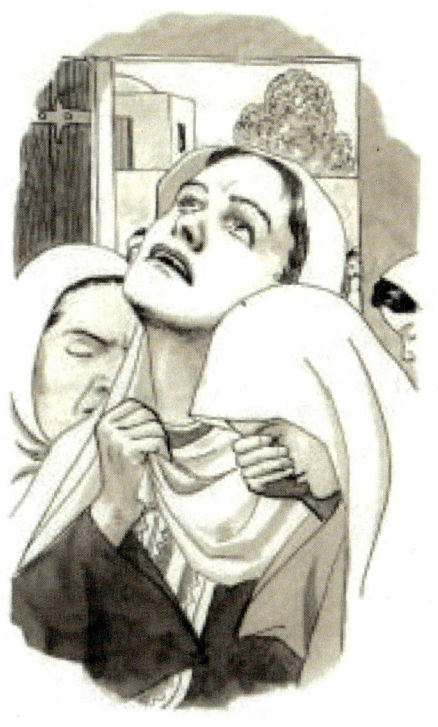
He sees much weeping and wailing

Little girl, I say unto you, Arise!

forward and tell everything because she had tried, as it were, to "steal" His power, which she thought was even in His robe. He wanted her to understand that she was healed not because of some magic in His clothes, but only because He had allowed His power to go from Him. Then He said to her gently: "Daughter, your faith has cured you; go in peace."

All this time Jairus stood by, waiting for Jesus. But before the Lord had finished talking to the woman, men came to Jairus with the sad news: "Your daughter is dead. Why do you still trouble the Master?" Jesus, however, turned to Jairus and said, "Do not be afraid. Only believe."

He then walked on with the ruler, taking just Peter, James, and John with Him. When they got to the house, they found a crowd already weeping and wailing for Jairus' daughter. Sending them all out, Jesus took the child's mother and father and His three disciples and went into the room where the child's body lay.

Then, taking the girl by the hand, He said, "Little girl, I say unto you, Arise!" To the amazement of everyone in the room, the twelve-year-old child got up and started walking! Understandingly, Jesus had the parents give the little girl something to eat. He then told them not to tell anyone what had happened. But news of this amazing miracle still spread throughout all that part of the country. (Mark 5:21-43; Matthew 9; Luke 8)

They uncovered the roof where He was   *They let down the bed*

THROUGH THE ROOF

The Lord Jesus had gone into the synagogues in all Galilee preaching and casting out demons. News of His wonderful words and works travelled fast, and many people soon came to Him.

After some time, He went back to Capernaum (see map), a city of Galilee where He had already worked many miracles. As soon as the people heard that He was back, they hurried to where He was staying. So many people crowded into the house, that there was not a bit of room left, not even around the door. This time some scribes and Pharisees were there, too. As teachers and rulers of the Jews, they had come from many cities — even from Jerusalem — to see this Jesus. They wanted to know what He was saying and doing to cause so many people to follow after Him.

While Jesus was talking to the crowd inside, four men came toward the house, carrying a thin mattress on which lay a very sick man. When they reached the door, they saw that they could not possibly push their way through the crowd. How disappointed they were! They were so sure that Jesus could heal their friend.

Then they had an idea. They carried the man on his bed up the outside stairs to the flat roof of the house. First they took away some of the tiles of the roof and then dug at the ceiling until they had made a large hole. Through this

Some of the scribes were sitting there

And he rose up immediately

opening they gently let down the bed by means of ropes right in front of Jesus.

Neither the four friends nor the man himself said anything. They waited to see what Jesus would do. Seeing their faith, Jesus said to the man, "Be of good courage, son, your sins are forgiven." The Lord could see that this poor man's soul needed healing too.

Although they did not say anything, the scribes and Pharisees thought to themselves: "How can this man talk like that? No one except God can forgive sins!"

Knowing what they were thinking, Jesus said to them: "Why do you question these things in your hearts? Which is easier, to say to the paralytic, 'Your sins have been forgiven you!' or to say, 'Arise, and take up your bed and walk'?" Which was easier? One who was only a man could not do either. But God could do both. If Jesus could heal this man with just a word, that would prove that He was God and so had the power to forgive the man's sins, too.

Jesus then told the rulers: "That you may know that the Son of man has authority on earth to forgive sins, I say unto you, (here Jesus turned to the paralytic), Arise! and take up your bed and go to your house."

The sick man got right up and, taking his bed, walked out of the house. As the surprised onlookers made way for him, they praised God and said, "Never have we seen anything like this before!" (Mark 2:1-12; Matthew 9; Luke 5)

His disciples were hungry

The Pharisees said to Him, Behold!

JESUS AND THE SABBATH

One Sabbath day, as Jesus and His disciples were walking through a grainfield, the Pharisees were watching them carefully to see if they could find fault with them. The disciples, being hungry, picked some of the grain. Rubbing it in their hands, they began to eat it. Now according to the Pharisees' rules, picking and rubbing grain, even in such a small amount, was said to be harvesting, and such work was not allowed on the Sabbath. So they went to Jesus and said: "Behold, your disciples are doing what it is not lawful to do on the Sabbath day."

The Pharisees were wrong. After all, the disciples were not harvesting, but just picking a little grain to eat on the way. But even if that could have been called working, it was needful because they were hungry. And needful work on the Sabbath is not sinful.

Jesus then tried to show them that even in the Old Testament some laws had been set aside in cases of need. For example, only the priests, He said, were allowed to eat the showbread in the tabernacle. Yet once when David and his followers were very hungry, the priest himself gave them some of the showbread to eat.

Besides, Jesus continued, the priests in the Temple work every Sabbath day. But because it is needful work, they are not breaking God's Law in doing it.

The Pharisees were very careful to keep outwardly every small part of the

Is it lawful to heal on the Sabbath?

Stretch out your hand!

Law. Yet because they did not have love and mercy in their hearts, God was not pleased with their outward obedience. Jesus told them. "If you had known what this means, 'I will have mercy and not sacrifice,' you would not have found fault with those who have done no wrong," that is, with His disciples.

On another Sabbath day, when Jesus was teaching in a synagogue, there was a man there whose right hand was withered. Still trying to see if Jesus would do something wrong, the Pharisees asked Him, "Is it lawful to heal on the Sabbath day?"

Jesus answered: "Is it lawful on the Sabbath day to do good, or to do harm, to save a life or to kill? Shall there be a man of you who shall have a sheep, and if it fall into a pit on the Sabbath, will he not lay hold on it and lift it out? How much better, then, is a man than a sheep? Wherefore, it is lawful on the Sabbath to do good." Then turning to the man He said, "Stretch out your hand!" And when he stretched it out, it became whole again.

Jesus did not want to do away with the Law of God. He was very careful to keep it in all matters. But He wanted the Pharisees to see that works of necessity and works of mercy could be done on the Sabbath without breaking the Law.

But the Pharisees could not understand this. They became so angry with Him that they had a meeting that very Sabbath day to find a way to kill Him. (Matthew 12:1-14; Mark 2- 3; Luke 6)

A woman brought a box of ointment *She began to wash His feet*

ANOINTED BY A SINFUL WOMAN

A Pharisee named Simon once invited the Lord Jesus to dinner at his house. It was the custom in Palestine in those days for the host to welcome his guest with a kiss and then to bring water to wash his dusty feet. However, when Jesus arrived for dinner, Simon neither kissed Him nor brought water for Him to wash His feet. The Lord noticed how impolite Simon was to Him, but He said nothing.

As Jesus and the other guests were having dinner, lying on their couches around the U-shaped table, a woman came into the room carrying a box of ointment. It was well known in the city that this woman had led a very sinful life. But after having heard Jesus preach, she had changed completely. She was truly sorry for her sins and felt that God had forgiven her. When she heard that Jesus was at Simon's house, she decided to go there and show Him her thankfulness and love.

The woman said nothing when she came in, but stood at Jesus' feet and began to weep. She wept so hard that the tears fell upon His feet, washing off the dust that Simon had failed to wash off with water. Then, wiping His feet with her long hair, she kissed them lovingly and anointed them with the costly ointment which she had brought along. She felt so unworthy because of her past sins that she did not dare to use the ointment upon the Lord's head. But she was happy to be able to pour it out upon His feet.

For she is a great sinner

Do you see this woman?

All this while, Simon was watching her. How could Jesus allow such a woman to touch Him in that way? Simon thought that if He were really a prophet, He would know that she was a great sinner.

The Lord knew what Simon was thinking and said to him, "Simon, I have something to say to you." The Pharisee replied, "Master, speak." "There were two men who owed money to a certain lender," Jesus began. "The one owed five hundred denaries, and the other fifty. But since neither one had anything with which to pay him back, the lender forgave them both. Which of them, then, do you say will love him most?" Simon answered, "He, I suppose, to whom he forgave the most."

"You are right," said Jesus. Then, turning to the woman, He said to Simon: "Do you see this woman? I entered into your house and you gave Me no water for My feet, but she has washed My feet with tears and wiped them with the hairs of her head. You gave me no kiss, but since I came in this woman has not stopped kissing My feet. You did not anoint My head with oil, but this woman has anointed My feet with ointment.

"Because of this I say unto you, she loves much because her sins, which are many, have been forgiven. But he to whom little has been forgiven loves little." Jesus then kindly said to the woman, "Your sins have been forgiven. Go in peace." (Luke 7:36-50)

The birds of the air came and ate it   *The sun arose and scorched it*

FOUR KINDS OF SOIL

Wherever the Lord Jesus went, the crowds followed Him. If He tried to go away to a quiet place, they soon found out where He was. The sick tried to get as near to Him as possible, hoping to be healed just by touching Him. And at times He could not even eat because of the people coming to Him.

Once, by the Sea of Galilee, such a huge crowd gathered around Jesus that He decided to get into a small boat and push out a little way from the shore. From there He could teach the people without being pushed and shoved.

His disciples must have been happy to see such great numbers coining to hear their master. But it would not always be like this. Already the scribes and Pharisees were showing their dislike for Jesus. Many more people would soon turn away from Him, too. And finally the Jews as a nation would crucify Him. Jesus told the parable of the sower so that His disciples would understand that the Gospel will not be received in the same way by everyone.

The sower went out to sow. As he was sowing, some seed fell by the side of the road, and the birds came and ate it up. Other seed dropped upon stony ground, where only a thin layer of earth covered the rock. It sprang up immediately because the earth was not deep. But when the sun came up, the grain withered away because it had no root. Still other seed fell among thorns.

The thorns grew up and choked it   *Another fell into the good ground*

As the grain grew, the thorns grew faster and choked it so that it bore no fruit. Finally, some seed fell into good ground and, growing up, it bore fruit — some thirty-fold, some sixty-fold and some a hundred-fold. Later on, when the disciples were alone with Jesus, they asked Him the meaning of the parable. He explained it in this way:

The seed is the Word of God, which is sowed by the Lord Himself and His servants. Those people who hear the Word but have no room for it in their hearts are like hard-packed paths. The Word does not even take root; Satan soon snatches it away.

Others are like the rocky ground, where there is not much earth. They immediately receive the Word with joy. But there is no depth to their faith. As soon as troubles come because of the Word, their faith dies.

Still others, like the thorny ground, receive the seed of the Word. It starts to grow in their hearts. But soon the worries, good times, and riches of this world crowd the Word and choke it out.

However, those in whom the Word grows well, without withering or being choked out, are like the good ground. There may be differences in the amount of fruit produced. Some may bear only thirty times as much, some sixty, and some even one hundred times as much. But as long as the Word does grow and produce fruit, they are called "good ground." (Mark 4:1-20).

A woman of Samaria comes

Sir, give me this water

THE SAMARITAN WOMAN

Once, while passing through Samaria, Jesus and His disciples came to Jacob's well, just outside the city of Sychar (see map). The disciples went on into the city to buy some food while their Master sat down beside the well to rest.

Soon a Samaritan woman came to the well to draw water. Since the Lord was thirsty and had no jar with which to draw water for Himself, He asked the woman, "Give me some water to drink." The woman was amazed. She could tell from the way Jesus spoke that He was a Jew. Yet because the Jews would have nothing to do with the Samaritans, she asked, "How is it that you, being a Jew, ask a drink of me, a Samaritan woman?"

The Lord replied, "If you had known who it is who asked you for a drink, you would have asked Him, and He would have given living water to you." By "living water," Jesus meant spiritual life. But the woman thought He was speaking about bubbling spring water. "Sir," she replied, "you have nothing to draw with, and the well is deep. From where, then, do you have the living water?"

Jesus then told her: "Everyone that drinks of this water will thirst again. But whoever drinks of the water which I will give him will never thirst." Again the Lord was talking about spiritual life which would satisfy the thirst of the soul. But again the woman misunderstood Him. She replied, "Sir, give me this water so that I may not thirst, nor come here to draw."

The woman left and went away

They asked Him to stay with them

Before the woman could believe in Jesus, she had to realize how sinful her life had been. So Jesus said to her, "call your husband and come back here." "I have no husband," she answered with a half-truth in order to hide her sin. But Jesus was not fooled. "You are right," He said. "You have had five husbands, and now he whom you have is not your husband." The woman was amazed that Jesus knew all about her. "Sir," she answered, "I see that you are a prophet!"

Feeling ashamed of her sin and wanting to change the subject, the woman then asked this "prophet" a question about worshipping God. By the wisdom and understanding with which Jesus answered her question, He reminded her of what the Christ was to be like. So she said, "I know that when Christ comes, He will tell us all things," Jesus replied, "I am He!"

At that moment, the disciples returned with the food they had bought. They were surprised that their Master was talking with a Samaritan woman, but they said nothing. Leaving her waterspot at the well, the woman hurried into the city to tell the people that she had found the Christ. Many of the Samaritans followed her back to the well and asked Jesus to stay with them for a while. After the Lord stayed and preached to them for two days, they said to the woman, "We no longer believe because of your saying, for we ourselves have heard, and we know that this is truly the Saviour of the world." (John 4:1-42)

A man sowing good seed in his field   *His enemy came and sowed tares*

THE PARABLE OF THE TARES

The Lord Jesus often taught the people by means of parables. A parable is an earthly story with a heavenly meaning. It is a story taken from everyday life to teach some truth about God.

When His disciples asked Him why He taught in parables, Jesus answered: "It has been given to you to know the mysteries of the kingdom of Heaven, but it is not given to them (the unbelieving crowds). Because of this, I speak to them in parables, because seeing they do not see, and hearing they do not hear, nor do they understand. But your eyes are because they see; and your ears, because they hear."

Jesus then told such a parable to the people.

A man once sowed some good seed in his field. But when it was dark and everyone was asleep, his enemy came and sowed tares, or weeds, right in among the wheat. Then he crept away.

When the wheat started to grow and bear fruit, the master's servants noticed the weeds. There was not just the usual amount, but a very great number of them.

The servants then came to the master and said: "Sir, did you not sow good seed in your field? Where then, do all these weeds come from?" The master answered, "An enemy has done this."

Sir, did you not sow good seed?   *Gather first the tares, and bind them*

Then the servants asked, "Do you want us to go and pull them up?" "No," answered the master, "for while you are pulling up the weeds, you may uproot the wheat also. Let both grow together until the harvest. Then I will tell the reapers to gather first the weeds and tie them up to be burned. But the wheat they shall put into my barn."

Later that day when the disciples were alone with Jesus, they asked Him to tell them the meaning of this parable. He explained that He, the Son of man, was the One who sowed the good seed. The field was the world, and the good seed were the sons of the kingdom (or the sons of God). The weeds were the sons of the devil, and the devil himself was the enemy who sowed them. The harvest was the end of the world, when the angels would be sent forth as reapers.

In the world there are always two kinds of people: those who believe the Gospel (the good seed) and those who do not (the weeds). God lets them live side by side, the good and the bad. It does not seem as though He is ever going to weed out the unbelievers, for they often seem to go unpunished in this life. But at the end of the world, Christ, the Judge, will send forth His angels. As the reapers gather up the weeds and throw them into the fire, so the angels will gather up the unbelievers and cast them into the fire of hell. But those who have believed in the Lord Jesus will be gathered up like the wheat and brought into Heaven, where they will shine forth as the sun. (Matthew 13:24-30, 36-43).

It is not lawful to have your brother's wife   *And the daughter came in and danced*

A BIRTHDAY PARTY

There was much talk in King Herod's court about this Jesus who was performing so many miracles. Some said, "It is Elijah." Others thought He was just another prophet. But Herod said, "John the Baptist, whom I beheaded, is risen from the dead." He had this strange idea because He was still greatly troubled by the dreadful way in which he had caused John to be killed. When news of Jesus reached him, he was sure that this miracle-worker must be John, come back from the dead.

This is how it happened that John the Baptist was beheaded.

Herod had done a very sinful thing by marrying his brother's wife, Herodias. It would have been easier and safer for John not to have said anything to the king about it. But he knew that God wanted His prophets to tell the people — even kings about their sins. So he went boldly to Herod and said, "It is not lawful for you to have your brother's wife."

Herodias hated John for this. If she could have had her way, she would have had him killed at once. Herod had him put in prison, but he would not allow him to be killed. One reason was that he was afraid of the people, for they believed that John was a prophet. Another reason was that Herod himself thought John was a holy and righteous man and even listened to him gladly.

So while John remained in the dark, lonely prison, Herodias waited for a

I desire the head of John the Baptist *He brought his head upon a platter*

chance to get rid of him. Then came Herod's birthday. He gave a great banquet to which he invited the lords and chief captains of his kingdom. While they were feasting and drinking, Salome, Herodias' daughter, came in and danced in a shameful way before all those men. But she pleased Herod and his guests so much that the king unwisely promised, "Whatever you may ask me I will give you, even unto half of my kingdom."

Salome quickly went out and said to her mother, "What shall I ask for?" Herodias was overjoyed. Here was the chance she had been waiting for! "Go," she told her daughter, "and ask for the head of John the Baptist."
The girl hurried back into the great hall and, standing before the king, said, "I desire that you give to me at once the head of John the Baptist on a platter." Not a diamond necklace or a beautiful silken gown or even a marble palace, but the head of a prophet of God!

Now the king was sorry and knew that he should never have made such a foolish promise. But he was afraid of what his guests would think if he broke his word. So he ordered one of his guards to bring John's head. The guard went to the prison and soon returned to the hall, carrying the prophet's head on a large platter. Taking her bloody reward, the girl left the banquet hall and went back to give it to her cruel mother. (Mark 6:14-29; Matthew 14; Luke 9)

Jesus made them get into a ship *It is a ghost!*

JESUS WALKS ON THE WATER

Jesus had just performed a great miracle, He had fed over five thousand people with just five loaves of bread and two fishes. And after they had all been filled, there were still twelve baskets full of bread and fish left over.

The people were so amazed at this miracle that they thought that Jesus must be the Messiah they had been waiting for. For who else could have done such a marvelous thing! They became so excited that they wanted to make Him king right away and would even use force if they had to.

Jesus, however, had not come to overthrow the Roman government and become king over Palestine. His kingdom was a heavenly one. Because He could not let the excited crowd go ahead with their plan, He first told His disciples to go by ship across the Sea of Galilee. Then He sent the crowds home.

It was getting dark now. Jesus went up into a mountain alone where He prayed many hours to His heavenly Father.

Meanwhile, a storm had come up on the lake where the disciples were rowing. They pulled and pulled on the oars, but because a strong wind was blowing against them, they were not making much progress. Towards morning Jesus came to them, walking on the rough sea. When the disciples saw Him, they became afraid and cried out, "It is a ghost!" But Jesus spoke to them, saying: "Be of good courage, it is I, do not be afraid."

Then Peter, who so often spoke or acted first even before he thought what

Peter walked upon the waters

Beginning to sink, he cried out

he was doing said: "Lord, if it be Thou, tell me to come to Thee upon the waters." And Jesus said, "Come."

Peter quickly stepped over the side of the boat, and looking toward Jesus, he, too, began to walk upon the waves. His faith in the power of his Lord held him up. But then he looked at the stormy sea around him and became afraid. His faith was shaken and he began to sink. Realizing once more his need of Jesus, he cried out, "Lord, save me!" And the Lord Jesus, always ready to forgive and help, stretched out His hand and took hold of him. You of little faith," He said to Peter, "why did you doubt?"

The moment the two of them got into the boat, the wind stopped and the sea was calm once more.

Such wondrous things were happening that night! The Lord had come to them, walking on the water. Peter, too, had been able to walk upon the waves. And now the sea was suddenly peaceful. Mark tells us that because of the hardness of their hearts they were surprised at Jesus' mighty power over the sea. Yet they should not have been surprised, for just the day before, they had seen this power multiply the bread and fish to feed more than five thousand people. And Jesus had worked other miracles before that. How slow his own disciples were to understand! But after seeing His power again that night, they worshipped Him, saying. "Truly, Thou art the Son of God." (Matthew 4:22-33)

They ran together on foot *Send them away*

FIVE LOAVES AND TWO FISHES

The Lord Jesus had sent His disciples out two by two to preach the Gospel and heal the sick. Now that they were back in Capernaum again, they had so many things to tell Jesus about what had happened on this first missionary journey. But they were tired, too, and could get no rest there in Capernaum. So many people were coming and going that they could not even find time to eat. Then Jesus said to them, "Come apart into a desert place and rest a little while."

So they all got into a boat and headed northeast across the Sea of Galilee to a lonely spot near Bethsaida Julias. However, the people saw in what direction they were rowing and, by running along the shore, were able to get there ahead of the boat. On the way they were joined by others from the cities through which they passed. When Jesus and His disciples stepped out it of the boat, instead of finding a quiet spot where they could rest, they saw a huge multitude of people waiting for them. But the Lord was not angry. His heart was filled with pity for these people, for they were as sheep without a shepherd.

He sat down upon the hillside and began to heal their sick and to teach them many things about the kingdom of God. The people listened with such interest that they did not realize how late it was getting to be. Finally His disciples came to Him saying: "It is getting late. Send them away that they

Here is a little boy

They took up twelve baskets full

may buy bread for themselves in the nearby farms and villages." The Lord, wanting His disciples to understand what a great miracle He was about to perform, said to them, "You give them something to eat." But Philip replied, "Two hundred denaries worth of loaves are not enough for each of them to have a little." Andrew then spoke up: "Here is a little boy who has five loaves and two small fishes. But what are these among so many people?" Jesus told them, "Make them sit down in companies of fifties." When everyone had sat down in groups on the soft green grass, the disciples could easily count them. There were five thousand men there, besides the women and children!

Jesus then took the five loaves and two fishes and, looking up, He gave thanks to His heavenly Father. After breaking the bread, He gave it to His disciples to pass around. As they went through the crowd handing out the bread and fish, they found to their surprise that there was always enough for the next group. And after everyone had had plenty to eat, they were still able to take up twelve baskets full of uneaten pieces. That was even more than they had started out with!

How excited the people became! Surely one who could perform such a miracle must be the Messiah! They wanted to make Him king right away. But because Jesus did not want to be the sort of earthly king they wanted, He sent them back to their homes. (Mark 6:30-46; Matthew 14; Luke 9; John 6)

Do you want to become well?   *Instantly the man was made well*

THE LAME MAN AT BETHESDA

Just outside the great wall of Jerusalem, near the Sheep Gate, there was a pool called Bethesda. Beside the pool were five porches, where many suffering people were lying. Some were lame, some were blind, some were sick. But all were lying there hoping to be made better. For at certain times, when the pool became stirred up, the first person to get into the water was healed.

One Sabbath day Jesus was walking through these porches. His heart was moved with pity to see so much suffering. Then He stopped beside a man who for thirty-eight years had not been able to walk. The man had lain there so long that he had lost all hope of ever being healed. Looking down at him, the Lord asked, "Do you want to become well?" For a moment the man's eyes brightened. But then he said, "Sir, I have no man to put me into the pool when the water has been stirred up. But while I am coming, another goes down in front of me."

Jesus then said to him, "Arise! Take up your bed and walk." At once the man was completely healed! He stood right up, picked up the mat he had been lying on, and walked joyfully away.

Some Jews soon stopped him. "It is the Sabbath," they told him. "It is not lawful for you to carry your bed." These men did not care at all that this man was now walking for the first time in thirty-eight years. Their only thought was that

It is the Sabbath *Jesus finds him in the Temple*

he was breaking one of their man-made additions to Moses' Law. The man replied, "He who made me well said to me, 'Take up your bed and walk.'" Surely, he thought, One who could perform such a miracle of healing also knew what was right for him to do. "Who is the man?" they asked him. But the man could not tell them, for he did not know Jesus' name.

Some time later, Jesus found the man in the Temple. Although He had healed his body, He had not yet spoken to him about his soul. The Lord said to him, "Behold!" You have become well. Sin no more so that a worse thing does not happen to you.

Happy to know now who it was who had healed him, the man went back and told the Jews that it was Jesus. The Jews became angry at the Lord, not only for healing a man on the Sabbath, but also for telling him to carry his mat on the Sabbath. The Lord, however, said to them, "My Father works until now, and I work." By this He meant that just as God His Father works on the Sabbath, for example, by causing the sun to shine on that day as on every other day, so He God's own Son could do His work on the Sabbath, too. This made the Jews so angry that they plotted to kill Him. For not only had He broken the Sabbath, according to them, but by calling God "His Father," He had made Himself equal with God. (John 5:1-18)

Have mercy on me, O Lord *His disciples said, Send her away*

A HEATHEN WOMAN'S FAITH

There were times when the Lord Jesus wanted to get away from the crowds and be alone with His disciples. One such time He and His disciples crossed over the northern border of Galilee and came into the land of Tyre and Sidon (see map). He had hoped no one would find Him there. But news of His wonderful works had spread even to this heathen country, and Mark tells us that "He could not be hid."

A certain woman of Canaan, whose daughter was very sick, soon learned that Jesus was there. Because the Jews usually had nothing to do with the heathen, she knew that Jesus, who was a Jew, might not even pay any attention to her. But her daughter was so sick that she decided to go to Him anyway and ask for help. So she hurried to where He was staying and, falling down at His feet, cried, "mercy on me, O Lord, Son of David, for my daughter is in the power of a devil."

Jesus did not say a single word in answer to her pleas. But she kept right on begging Him to make the evil spirit go out of her daughter. Finally, the disciples grew tired of hearing her and said to their Master, "Send her away, for she cries after us." They hoped that Jesus would heal her child just to get rid of her. But the Lord did not do what they asked because He never performed His miracles just to get rid of someone. Besides, He had come into the world to

The little dogs eat of the crumbs *Her daughter . . was made whole*

bring salvation to the Jews first, and not to the heathen. Only when the Jews made it clear by crucifying Jesus that they would not have Him, would the Gospel be preached freely to the Gentiles.

The woman, however, did not give up. Humbly worshipping Him, she pleaded, "Lord, help me." Then Jesus answered, "It is not good to take the children's bread and throw it to the dogs." That seemed like a strange thing for Him to say! But the woman understood what He meant. The children's bread was the Gospel of salvation and belonged first to the Jews. At this time, at least, it was not meant for the heathen, who were called "dogs" by the Jews.

But she did not become angry or even give up hope. Instead she replied, "True, O Lord, but even the little dogs eat of the crumbs which fall from the table of their masters." She was not asking for the great blessings which were promised to the Jews. But she hoped that as a dog is allowed to lap up the crumbs under the table, so she, a heathen, could receive just a bit of Jesus' mercy, even though it was meant for the Jews.

The Lord then answered her: "O woman, great is your faith! Be it done to you as you wish." Thankfully the women hurried home and found that her daughter had been healed. (Matthew 15:21-28; Mark 7)

And they bring to Him a deaf man   *Instantly his ears were opened*

THE DEAF HEAR AND THE BLIND SEE

The Lord Jesus performed many miracles of healing during His ministry. Never did He perform them as magic tricks just to amuse the crowds. He used them to show His own power and glory as the Son of God and to help people who were suffering. He also used them to cause people to believe in Him for the first time, or else to believe more strongly in Him.

To help people's faith, Jesus used different ways of healing. Because He knew the hearts of all men, He knew each person's own spiritual need and the way of healing which would be the most helpful for that need. In the case of the Canaanite woman, He healed her daughter without even going near her. He freed the Gerasene man from the demons with just a word. At other times He used such things as clay or mud, even though these had no healing power in themselves. Let us look at two more miracles of healing to see just how the Lord worked in different cases.

One time some people brought to Jesus a man who was not only deaf but who also spoke with great difficulty. These people asked Jesus to lay His hands upon him to heal him. However, because this man had not come to Jesus by himself, but had been brought by others, the Lord wanted to awaken hope and trust in his heart before He actually healed him.

They bring unto Him a blind man   *He was restored and saw every man*

Jesus took him away from the crowds so that they would not be disturbed. Then, since the man was deaf, Jesus spoke to him in sign language. He put His fingers into the man's ears and, wetting His finger, touched his tongue. By these actions Jesus did not heal him, but told him that He was about to make both his ears and tongue better. Then Jesus looked up to heaven and sighed, showing that the healing would come from God. Finally He said, "Be opened." At the command of the Lord, the man could immediately hear and talk.

Shortly after this, a blind man was brought to Jesus to be healed. The Lord could easily have given him his sight right away, without even touching him. But He did not. First He took him by the hand and led him out of the village, away from the crowds, as He had done with the deaf man. Then, wetting His fingers, He touched the man's eyes and said, "Do you see anything?" The man looked up and said, "I see men, for I see them as trees, walking." He was beginning to see a little, but not very clearly as yet. The dark forms of people seemed only like tree trunks to him. Jesus touched his eyes again. And this time the man could see everything plainly.

This is the only case in the Bible where Jesus healed a man in two steps instead of all at once. Exactly why He did so we cannot be sure, but, as in Jesus' other miracles of healing, it was probably more helpful for the blind man's faith to do it that way. (Mark 7:31-37: 8:22-26)

Go! Wash in the pool of Siloam

We know that this is our son

A BLIND MAN IS HEALED

On another Sabbath day, Jesus and His disciples passed a beggar who had been born blind. Bending down, Jesus spit upon the dusty ground and made a little clay which he spread upon the blind man's eyes. Then He said to him, "Go! Wash in the pool of Siloam." The beggar obeyed Jesus, and, making his way to the pool, washed the clay from his eyes. To his great amazement, he could see for the first time in his life

When he returned home, his friends and neighbors were amazed, too. Some even thought that it must be someone else who looked like him, for how could anyone who was blind now see? But the man told them that he was indeed the same person and that a man called Jesus had healed him.

Because this miracle had taken place on the Sabbath, the man was brought before the Pharisees. "How did you receive your sight?" they questioned him. The man related to them how Jesus had healed him. This started the Pharisees arguing. Some of them said, "This man (Jesus) is not of God because he does not keep the Sabbath," that is, their idea of Sabbath. But others replied, "How can a man who is a sinner do such miracles?" So they asked the man who had been blind, "What do you say about him?" Coming to understand more clearly that Jesus was not an ordinary man, he answered, "He is a prophet."

I was blind, but now I see

I believe, Lord

The Pharisees, however, would not believe any good about Jesus. Perhaps this whole miracle was a trick. Maybe the man had never even been blind. Calling in his parents, they asked them if he had been blind, and if so, how it was that he now saw. The parents, not daring to give praise to Jesus for fear of being put out of the synagogue, answered: "We know that this is our son, and that he was born blind. But how he now sees, we do not know. Ask him."

Even when it became plain that Jesus had performed a great miracle, the Pharisees still would not believe. Calling the man again, they said, "Give glory to God; we know that this man is a sinner." "I do not know if He is a sinner," the beggar answered. "One thing I do know, that I was blind but now I see."

The Pharisees kept on arguing against Jesus. But the more they spoke against the Lord, the clearer and stronger the man's faith in Him became. Finally he said bravely to the rulers: "We know that God does not hear sinners. Since the world began, it was never heard that anyone opened the eyes of one who was born blind. If this man were not from God, he could do nothing." At that, the furious Pharisees put the man out of the synagogue forever.

Jesus heard what had happened and came to him. "Do you believe on the Son of God?" He asked him. "Who is He, Lord, that I may believe on Him?" "I am He," replied Jesus. Falling down before Him, the man said, "I believe, Lord!" (John 9:1-38)

Peter and James and John   *And behold! . . . Moses and Elijah*

JESUS IS TRANSFIGURED

The Lord Jesus once asked His disciples, "Who do you say that I am?" Peter replied, "Thou art the Christ, the Son of the living God!" From then on, Jesus began to show His disciples more fully what His work would be as the Son of God. He told them that He must go to Jerusalem and suffer many things there. He would be killed and then would rise the third day. He also told them that one day He would come back in glory with His angels.

A week later, Jesus went up into a high mountain to pray, as He often did when He did not want to be disturbed. This time He took Peter, James, and John with Him.

As He was praying, He was transfigured before them. His face began to shine as the sun, and even His clothes became dazzling white. These three favorite disciples were seeing something that no man had ever seen before: some of the heavenly glory of the Son of God. Not all of it, but as much as they were able to stand and enough to prove to them again that Jesus was indeed the Christ.

Then suddenly Moses and Elijah, two great men of God who had lived hundreds of years before, came back from the dead and appeared to the disciples on the mountain! There they stood talking with the Lord about His coming death at Jerusalem.

A bright cloud overshadowed them

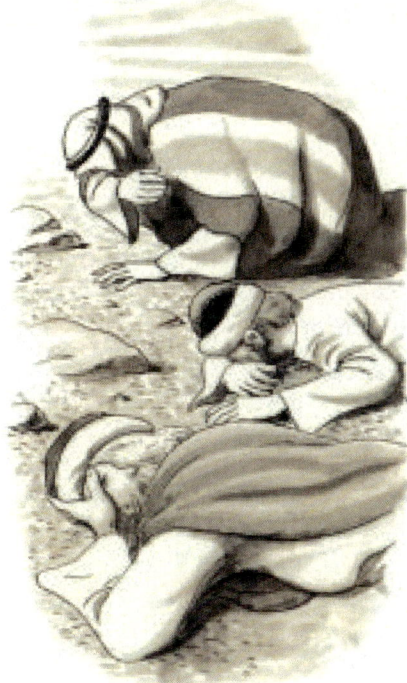
The disciples fell and were terrified

    The disciples were both amazed and afraid at what they saw. Again it was Peter who spoke up: "Lord, it is good for us to be here. If it pleases Thee, let us make here three tabernacles: one for Thee, and one for Moses, and one for Elijah." Peter meant well. But what a foolish thing for him to say! What good would it do for Jesus to stay on a mountaintop to be enjoyed by three disciples? How would He save His people if He did not go to Jerusalem to die on the cross?

    While Peter was still speaking, a bright cloud came upon Jesus, Moses, and Elijah and hid them from the disciples. Then from the cloud the voice of God the Father said: "This is My beloved Son, in whom I am well pleased: hear Him." At the sound of God's voice, Peter, James, and John fell to the ground, very much frightened. But Jesus came and touched them, saying, "Rise up, and do not be afraid." When they looked up, they saw only the Lord. Moses and Elijah had disappeared as suddenly as they had come.

    As they were coming down from the mountain, Jesus commanded them: "Tell no one what you have seen until the Son of man is risen from the dead." Jesus did not want His glory and power to be made known to the crowds at this time. For this would excite them into making Him, king. And He came not to be an earthly king, but to die for His people. (Matthew 17:19; Mark 9; Luke 9)

A priest passed by on the other side   *A Samaritan bound up his wounds*

THE GOOD SAMARITAN

The scribes were Jews who studied and explained the Law which God had given to Moses. These men often questioned Jesus to see if His teachings agreed with their explanation of the Law.

One of them once asked Jesus, "Master, what shall I do to inherit eternal life?" This scribe thought he knew the answer, but he wanted to see what Jesus would say. The Lord replied, as He so often did, with another question. "What is written in the Law?" Jesus had not come with any strange, new teaching. He was only trying to make the people understand what the Law which God had already given them really demanded.

The scribe answered, "You shall love the Lord your God with all your heart and with all your soul and with all your strength and with all your mind; and your neighbor as yourself." "You have answered right," replied Jesus. "Do this and you shall live." He who loves God and his neighbor perfectly will have eternal life. But he who thinks he can do so has not understood his own sinfulness.

The lawyer then asked Jesus, "Who is my neighbor?" The scribes had explained that their neighbors were only their fellow Jews who loved them. All the rest were enemies and could be hated. Such an explanation made it much easier to obey the Law.

Jesus then told this story to show the scribe that a neighbor is not just

He brought him to an inn

Take care of him

someone who loves us, but anyone who needs our help.

    A certain man traveling on the lonely, dangerous road from Jerusalem to Jericho was attacked by robbers. After taking all that he had, the robbers beat him and left him lying by the side of the road half dead. Soon a priest came along. He was a person who would be expected to show some pity toward the wounded man. But when the priest saw him, he passed by on the other side without giving him any help. Then a Levite came along and he, too, passed by on the other side.

    Finally another traveler drew near. He was a Samaritan, one of those people whom the Jews hated and looked down upon. Yet this Samaritan was moved with pity when he saw the helpless man lying in the road. He went to him and poured oil and wine on his wounds and bound them up as well as he could. Then, carefully helping the man onto his own donkey, he walked along beside him until they came to an inn. There the Samaritan put him to bed and took care of him. The next morning, however, he had to continue on his way. But before he left, he gave two denaries to the innkeeper, saying, "Take care of him, and if you should have to spend more than this on him, I will repay you when I come back."

    Jesus then asked the lawyer, "Who, then, of these three seems to you to have been a neighbor to him who was attacked by the thieves?" The scribe replied, "He who showed mercy to him." And Jesus said unto him, "Go! and do likewise." (Luke 10:25-37)

A friend of mine has come

Friend, lend me three loaves

ASK, AND IT SHALL BE GIVEN TO YOU

Even though Jesus was the eternal Son of God and was without any sin, He felt the need of going to His heavenly Father often in prayer. Sometimes He would even spend a whole night praying. Seeing how often and how earnestly their Lord prayed, the disciples realized how poor and weak their own prayers were. They prayed, of course, but they did not know really how to pray as Jesus did. So once after He had finished praying, one of His disciples asked Him, "Lord, teach us to pray."

Jesus then gave them again the "Lord's Prayer," which He had taught the people in the Sermon on the Mount; He did not mean that they should always pray those same words. Sometimes they should. But at other times they should use the "Lord's Prayer" as an example or model for prayers of their own.

But knowing what to pray for was not all Jesus' disciples needed to know. They did not pray as He did partly because they did not really believe that their prayers would do much good. So Jesus told them a parable to teach them that God does hear and answer those who pray earnestly for something they really need.

Suppose, He said, a friend of yours arrived at your house unexpectedly at midnight, after having traveled a long way. He was tired and hungry, but it happened that you were all out of food. So you went to another friend of yours

He will rise and give

Will he give him a serpent?

at that late hour and, knocking at his door, asked, "Friend, lend me three loaves, for a friend of mine has come from a journey unto me, and I have nothing to set before him." Even though he and his family were all in bed and the doors locked, he would get up and give you what you needed — if not for friendship's sake, then at least to get rid of you so that you would not disturb him any more. If, then, said Jesus, such a man would give you what you asked for, how much more readily will your loving God give His blessings to you if you ask Him for them! "Ask," urged Jesus, "and it shall be given to you. Seek, and you shall find. Knock, and it shall be opened unto you."

The Lord then further encouraged His disciples with another example. If a hungry boy should ask his father for a loaf of bread, surely that father will not give his son a stone instead. Or if the boy should ask his father for a fish, certainly he will not give him a snake. Or if the son should ask for an egg to eat, his father surely will not give him a dangerous scorpion instead of an egg.

Earthly fathers, said Jesus, although they are sinful, are willing to give good things to their children when they ask for them. If that is true of sinful, earthly fathers, how much more true is it of your heavenly Father! He is more than willing to give all good gifts to you, who are His children, when you ask Him. (Luke 1:1-13)

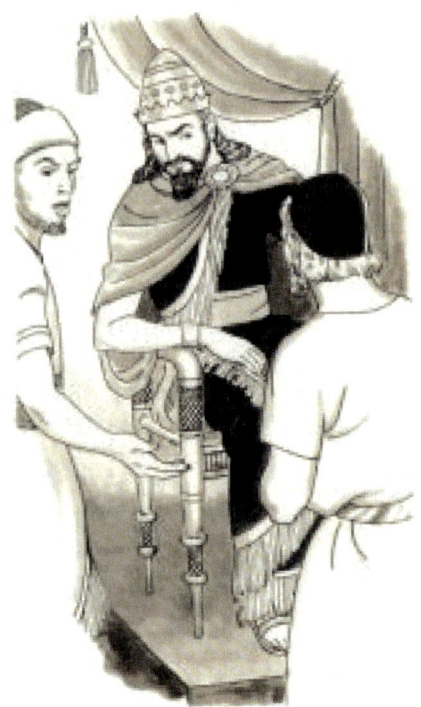 

There was brought to him one debtor   *Lord, have patience with me*

THE UNMERCIFUL SERVANT

One day Peter asked the Lord Jesus: "Lord, how often shall my brother sin against me, and I forgive him? Until seven times?" Jesus answered: "I do not say to you, 'Until seven times,' but, 'Until seventy times seven.'" In other words, our hearts should be so filled with love that we should not even keep track of the number of times that we have forgiven.

Then Jesus told His disciples a parable about forgiving. A king once began to settle his business accounts with his servants. One servant who was brought before him owed him ten thousand talents. This was such a huge amount of money that no ordinary person could ever repay it in his whole life. And what was worse, this man had no money at all with which he could even begin to repay the debt. So the king commanded that the man be sold, and also his wife and children, and everything that he had. Whatever money was received from the sale would go to the king in payment of the debt.

The servant then fell down on his knees before the king and said, "Lord, have patience with me, and I will pay you all." The king, being a kind man, felt sorry for his servant. He changed his mind and told him that he would not have to pay back the debt at all. Then he let him go.

After the servant left the king, he met a fellow servant who owed him one hundred denarii, which was only a very small amount of money. Grabbing the

He took him by the throat   *He delivered him to the tormentors*

poor fellow by the throat, he said, "Pay me what you owe me. The fellow servant fell down before him and begged, "Have patience with me, and I will pay you all." This was exactly what the first servant had asked the king, even though his debt was so large that he never would have been able to repay it. And the king had let him go free. But now when this second servant whose debt was so small, begged for a similar chance to repay, the first servant showed him no mercy. He had him thrown into prison until he should pay everything.

Some fellow servants saw what happened and, feeling sorry for the second servant, hurried to tell the king. Then the king called the first servant back to him and said: you wicked servant! I forgave you all that debt because you begged me. Shouldn't you also have pitied your fellow servant, even as I had mercy on you?" He was so angry with him that he turned him over to the tormentors until he should pay everything that he owed. That meant that for the rest of his life he would be in pain and suffering.

Jesus ended this story by saying, "Even so shall My heavenly Father do to you, unless each one of you forgives his brother from his heart." For if our heavenly Father forgives us the many great sins which we commit against Him every day, then surely we should forgive the few small sins that others commit against us. (Matthew 18:21-35)

He is a thief and a robber   *The doorkeeper opens to him*

THE GOOD SHEPHERD

There were many flocks of sheep in Palestine in the days of Jesus. Each flock had its own shepherd, who knew every one of his lambs and sheep by name. At night, the shepherd would usually bring his sheep to a sheepfold. There, behind the stone walls, the flocks of several shepherds would often be kept together, safe from wolves and robbers. Then in the morning, the shepherd would come to the door of the sheepfold and call his sheep to go out to the green pastures. They knew their shepherd's voice so well that they would come to him right away. But if a stranger tried to call them, they would not follow him, because they did not recognize his voice.

David, who had been a shepherd himself, used this picture of the shepherd and his sheep when He wrote: "The Lord is my Shepherd, I shall not want. He makes me to lie down in green pastures" (Psalm 23).

Jesus used this same picture when He said:

"He that does not enter in by the door to the sheepfold, but climbs up some other way, the same is a thief and a robber. But he that enters in by the door is the shepherd of the sheep. The door keeper opens to him, and the sheep hear his voice, and he calls his sheep by name, and leads them out. And the sheep follow him because they know his voice. But they will not follow a stranger, but will flee from him because they do not know the voice of strangers. The thief

He goes in front of them   *The hired servant runs away*

comes that he may steal and kill and destroy. I am come that they might have life, and might have it abundantly."

    Jesus told this parable because the blind man whom He had just healed was one of His sheep. The Pharisees, like thieves, had tried to steal him away by making him follow them instead of the Lord. But they had failed. Their voices were strange to him and he would not follow them.

    The Lord then went on: "I am the Good Shepherd! The Good Shepherd lays down His life for the sheep. But the hired servant, who does not own the sheep, sees the wolf coming and leaves the sheep and runs away. And the wolf catches them and scatters the sheep."

    Jesus had compared the Pharisees to thieves who climbed up over the sheepfold to steal the sheep. Now He compares them to hired servants, who took care of the sheep only for the pay they received. They did not own the sheep and therefore did not care what happened to them. When a wolf attacked the flock, they would not stay to fight off the wild animal, but would run for their lives, leaving the sheep to be killed or scattered. In such cases, those hired servants were not much better than the thieves.

    The Good Shepherd, however, was so different! He knew and loved His own sheep, and His sheep knew Him. He took good care of them and was even willing to die in order to save them. (John 10:1-18).

He sent him into his fields　　　　*His father fell on his neck*

THE PRODIGAL SON

Jesus received gladly all the sinners who came to Him. But the scribes and Pharisees complained about this, for they thought that Jesus, like themselves, should have nothing to do with sinners. So the Lord told them a story to teach them that if God is willing to forgive those who truly repent of their sins, then they should not find fault with God for His mercy. Rather, they should be happy when a sinner repents.

This is the story Jesus told:

A certain rich man had two sons. The younger one asked his father to give him his share of the inheritance. When his father had done so, the young man took all his money and went away to a far country. There he spent it freely in wild living until it was all gone. He then began to suffer hunger. But because there was a famine in the country at that time, there was little food or work to be had anywhere. At last a man gave him work taking care of his pigs. But even then he was so hungry that he wished he could eat the husks that were fed to the pigs.

The young man had thought he would find happiness by leaving his father and doing just as wanted. But because of his sins, he was now hungry, ragged, and lonely. Then he thought of home. "How many hired servants of my father," he thought, have more than enough bread, and I am dying here of hunger? I will arise and go to my father and I will say unto him, "Father, I have sinned against

And they began to be merry

His father entreated him

Heaven and before you, and I am no longer worthy to be called your son. Make me as one of your hired servants."

Truly sorry for what he had done, he made the long trip back home. While he was still some distance from his house, his father saw him and ran to meet him. He was so glad to see his son back again thin, ragged, and dirty though he was that he hugged and kissed him lovingly. Before his son could finish telling him how unworthy he was, his father had ordered the best robe, a ring, and some shoes to be put on him. He also gave orders to kill the fattened calf at once for a feast in his honor.

The elder son, meanwhile, had been working in the field. Coming back and hearing music and dancing, he called one of his servants to find out what was going on. When he learned that all this merry making was in honor of his brother who had come back, he was angry and would not even go into the house. His father, therefore, went out and begged him to come in. The elder son, instead of being happy because his brother had left his sinful life to come home, complained of the attention his father was giving him. But his father rebuked him lovingly, saying you are always with me, and all that is mine is yours. But it was right for us to make merry and rejoice, because your brother was dead, and is alive again; and was lost, and now is found. (Luke 15:11-32)

Making merry every day   *Lazarus was laid at his gate*

THE RICH MAN AND LAZARUS

It is not a sin to be rich. Some of the great saints in the Bible Abraham, Job, and David were very rich men. Yet the Bible often warns against the dangers of riches. People who have everything they want often feel that they do not need God. And sometimes they spend all their money on their own pleasures without helping the poor at all. Jesus once told a story about a rich man as a warning to all "lovers of money."

There was a certain rich man who dressed in purple and fine linen and feasted every day on the best food that money could buy. At this man's gate lay a pitiful-looking beggar named Lazarus. He was thin and ragged and his body was covered with open sores which the dogs came and licked. Not being able to walk, he lay there day after day hoping to be given a few crumbs from the rich man's table. But although the rich man saw Lazarus every time he rode through the gate, he never showed him any kindness.

At last the beggar died. And because he had believed in God, his soul was carried to Heaven by the angels and brought into the presence of Abraham, the father of all believers. His body probably received no more care then than it had while he was living.

The rich man also died. We can be sure that his body was buried in a grand and costly manner. But because he had never loved God, his soul went to hell.

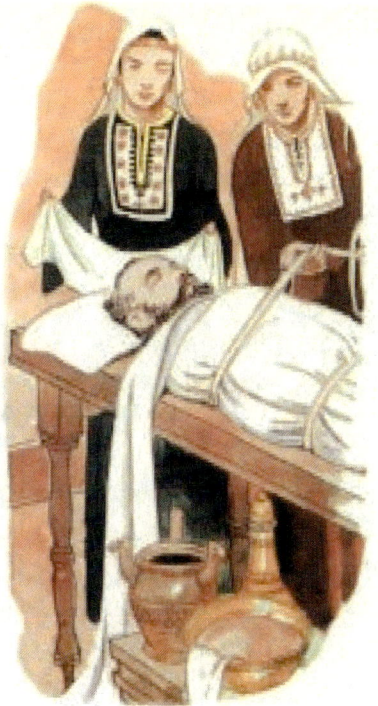

The beggar died *The rich man also died*

Suffering great pain there, he looked up and saw Abraham far away, with Lazarus close to him. Then he cried out, "Father Abraham, have mercy on me, and send Lazarus, that he may dip the tip of his finger in water and cool my tongue; for I am tormented in this flame." Souls, of course, do not have tongues or fingers and cannot be burned by fire. Nor can souls in hell talk with those in heaven. But the Lord Jesus spoke this way to make us understand what a fearful place hell is. The souls there are not asleep, but suffer torment all the time.

Abraham replied to him, "Son, remember that you received your good things in your lifetime, and Lazarus likewise his evil things. But now he is comforted and you are suffering. Besides, there is a great gulf between us so that no one can cross from one place to the other."

The man who had been rich then begged Abraham to send Lazarus to warn his five brothers so that they would not come to that place of torment, too. But Abraham replied, "They have Moses and the Prophets; let them hear them." He answered, "No, father Abraham, but if one should go to them from the dead, they will repent."

But that was not true. God's message in the Old Testament was warning enough. No miracles would change their unbelieving hearts. "If they do not hear Moses and the Prophets," replied Abraham, "they will not be persuaded even though one should rise from the dead." (Luke 16:19-31)

The Master calls you   *My brother would not have died*

LAZARUS RAISED FROM THE DEAD

Once, while the Lord Jesus was preaching in the land east of the Jordan River, Mary and Martha, two sisters who were good friends of His, sent word to Him that their brother Lazarus was very ill. Knowing that the Jews in Jerusalem had just lately tried to stone Jesus, the sisters had not asked Him to endanger His life by coming to their home in Bethany, which was just two miles from that city. Yet they hoped that He would do something for their sick brother.

The Lord, however, stayed two more days where He was. Then He told His disciples that Lazarus had died and that He was going to him.

By the time Jesus drew near to Bethany, Lazarus had been in the tomb four days. As soon as Martha heard that her Lord was coming, she left the house and went out of the village to meet Him. Full of sorrow, she said, "Lord, if Thou hadst been here, my brother would not have died. But I know even now that whatsoever Thou mayest ask of God, God will give Thee." Martha believed that Jesus could have healed her brother while he was alive. But she really did not think that He could raise him from the dead after so many days. For when Jesus said, "Your brother will rise again," Martha answered, "I know that he will rise again in the resurrection in the last day" (the day of Judgment).

"I am the Resurrection and the Life," Jesus told her. "He that believes on

Take away the stone *He who had been dead came forth*

Me, though he die, yet shall he live. Do you believe this?" In faith, Martha answered, "I have come to believe that Thou art the Christ, the Son of God, who comes into the world."

Saying this, Martha hurried home and told Mary secretly, "Master is come and calls you." As Mary slipped out of the house, the Jews who had come to comfort the sisters saw her leave. Thinking that she was going to the grave to weep, they followed her. When they came to where Jesus was waiting, Mary fell down at His feet and sobbed, "Lord, if Thou hadst been here, my brother would not have died." Seeing the great sorrow which Lazarus' death had caused, Jesus Himself was troubled. And He, too, wept.

"Where have you laid him?" He asked. They led the way to the cave where Lazarus was buried. A large stone had been rolled in front of the opening. "Take away the stone," He commanded. But Martha said, "Lord, by this time the body is rotting, for he has been dead four days." But Jesus replied, "Did I not say to you that if you would believe you would see the glory of God?" After the stone was rolled away, Jesus lifted up His eyes and gave thanks to the Father. Next He called out with a loud voice, "Lazarus, come forth!" Everyone watched and waited. Then, to their great amazement, Lazarus came forth out of the grave, still bound in the linen cloths in which he had been buried. And Jesus commanded, "Loose him and let him go." (John 11:1-44)

He sent them into his vineyard *Others standing idle in the marketplace*

THE LORD OF THE VINEYARD

A rich man, who thought that he had kept all the commandments of God, once came to the Lord Jesus and asked, "Good Master, what good thing shall I do that I may have eternal life?" Jesus, knowing the hearts of men, said: "If you desire to be perfect, go, sell what you have, and give to the poor. And come, follow me." Hearing this, the young man turned away sorrowfully. For he loved his riches too much to give them up, even for Jesus.

Seeing this, Peter, perhaps a bit proudly, said to the Lord: "Behold, we left all things and followed Thee. What then shall we have?" Jesus answered that those who had left homes and families and lands for His sake would indeed receive a great reward. But He warned Peter and the disciples not to think too much about their reward, for many who are now first shall be last; and the last shall be first." Many who think that they will receive the greatest reward in the day of Judgment will be surprised. Others who have not been able to work as hard or as long for the Lord may receive a greater reward than they.

To help His disciples understand this, Jesus told them another parable. Early one morning the owner of a certain field of grapevines (a vineyard) went out to hire some men to work for him. He made an agreement with them to pay them a denarius for the day's work. Later, at about nine o'clock, he found more workers standing around the marketplace doing nothing. To these he said, "You

Each received a denary *They grumbled against the master*

go also into the vineyard, and whatever is right I will give you." And they went. Again, at noon, at three, and even as late as five o'clock he hired more men to work in the vineyard.

At six, when it was time to stop work, the owner of the vineyard said to his steward, or overseer, "Call the workers, and pay them their wages, beginning from the last unto the first." The ones who had been hired at five o'clock stepped up and were given a denarius. A denarius, you remember, was what the owner had agreed to pay those whom he had first hired. When the first workers came to the steward, they thought they would receive more than a denarius, for they had worked longer than all the others. But they, too, were each given a denarius. Then they began to grumble against the owner and said to him:

"These last have worked one hour, and you have given them the same amount of money that you gave to us, who have worked all day." But the owner replied to one of them: "Friend, I do you no wrong. Did you not agree with me for a denarius? If I wish to give to these last ones what I give to you, isn't it my right to do what I please with what is mine?"

No worker received less than he had agreed to. But because of the goodness of the owner's heart, some received even more. In a similar way, God is free to give rewards as He wishes. (Matthew 20:1-16)

A man planted a vineyard

He let it out to husbandmen

THE WICKED FARMERS

In the Temple one day Jesus told a parable to warn the chief priests and elders against their unbelief.

A man once planted a fine vineyard and set a hedge around it to keep out robbers and animals. He also dug a hole in the ground for the winepress and built a tower from which the watchman could keep guard. Then, before going away to another country, he rented his vineyard to some farmers. As payment, these men agreed to give the landlord some of the fruit at harvest time.

When the grapes were ripe, the owner sent one of his servants to get his share of the fruit. But instead of giving him any, the farmers beat the servant and sent him back empty-handed. The landlord then sent another servant, and this one, too, they mistreated. When the owner sent a third servant, the farmers seized him and killed him. No matter how many servants the owner sent, he did not receive any fruit, because the farmers either beat or stoned or killed each one.

The master finally decided to send his own beloved son, thinking that if the farmers would not honor his servants, they would certainly respect his son. But when those wicked farmers saw the son coming, they said to each other: "This is the heir. Come, let us kill him and the inheritance will be ours." So, catching hold of him, they killed him and threw his body out of the vineyard

They beat him and sent him away empty *Come, let us kill him*

Jesus then asked, "What will the owner of the vineyard do to those wicked farmers?" Angry at the way the farmers had acted, the chief priests and elders replied, "He will come and destroy them and rent the vineyard to others who will give him the fruits at harvest time.

Then they realized that Jesus was talking about them. Isaiah had often spoken of Israel as the Lord's vineyard. Jesus meant, then, that they were the wicked farmers who should have given fruits to the Lord, love and service. Formerly God had sent His servants, the prophets, to warn them whenever they failed to do so. But they had mistreated and killed these messengers.

Now, Jesus was saying, He was the beloved Son whom God was sending because they had paid no attention to the prophets. But they were not treating Him any better. In fact, He foretold that they would kill Him, even as they had killed the prophets. As punishment, Jesus had said that God would take His kingdom away from them and give it to the Gentiles, who would bring forth fruits at the proper time.

The chief priests and scribes understood the warning perfectly. But instead of turning from their unbelief, they only became more bitter against the Lord. They would even have tried to take Him prisoner right then, but because they feared the people, they did not do so.
(Mark 12:1-12: also Matthew 21 and Luke 20)

Why do you untie the colt?   *Many spread their robes*

HOSANNA TO THE SON OF DAVID

Jesus' raising of Lazarus caused so many people to believe in Him that the chief priests and Pharisees became very worried. If they did not do something right away, everyone would follow after Him! But what should they do? After holding a meeting, they decided that He must die. They gave the order that anyone who knew where He was should tell them so that they might capture Him. Jesus, therefore, left Jerusalem with His disciples and went to a quiet town where He would be out of danger.

However, the time for the Passover Feast was drawing near. As the Jews streamed into Jerusalem from every part of the country, the one question they asked was "Will Jesus come to the feast?"

The Lord knew that to go to Jerusalem at this time would mean certain death. Yet He knew, too, that His "hour" had come. It was His Father's will that He should now die for His people. So He left His place of safety and started out for the feast at Jerusalem.

When the Lord reached the Mount of Olives, just outside the city, He sent two of His deputies into a nearby village. "When you enter the village," He told them, "you will find a young ass tied, upon which no man has ever sat. Untie it, and bring it to Me. And if any man ask you why you are doing this, say, The Lord needs it." The disciples went and, finding everything as Jesus had said, brought the colt back for their Master to ride on.

Others spread branches   *Master, rebuke your disciples*

Before His death, Jesus wanted the Jewish people to know that He was the Messiah the great King of Israel whom God had promised to send to His people. This time He would not enter Jerusalem unnoticed, followed by only a handful of disciples. He would ride in as a King, surrounded by joyous crowds.

As He started down the Mount of Olives, the crowds who had gathered around Him grew wild with excitement. Joyfully they spread their robes on the dusty road as a carpet for their King. Others cut down branches from palm trees to spread in the way or to wave before Him. Then they burst out into happy praise, singing: "Hosanna to the Son of David! Blessed is He who comes in the name of the Lord. Hosanna in the highest!"

There were some Pharisees in the crowd who did not like to hear Jesus being called the Messiah, the Son of David. "Master," they said to Him, "tell your disciples to be quiet." But Jesus answered them, "I tell you, if these are silent, the stones will cry out."

Thus the Lord Jesus rode into Jerusalem greeted on all sides as King. However, He did not come as a mighty king who would drive out the Romans; but rather, as the Prince of Peace, "meek, and riding upon an ass" (Zech. 9:9). Soon the crowds would realize that He was not the kind of earthly King they had hoped for. And within five days those who had joyfully sung "Hosanna!" would angrily shout, "Crucify Him!"

(John 11, 12; also Matthew 21, Mark 11, and Luke 19)

Give us some of your oil *No, lest there be not enough for us*

THE WISE AND FOOLISH VIRGINS

During the last few days before the Lord Jesus was crucified, He spent much time with His twelve disciples. There were still so many things He wanted to explain to them before His death.

Knowing everything that would happen, Jesus told them that He would soon be delivered up to be crucified. But He comforted them also by saying that at the end of the world He would come back again, with His angels, "on the clouds of the sky with power and great glory." Then He would sit on His throne, and all nations would be brought before Him. He would separate them one from another, as the shepherd separates the sheep from the goats. The sheep (that is, the righteous) would enter into everlasting life, but the goats (the unrighteous) would go to everlasting punishment.

Jesus told His disciples that before that time came there would be wars and rumors of wars, famines and earthquakes. Many false prophets would try to fool the people. And the Gospel of the kingdom would be preached in the whole world. These things would have to happen first. But as for the exact day and hour of His return, Jesus said: "No one knows, not even the angels of Heaven, but My Father only. Watch therefore, for you do not know in what hour your Lord comes." To help His followers understand that they must always be ready and waiting for Him, the Lord then told the parable of the wise and foolish virgins.

And they went in with him *Lord, Lord, open to us*

There were ten virgins who were to take their lamps and go out to meet a bridegroom. Five of these virgins were foolish because they had no oil with them for their lamps. The other five wisely carried an extra supply along with them. Since the bridegroom did not come right away, the virgins grew tired and fell asleep.

But suddenly, at midnight, there was a cry: "Behold, the bridegroom is coming. Go out to meet him." The virgins quickly got up and trimmed their lamps. But the five foolish ones found that their oil was almost all gone. They said to the other virgins, "Give us some of your oil, for our lamps are going out." But the wise virgins answered: "for if we do that, there may not be enough for you and us. Go rather to those who self, and buy your own."

The foolish virgins hurried away to buy some oil, and while they were gone, the bridegroom came. Those who were ready went in with him to the wedding feast, and the door was shut. Coming back and finding the door already shut, the foolish virgins called out, Lord, Lord, open to us." Then the answer came to them, " I do not know you."

"Watch, therefore," said Jesus, "for you do not know the day nor the hour in which the Son of man comes." When He does come, it will be too late to start getting ready. And those who are not ready will be shut out of Heaven. (Matthew 24-25)

A king who made a wedding feast *Paying no attention, they went away*

THE WEDDING FEAST

Jesus' life on earth was almost over. For three years He had healed and preached and taught. Multitudes had followed Him and many thought that He was a great prophet. But the leaders of the Jews the chief priests, scribes, and Pharisees had become His bitter enemies. They were jealous of Him because so many of the people were following Him. But more than that, they did not believe that He was the Son of God, as He said He was. They thought He was taking upon Himself the honor which was due to God alone.

The Lord Jesus, meanwhile, was speaking out more sharply than ever against these Jews. Here is one of the parables He used to show them how great their sin of unbelief was.

A king once gave a wedding feast for his son. He sent his servants to tell those who had been invited that it was now time for them to come. But they refused to come. Then he sent some more servants to them with the message: "have prepared my dinner; my oxen and fatlings are killed, and all things are ready. Come to the wedding feast." But the guests paid no attention to this invitation, either. They went right on with their farming, selling, or whatever they were doing. Some of them even murdered the messengers. The king became so angry at this that he sent his armies to kill these murderers and to burn their city.

Then the king told his servants: "The wedding feast is indeed ready, but

And the wedding feast was full of guests

Take him away and throw him out

those who had been invited were not worthy. Go therefore into the highways and invite everyone you find to the feast." The servants did as they were told, and the wedding was filled. When the king came in to look at the guests, he found them all dressed in the special clothes worn at weddings all, that is, except one man. The king said to him, "Friend, how did you come in here without a wedding garment?" But when the man had nothing to say for himself, the king commanded his servants to tie his hands and feet and throw him into the outer darkness.

    The Pharisees were now more bitter than ever against the Lord, for they realized that in this parable Jesus was talking about them. They were the ones, He said, who had paid no attention to God's invitation to enter the kingdom of Heaven and had even killed His messengers, the prophets. They were angry to hear Jesus say that they would be punished and that others (the Gentiles) would be invited into the Kingdom in their place. They thought that nothing could change their favored position as God's people. But how mistaken they were! No one can keep on refusing to obey God and still expect to be in the kingdom of Heaven. Even the man who had been invited in the place of the disobedient Jews was thrown out of the feast because he refused to wear the proper clothes. Those clothes were the white robes of Jesus' righteousness, given to all who ask Him for them in faith. (Matthew 22:1-14)

He was trying to see Jesus *He climbed up into a sycamore tree*

ZACCHEUS

There lived in Jericho a rich man named Zaccheus, who was one of the chief tax collectors. Although he was hated along with all the other tax collectors, he had probably gotten most of his wealth in an honest manner. However, there were probably some people from whom he had demanded more taxes, or customs, than he should have.

One day the Lord Jesus was passing through Jericho on His way to Jerusalem. As always, great numbers of people were following Him, and crowds lined both sides of the street along which He was travelling.

Zaccheus, too, wanted to see the Lord, for he had heard much about Him. He had heard of His wonderful miracles and especially of how kind and forgiving He was to sinners. Jesus was so different from all the priests and scribes and Pharisees! But as Zaccheus came up behind the people, he could not see anything because he was so very short. No matter where he tried to peek through, there was always someone taller than he in the way.

But Zaccheus would not give up. He ran on ahead to a spot where he knew Jesus would have to pass. Then, rich and important though he was, he climbed up into a sycamore tree and sat in the branches waiting for Jesus to come along. He was so eager to see Him that he did not care how foolish people would think he looked up there in the tree.

When the Lord came near, He looked up and said, "Zaccheus! Hurry. Come

Zaccheus, Hurry, Come down!   *I give half of what I owe*

down, for today I must stay in your house."

How was it possible! The Lord wanted to stay in his house! This was much more than he had dared to hope for! Zaccheus excitedly scrambled down and took Jesus with him to his beautiful home.

The people were surprised, too, that Jesus would go to the house of a tax collector. Thinking that He should have nothing to do with such people, they murmured against Him, saying, "He has gone in to stay with a sinful man!" They did not understand that Jesus had come "to seek and to save that which was lost." He was more interested in sinners than in saints, for, as He had said: "They who are well do not need a doctor, but they who are sick. I did not come to call the righteous, but sinners, to repentance."

The Lord had shown love and forgiveness toward Zaccheus and had worked a great change in his heart. Now everything would be different. No longer would he be greedy about money. He promised to give half of what he earned to the poor. And to make up for any cheating in the past, he would give back to those whom he had wronged four times as much as he had taken from them.

Jesus then said, "Salvation is come to this house today, because he also is a son of Abraham." The Lord did not mean that Zaccheus was a son of Abraham because he was a Jew, but because he now believed, for Abraham was called the father of all believers. (Luke 19:1-10)

I am not as other men are *Be merciful to me, a sinner*

TWO PRAYERS AND TWO GIFTS

Two men, said Jesus, went up into the Temple to pray. One of them was a Pharisee, that is, a Jew who was very careful to keep every part of Moses' Law outwardly, at least. The other man was a publican, that is, a Jew who collected taxes for the hated Roman government. For this and also because they usually became rich by demanding more money than they were supposed to, the publicans were greatly disliked.

The Pharisee stood in the Temple and prayed with outstretched arms, looking up to Heaven: "God, I thank Thee that I am not as other men are, robbers, unrighteous, adulterers, or even as this tax collector. I fast twice in the week and give a tenth of all that I get."

Actually, what the Pharisee had said was not a prayer at all. He did not confess his sins unto God, for he thought that he had none. According to him, all other men were sinners, but not he! He found no need to ask God for forgiveness. To the contrary, he wanted to tell God how much more he had done again, outwardly than the Law demanded. Fasting was not even required, but he fasted twice in the week. He also gave to God a tenth of everything he received, even of things which were not required by the Law. So instead of praying to God, he was praising himself.

The tax collector also stood and prayed. But he felt so sinful before God that he did not even dare to look up to Heaven, as the custom was. He bowed his

Rich men putting in their gifts

A poor widow putting in two mites

head humbly and beat his chest in sorrow, saying, "God, be merciful to me, a sinner." He realized that he had done nothing to deserve God's favor. If he was to be saved, it would be only because of God's mercy.

Each man received what he had prayed for. The Pharisee had asked God for nothing, and he got nothing. He returned home as proud as ever and still in his sins. The tax collector had asked for God's pardon, and he received it. "For," said Jesus, "everyone that sets himself up high shall be brought down low; and he that puts himself down low shall be set up high."

Another time, Jesus was watching the people bring their gifts to the Temple. Some rich men came up first and put their money into the offering boxes. Then Jesus saw a poor widow drop just two small coins into the box. Turning to those who were with Him, He said, "Truly I say unto you, that this poor widow has put in more than all of them."

The rich men had indeed given much, explained Jesus, but their giving was no hardship for them. They still had plenty of money left. The widow, on the other hand, had given everything she had. Not a penny did she have left with which to buy bread the next day! In God's sight, it was not how much they gave that counted, but how much they kept back for themselves. That is why He said that the widow's two coins were worth more than the gifts of all the rich men. (Luke 18:9-14; 21:1-4)

He overthrew the money-changers table   *And the seats of those selling doves*

A DEN OF THIEVES

On the Sunday before His crucifixion, the Lord Jesus rode into Jerusalem as King. Joyful crowds spread clothes and palm branches before Him and shouted, "Hosanna to the Son of David." After a little while, Jesus went back again to the peaceful village of Bethany to spend the night at the home of one of His friends.

On Monday morning Jesus and His disciples again went to Jerusalem. Walking up to the beautiful Temple, they entered the Court of the Gentiles. What an uproar they found in the house of God! Everywhere men were sitting at tables and benches carrying on business. Money-changers were jingling their coins and calling out that they would exchange Roman, Greek, and other money for the Jewish coins which everyone needed for the Temple tax. Others were busy selling doves and pigeons to be used for the sacrifices in the Temple. Formerly, this business had been carried on outside the Temple. But little by little the merchants had moved inside, so that the Court had become as busy and noisy as a marketplace.

When Jesus looked upon the scene, His heart was filled with a holy anger against these people who showed so little respect for God's house. He strode across the Court, turning over the tables of the money-changers and spilling their coins all over the floor. He upset the benches and began to drive out those

The people all hung on Him, listening

They began seeking how to destroy Him

who were selling doves. No one dared to stop Him from what He was doing, and no one tried to make excuses. As the merchants were picking up as much as they could and were hurrying out of the Temple, Jesus said to them, "Is it not written, "My house shall be called a house of prayer for all nations'? But you have made it a den of thieves."

When the chief priests and scribes heard what had happened, they became furious at Jesus. They were the ones who were supposed to be in charge of the Temple, but Jesus had acted as if He were in charge. By driving out the merchants, Jesus was not only taking upon Himself authority which they thought did not belong to Him, but He was even blaming them for not keeping order.

They were also angry because so many people were following after Him. During that last week of Jesus' life, crowds came to the Temple early each morning and sat there listening to His every word in great amazement. And when the children in the Temple sang, "Hosanna to the son of David," Jesus did not stop them, as the chief priests thought He should have, but received their praise.

Everything; Jesus' authority over the merchants, His wonderful teaching and healing, and His willingness to be called the Son of David, pointed to the fact that He was indeed the Messiah, the Lord of the Temple. But the chief priests and rulers were so blinded by their unbelief that they could not see in Him the Messiah. They could think only of how they might kill Him
(Matthew 21:12-16; Mark 11:15-18; Luke 19:45-46)

Strike the door posts with blood   *Lord, is it I?*

THE LAST SUPPER

Hundreds of years before Jesus was born while the Israelites were still slaves in the land of Egypt, God commanded each Israelite family to kill and eat a lamb and to sprinkle its blood on the upper door post and on the two side posts of their house. That night God went through the land killing all the first-born of the Egyptians, but "passing over" every Israelite house which had blood on the door. In fear and anger, King Pharaoh sent for Moses, even though it was the middle of the night. He commanded him to take the Israelites and get out of Egypt at once.

Every year after that, the Jews celebrated the feast of the Passover to remember how God had set them free and had saved their first-born from death because of the blood of the Passover lamb. But that lamb only pointed forward to Jesus, the true "Lamb of God who takes away the sins of the world" (John 1:29).

The night before the Lord Jesus was crucified, He and His twelve disciples came together in a large upper room in Jerusalem to celebrate this Passover feast. While they were eating, Jesus said, "Truly I say unto you that one of you will betray Me." The disciples looked up in surprise. They knew that Jesus had many enemies, especially among the scribes and Pharisees. But could one of their own trusted group be an enemy too?

Is it I, Master? *He immediately went out*

Very sorrowfully, each one asked Him, "Lord, is it I?" Jesus answered: "He who dips his hand with Me in the dish will betray Me. Truly the Son of man goes, as it has been written concerning Him, but woe unto that man through whom the Son of man is betrayed!"

Then, like the others, Judas Iscariot also asked, "Is it I, Master?" But he knew the answer very well, for the chief priests had just paid him thirty pieces of silver to betray Jesus. When Jesus answered him, "You have said," Judas quickly left the room and went out into the night to carry out his wicked plan.

The disciples had either not heard or not understood what their Master had said to Judas, for they went right on with their eating. Jesus then took some bread, and when He had given thanks, He broke it and gave it to His disciples, saying: "Take, eat; this is My body which is given for you. This do in remembrance of Me." Next He took a cup of wine and, again giving thanks, said to them: "All of you drink it, for this is My blood of the new covenant which is being poured out for many for the forgiveness of sins."

When Jesus was crucified, He offered Himself as a sacrifice for the sins of many. From that time on, Christians have celebrated the Lord's Supper instead of the Passover. By eating the bread and drinking the wine, they remember that Jesus' body and blood were given to save sinners from their sins.
(Matthew 26:17-29; Mark 14; Luke 22; John 13)

Lord, where dost Thou go? *Every one that bears fruit*

JESUS' LAST WORDS TO HIS DISCIPLES

The night before Jesus was crucified, you remember, He and His twelve disciples gathered in the upper room to celebrate the Passover Feast. After Judas had left the room, Jesus began to explain many precious things to His disciples.

He told them that in a little while He would leave them. The disciples were amazed and sorrowful. "Lord," asked Peter, "where dost Thou go?" Jesus answered, "Where I go you are not able to follow now, but you shall follow Me afterwards." He then explained that He was going back to His Father in Heaven. This should not make His disciples sad. For He was going to prepare a place in Heaven for them, so that where He was, they could go, too. Thomas said to Him, "Lord, how can we know the way?" Jesus replied, "I am the Way, the Truth, and the Life. No man comes to the Father but by Me" (John 14:6).

The disciples were still sorrowful to think that their Lord would no longer be with them. What could they do, which way could they turn without their Master? But then Jesus told them that He would not leave them alone. He and the Father would send the Comforter the Holy Spirit to be with them forever. In fact, it would be even better for them that Jesus did go away. For the Comforter being a Spirit, could be with all believers everywhere at the same time. This

He takes away every branch not bearing fruit   *He that remains in Me bears much fruit*

Comforter, said Jesus, "will teach you all things, and will bring to your memory everything that I said unto you.

Jesus also told His disciples that after His death there, would be an even closer relationship between Himself and them. "I am the true Vine," He said, "and you are the branches. As the branch is not able to bear fruit of itself unless it remains in the vine, so neither can you unless you remain in Me." There is no branch of a grapevine which can even live, let alone produce grapes, unless it is joined to the vine. The same is true of the souls of men. No one can have spiritual life, let alone produce the fruit of good works, unless he is in Christ. "He that remains in Me," said Jesus, "and I in him, he bears much fruit; for apart from Me you are not able to do anything." Jesus explained further that just as the farmer trims a fruitful branch so that it will produce even more grapes, so God purifies every true believer so that he, too, will bear more fruit. And just as the farmer cuts away and burns every unfruitful branch, so God will cast into hell all who seem to be believers, but who are really not since they do not bear fruit.

After many other words to His disciples, the Lord prayed to His Father that He would keep them in His care. Then together they left the upper room and started off for the garden of Gethsemane (John 13-17)

Sit here while I pray *Stay here and watch*

GETHSEMANE

While Jesus and his twelve disciples were eating their last Passover Feast, Judas, you remember, left the group when he realized that Jesus knew of his plan to betray Him.

After the supper, Jesus and His eleven remaining disciples walked to the garden of Gethsemane, where the Lord often went to pray. Leaving eight of them near the entrance, He took Peter, James, and John and went on farther into the garden.

Then Jesus began to be very troubled. Because He was truly God, He knew that His death was now only a few hours away. He knew, too, that besides the bodily pain of being nailed to a cross, His soul would have to bear the wrath of God against the sins of all believers. But because He was also truly man, He did not think He could bear this suffering. He told Peter, James, and John, "My soul is exceeding sorrowful, even unto death. Stay here and watch."

Going a stone's throw farther, Jesus fell down upon His face and began to pray, "My Father, if it be possible, let this cup pass from Me: nevertheless not as I will, but as Thou wilt." If there could be any other way for Jesus to save His people, He would rather do it differently. But if not, He would obey His Father's will completely and perfectly.

He Comes and finds them sleeping   *And there appeared an angel to Him*

In His great suffering, He went back to His three disciples, but found them sleeping. Waking them, He asked, "Could you not watch one hour? Watch and pray that you do not enter into temptation." Even these three favorite disciples had so little understanding of what their Master was going through that they could not keep awake to pray for Him and themselves.

Jesus turned again to His heavenly Father in prayer. He prayed in such agony that drops of blood actually rolled down onto the ground. "O My Father," He said, "if this cup cannot pass away from Me, unless I drink it, Thy will be done."

A second time Jesus went to Peter, James, and John and again He found them sleeping. The disciples did not know what to say to their Lord, for they were ashamed of themselves.

Once more Jesus left them to pray. He realized that in all His suffering He would have no comfort or help from men. Although it was His heavenly Father's will that Jesus should suffer like this for His people, His Father was the only One who could help Him in His agony. When Jesus came the third time to His disciples, He was no longer troubled and sorrowful. Calmly and willingly, He was going forth to His death in perfect obedience to His Father. "Behold! the hour has come near," He said to His disciples, "and the Son of man is betrayed into the hands of sinners." (Mark 14:32-42; Matthew 26; Luke 22)

Judas comes up with a great multitude

Simon Peter struck the servant

THE KISS OF JUDAS

On their way to Gethsemane, Jesus had told His eleven disciples, "All of you will be caused to stumble this night: for it has been written, "I will smite the shepherd, and the sheep shall be scattered abroad." Peter spoke up at once, "Even if all the rest will be caused to stumble, yet not I." His Master replied to him, "Verily I say unto you that this very night, before the cock crows twice, you will deny me three times." Peter was so sure of his faithfulness toward his Lord that he said even more positively, "if it were necessary for me to die with Thee, in no way will I deny Thee."

After Jesus had finished praying in Gethsemane, and had come for the third time to His disciples, He said, "Rise up, let us go. Behold! he who is betraying Me has come." At that very moment, Judas entered the garden, followed by a huge crowd armed with swords and sticks, and carrying torches and lanterns. The chief priests and elders had sent their own officers from the Temple guard to capture Jesus. Even some of the rulers themselves had come along to make sure that Jesus did not escape.

When Judas saw the Lord, he said, "Hail, Master," and went up and kissed Him. But his kiss was not a sign of his love for Jesus. Instead, it was the sign agreed upon ahead of time that this was the man to be taken prisoner. By this kiss, Judas, one of the twelve disciples, betrayed the Lord whose power and

Are you come out as against a thief?

And forsaking Him, they all ran away

glory he had seen daily for three years.

The soldiers then came forward and took hold of Jesus. Seeing what was happening, one of His disciples asked Him, "Lord, shall we strike with the sword?" But before His Master could answer, Peter drew his sword and struck a servant of the high priest, cutting off his ear. Ordering Peter to put his sword away, Jesus healed the servant's ear by touching it. Jesus told Peter that if He wanted help against this band of soldiers, He would call upon His heavenly Father, and He would send Him twelve legions of angels. But Jesus did not want help. He knew that the Scriptures must be fulfilled. It was the will of God His Father that He should be given over into the hands of sinners to be crucified.

But why had they come to this lonely spot by night with such an armed mob to get Him? "Are you come out as against a thief, with swords and sticks, to take Me?" Jesus asked the rulers. "was daily with you in the Temple teaching, and you did not lay hold on Me." But the rulers had not dared to take Him while He was in the Temple, for fear of the people. This was the only way they could arrest Him without causing an up roar.

As the soldiers tied Jesus and led Him back to Jerusalem, all of His disciples became frightened and ran away. Now that the shepherd was smitten, the sheep all scattered. (Mark 14:43-50; also Matthew 26, Luke 22, and John 18)

Are you the Christ?   *You also were with Jesus*

PETER DENIES HIS LORD

The Jewish rulers were so anxious to see Jesus put to death that they called a special meeting of the council in the middle of the night to question Jesus. The chief priests, elders, and scribes hurried to the high priest's palace, and the prisoner was brought in.

According to Jewish law, a man could not be punished unless at least two people agreed on what he had done. But of all the witnesses that were called in to tell lies about Jesus, no two agreed.

While all these false charges were being made against Him, Jesus did not once speak up for Himself. Finally, however, the high priest stood up and said to Him, "command you by the living God that you tell us whether you are the Christ, the Son of God." To this question, Jesus gave an answer. "I am!" He said. "And you will see the Son of man sitting at the right hand of power, and coming with the clouds of heaven."

The high priest tore his clothes in anger. This lowly prisoner before them not only dared to say that He was the kingly Messiah, but had added that He would come to judge the world! "What need do we have of any more witnesses?" he cried out. "You heard the blasphemy. How does it look to you?" The rulers all quickly agreed that He should die.

While Jesus was being questioned, Peter sat in the open court below, warming himself by a fire. After having first run away when his Master was taken

I do not know this man *And going out, he cried bitter tears*

prisoner, Peter later came back and followed Him at a distance to see what would happen. Sitting there among the servants and officers, Peter felt sure that no one would notice him. But one of the high priest's maids saw his face in the light of the fire and said, "You also were with Jesus the Nazarene."

Peter became frightened. If they found out that he was one of Jesus' disciples, they might arrest him, too! "I do not know what you are talking about," he answered roughly. Leaving the fire, he went out onto the porch and there he heard a cock crow. Another saw him and said to the men standing around, "This is one of them." But Peter denied and swore, "I do not know the man."

About an hour later, one of the high priest's servants asked, "Did I not see you in the garden with Him?" Another added, Truly you are also one of them, for your speech gives you away. More frightened than ever, Peter replied, cursing and swearing, "I do not know the man."

At that moment the cock crowed a second time and the Lord Jesus turned and looked down at His disciple. Then Peter remembered Jesus' words, "Before the cock crows twice, you will deny me three times." How weak and faithless he had been! Instead of helping his Lord in His suffering, Peter had only added to it by denying that he even knew Him. Ashamed and sorrowful, he went out and cried bitterly. (Mark 14:53-72: also Matthew 26, Luke 22)

They were accusing Him of Many things   *Are you a King?*

JESUS BEFORE PILATE

After Jesus was taken prisoner in Gethsemane, He was brought at once in the middle of the night before the Jewish rulers to be judged. As soon as He claimed to be the Son of God, they all agreed that He should die. For since they did not believe that He really was, they thought He was mocking God.

Under the Roman rule, however, the Jews were not allowed to punish anyone by death. So very early in the morning — before six o'clock they took Jesus to the Roman governor, Pilate, to have him sentence Jesus to death. But the Jews themselves would not go into the Roman palace. For according to their Law, they would become unclean by doing so and would then be unable to keep the feast days. So they left Jesus at the gate and stood in the court outside, where Pilate could talk to them from a balcony.

The Jews knew that it would not make any difference to Pilate if Jesus had broken their own Jewish Law. Therefore, they first tried to prove that He had plotted against the Roman government. They charged that He had forbidden people to pay taxes to the emperor (which was a lie) and that He claimed to be a king.

Pilate took Jesus inside and asked Him, "Are you a king?" The Lord answered that He was indeed, but not the kind Pilate was thinking about. His kingdom was not of this world. Otherwise, His servants would have fought for Him.

Herod rejoiced greatly

His wife sent a message

The governor went out again and said to the growing crowd, "do not find any fault at all in Him." The chief priests then angrily began to accuse Jesus of stirring up the whole country from Galilee to Judea. When Pilate heard that Jesus was from Galilee, he had an idea. Herod, the ruler over that province, happened to be in Jerusalem for the feast days. Pilate would send this Prisoner to him and get rid of this troublesome case!

Herod was very glad to have Jesus sent to him. For a long time he had wanted to see some of His miracles. But Jesus neither performed any miracles for Herod's pleasure nor answered any of the charges brought against Him. So back again He went to Pilate.

Now the governor did not know what to do! Neither he nor Herod had found Jesus worthy of death. He should have set Jesus free. But he feared what the excited Jewish rulers would do. Finally he thought of another plan. During the Passover, he usually set one prisoner free. This time he would let the people themselves choose between Jesus and another man named Barabbas. Pilate was sure that they would choose to free this kind Rabbi rather than Barabbas, who was a murderer and a thief! Appearing again before the crowd, Pilate asked, "Whom do you want me to release unto you? Barabbas or Jesus, who is called Christ?" At that moment a message came to him from his wife. In it, she warned him not to have anything to do with that just Man, Jesus, because she had a frightening dream about Him that night. (John 18-19; Matthew 27; Mark 15)
(Continued)

Release unto us Barabbas!   *He washed his hands*

SENTENCED TO DEATH

While Pilate was reading the message from his wife and wondering what to do, the Jewish rulers were stirring up the crowd to have Barabbas freed and Jesus crucified. So when Pilate again asked them which prisoner they wanted freed, they shouted, "Away with this man! And release unto us Barabbas." Pilate was amazed. "What, then," he asked, "do you want me to do with Jesus?" "Crucify him! Crucify him!" they shouted. "Why?" asked Pilate. "What evil did He do?" But the angry mob only shouted louder, "Crucify him!"

When the governor saw how useless it was to try to talk to the wild crowd, he called for a basin of water. Then, washing his hands before the people, he said, "I am innocent of the blood of this just man." But they only yelled back, "His blood be on us, and on our children."

Even though Pilate now thought that he was no longer to blame because he had washed his hands of the whole case, he was still troubled. He did not want to crucify a man who had done no wrong. Yet the mob was yelling for blood. Perhaps if he had Jesus whipped before their eyes, they would be satisfied and he could still release Him. So, on Pilate's orders, the Roman soldiers took off Jesus' robe and began to lash the Lord again and again with a short-handled whip. The metal pieces on the ends of the leather cords bit into His back, causing the blood to stream forth.

Pilate took Jesus and whipped Him *Hail, King of the Jews!*

Then, taking Him back inside the palace, the soldiers began to make fun of this "King." They made a crown of thorns and pressed it on His head. They threw a robe of royal purple over His bleeding back and put a reed in His hand for a scepter. Kneeling before Him, they jokingly said, "Hail, King of the Jews!" Then they spit upon Him and hit Him on the head.

Still wearing the purple robe and the crown of thorns, Jesus was again led out before the angry mob. "Behold!" said Pilate. "I bring Him out to you so that you may know that I do not find any fault in Him." The Jews shouted back, "We have a law, and according to our law, he ought to die, because he made himself the Son of God." Hearing that Jesus claimed to be the Son of God, Pilate became afraid and wanted even more to let Him go. But the clever Jews cried out, "If you let this man go, you are not Caesar's friend. Everyone who makes himself a king speaks against Caesar." These words also frightened Pilate. If the Jews reported to the emperor that he had released a man who claimed to be king, he could be called back to Rome and even killed!

The Jews had won. Pilate had declared again and again that he found no fault in Jesus. Yet when his own position and life were in danger, he was too weak to do what was right. He gave in to the angry, excited mob and ordered Jesus to be crucified. (John 18-19; also Matthew 27, Mark 15 and Luke 23)

Forced a certain one to carry   *His cross where they crucified Him*

JESUS IS CRUCIFIED

After Pilate had ordered Jesus to be crucified, the purple robe was taken off Him and His own clothes were put back on. A guard of four soldiers, commanded by a centurion, then led Him out of Jerusalem, followed by a great crowd of people. For a while Jesus bore His own heavy wooden cross on His bleeding back. But then the soldiers saw that He was growing too weak to carry it any farther. So they ordered a man named Simon of Cyrene who was just going into Jerusalem to carry the cross the rest of the way.

Around nine o'clock in the morning they arrived at a hill called Golgotha, or Calvary, where Jesus was to be crucified. The soldiers offered Him some wine mixed with myrrh to lessen the pain. But when Jesus tasted what it was, He would not drink any more, for He wanted to bear the full suffering of the cross with a clear mind.

The Roman soldiers took off Jesus' clothes again and, driving heavy spikes through His hands and feet, they crucified Him. Two robbbers were also crucified at the same time, one on each side of Jesus. There hung the holy Son of God on the shameful cross, between two thieves! Yet even then the Lord could pray for His enemies, "Father, forgive them, for they do not know what they do."

Pilate had commanded that above Jesus' cross the words "Jesus the Naaarean, the King of the Jews" should be written in Hebrew,

Come down from the cross!

They threw dice for them

Latin, and Greek. Not at all pleased with this sign, the chief priests went back to Pilate and asked him to change it. After all, they thought, this pitiful, suffering Prisoner was not their king! But Pilate refused to change it.

After the soldiers had crucified Jesus, they took His clothing and divided it into four parts, one for each soldier. Only His robe was left over and, not wishing to tear it, they drew dice for it. Thus they fulfilled what David had foretold would happen to the Christ when he said, "They parted My clothes among them, and for My robe they threw dice" (Ps. 22:18).

As the Lord hung there in pain and disgrace, the rulers of the Jews and even the passersby made fun of Him. "If you are the Son of God," they mocked, "come down from the cross." Others said, "He is the King of Israel; let him now come down from the cross, and we will believe on him." Jesus could easily have stepped down and destroyed every one of these mockers with just a word. It was not the nails which held Him there, but His love for the sinners for whom He was dying.

Even one of the robbers at His side mocked Him saying, "If you are the Christ, save yourself and us." But the other thief was coming to realize that this Jesus was indeed the King He had claimed to be. He said to Jesus, "Remember me, Lord, when Thou dost come in Thy kingdom." Seeing the robber's faith, Jesus replied, "Today you shall be with Me in Paradise." (John 19) (Continued)

He begged the body of Jesus   *Joseph laid it in his new tomb*

THE BURIAL OF JESUS

The Lord Jesus was dead. He had been nailed to the cross. For three hours He had suffered dreadful pain in His body. But He had suffered much more in His soul. God's anger against the sins of all believers was poured out upon Him during those three dark hours. At three o'clock He died.

What, now, was to become of His body? At six o'clock the Sabbath would begin. According to Jewish law, no dead body could be left on the cross overnight, and especially not over the Sabbath. The bodies of the two robbers who had been crucified with Him would probably be thrown into a common grave. But would the body of the Lord Jesus be treated in the same shameful way?

Not at all. It was given loving care by a rich man from Arimathea called Joseph. He was one of the rulers of the Jews and belonged to the council that had asked for Jesus' death. But Joseph had not agreed to their sinful demand. He really believed that Jesus was the Christ, yet because he was afraid of the Jews, he had not come out openly as one of Jesus' disciples.

Now, however, God made Joseph brave. He was no longer afraid of what the other members of the council would say or do. Going boldly to Pilate, the Roman governor, he got permission to take Jesus' body away. Then, with the help of Nicodemus (another ruler of the Jews who secretly believed in Jesus, too), Joseph wrapped the body in a new linen cloth.

They gathered together unto Pilate *They made the grave secure*

In a garden near the place where Jesus had been crucified, Joseph's own tomb had been cut out of the rock. There the two men carefully laid the body of their Lord. Then they rolled a heavy stone in front of the door of the tomb. While they were working; two of the women who loved Jesus were sitting in the garden watching.

The chief priests and Pharisees had gotten their wish. Jesus was out of the way! But on the next day, which was the Sabbath, they remembered something that worried them. They came to Pilate and said: Sir, we remember that that deceiver said while He was still living, "After three days I will arise." Command, therefore, that the grave be made secure until the third day. Perhaps His disciples will come by night to steal Him away and then will say to the people, "He is risen from the dead."

Pilate answered them, "Take a guard yourselves and go make the grave as secure as you know how."

So even though it was the Sabbath, the Jews took some soldiers to the garden. They put a seal on the stone so that no one could break into the tomb. Then they left the guard to watch over the grave. They were sure, now, that this "deceiver" would not trouble them again. He was dead and buried, and no one could steal His body away and then say that He had risen from the dead.
(Matthew 27:57-66: also Mark 15, Luke 23, and John 19)

Woman, behold your son! *Truly this Man was the Son of God*

THE DEATH OF THE SON OF GOD

Standing near the cross of Jesus there was also a group of women who looked on in great sorrow. One of them was Mary, His mother, with the disciple John beside her. Joseph, Mary's husband, was probably dead by this time. And Jesus' brothers had not yet come to believe in Him. Who, then, could take better care of His mother than John? Through His suffering, Jesus looked down at Mary and said, "Woman, behold your son!" And to His disciple He said, "Behold your mother!" John understood, and from that day he took Mary into his own home.

For three hours, the Lord had been on the cross. Then a strange thing happened. At twelve o'clock, when the sun should have been the brightest, darkness fell over the whole land. The mockers grew quiet and wondered. Jesus was now suffering a deeper kind of pain than that of the whip and the nails. God the Father, who had always been so close to His Son, now left Him. All, all alone, Jesus had to bear the Father's terrible anger against sin. He hung there on the cross between Heaven and earth, rejected by God and men. For three hours the darkness lasted. For three hours Jesus suffered hell to the fullest so that those who trusted in Him would never have to go there. Toward the end, He cried out in agony, "My God, My God, why hast Thou forsaken Me?"

Then He said, "I thirst." One of the soldiers dipped a sponge into some vinegar and, putting it on a stick, he reached it up to Jesus' dry lips.

Asked Pilate that their legs might be broken   *One of the soldiers pierced His side*

The Lord then cried out, "It is finished." His work of saving sinners through His whole life of suffering and now His bitter death was over. After saying, "Father, into Thy hands I commit my spirit," Jesus willingly died.

At the death of Christ, the world shuddered. The veil in the Temple was ripped from top to bottom. The earth shook, the rocks were split, and tombs were opened. The great crowd still standing near the cross was overcome with fear and wonder. And the centurion in charge of the crucifixion cried out, "Truly this Man was the Son of God."

Meanwhile, some of the Jews had gone again to Pilate. According to their Law, no dead body was to be left hanging on the cross overnight, and especially not over the Sabbath. If Pilate would allow the legs of these three men to be broken, they would die more quickly. Then the bodies could be taken down before sunset. Pilate this time gave his permission.

The soldiers, therefore, broke the legs of the two thieves. But when they came to Jesus and found that He was already dead, they did not break His. However, just to be absolutely sure that He was dead, one of them pierced His side with a spear.

It was all over. But instead of being a victory for the Jews, it was a victory for Jesus. By purposely dying on the cross, He had finished the work He had come to do. (John 19)

They found the stone rolled away *They bowed down their faces*

JESUS IS RISEN!

While Joseph of Arimathea and Nicodemus were carefully laying the body of their crucified Lord in the tomb, two women, you remember, sat in the garden watching. It was a loving, but hurried, burial, for at six o'clock the Sabbath would begin, and then no more work could be done.

What a long and sorrowful Sabbath that was! The Shepherd was dead and buried, and His sheep did not know which way to turn. Mary Magdalene and some other women, however, wanted to perform one last act of love for their Master. As soon as the Sabbath was over at six o'clock Saturday evening they prepared some spices. Early the next morning, they would go to the tomb and anoint the Lord's body better than the two men had time to do.

These women did not know that the chief priests had sealed the tomb and had left a guard there so that no one could break into it. If they had, they might not have gone back. But as they hurried along the dark streets early Sunday morning, they did wonder who would roll away the heavy stone for them.

When the women arrived, they saw to their great surprise that the stone was already rolled away and the tomb was open. They went in and looked around. The Lord's body was gone! What could this mean? Had someone come in the night and stolen it away?

Just then, they noticed two bright, shining angels. Frightened by these

They told all these things

The two were running together

heavenly messengers, the women bowed down to the ground before them. Then one of the angels spoke to them: Why do you look for the living among the dead? He is not here, but is risen. Remember how He spoke to you while He was yet in Galilee, saying, "It is necessary for the Son of man to be crucified and to rise again the third day."

Suddenly those words of Jesus came back to them. In their sorrow at His death they had forgotten all about them. But now they remembered. Then the angel went on: "Go quickly and tell His disciples, 'He is risen from the dead; and lo, He goes before you into Galilee. There you shall see Him." The women waited no longer. With fear and great joy, they left the tomb and hurried back to the city with their good news.

While Jesus was still with His disciples, He had told them many times that He would be crucified and would rise the third day. Yet when the women came to them and began to talk about an empty tomb, angels, and a risen Lord, the disciples did not believe them.

Peter and John, however, decided to go see for themselves. Together they ran to the tomb. John, being the younger, got there ahead of Peter and looked in. But he did not dare go into the tomb until Peter, who was bolder, arrived and went in first. There they saw the linen cloths that had been wrapped about Jesus' body. But the Lord Himself was gone! Could He indeed be risen, as the angel had said? (Luke 24:1-12; also Matthew 28, Mary 16, and John 20)

They were talking with one another

Have you not known?

ON THE WAY TO EMMAUS

In the afternoon of that first Easter Sunday, two of Jesus' followers started out from Jerusalem to go to the village of Emmaus, about seven miles away. They had much to talk about as they walked along the dusty road. Such sad and strange things had been happening the last few days. What could they all mean? There was so much they did not understand.

As they were going along discussing with each other, a Stranger came up and started walking with them. It was their risen Lord, but God caused them not to recognize Him. Jesus asked them what it was they had just been talking about that made them so sad. They turned to Him and asked, "Don't you know the things that have been happening in Jerusalem these last days?" The Lord replied, "What things?" They answered: "The things concerning Jesus the Nazarean, who was a prophet. Our leaders turned Him over to be crucified. But we had hoped that He would be the Saviour of Israel. Three days have passed since then. And now some women who went to the tomb this morning found it empty. They claim that angels told them that He is alive. Some of the disciples went and found everything as the women had said, but they did not see Jesus."

Then the Lord said to the two men: "fools, and slow of heart to believe all that the prophets have spoken! Was it not necessary for the Christ to have suffered these things, and to enter into His glory?" He did not scold them

Their eyes were opened and they knew Him   *They went back to Jerusalem*

for not having believed the women report or even for not having believed what He Himself had told them before He died. But they should have understood these things from the Old Testament. Starting with Moses and going through the prophets, Jesus explained how the Christ's suffering and death had all been foretold. The chief priests and rulers had not ruined His plans by crucifying Him. Rather, they had helped to fulfill His plans. For it was only through His death that He would save His people and become the mighty King who would rule forever and ever.

When they reached Emmaus, the two men begged the Stranger to spend the night with them. It was getting too late for Him to go on. And besides, they wanted to hear more of what He had to say. The Lord agreed and went into the house with them.

When they were all sitting around the supper table, Jesus took the bread and, after giving thanks, He broke it and gave it to them just as He used to do. At that very moment their eyes were opened and they recognized their Lord. At once He disappeared from their sight. How foolish of them, they thought, not to have recognized Him before! Who else could have taught them as He had done on the way?

It was already getting dark. But the disciples were so filled with joy that they hurried all the way back to Jerusalem that same evening to tell the others that they had seen Jesus! (Luke 24:13-35)

Why are you troubled? *My Lord and my God!*

JESUS APPEARS TO HIS DISCIPLES

The evening of that first Easter Sunday, the disciples met together, but behind locked doors for fear of the Jews. Suddenly, Jesus stood before their very eyes! He had come into the room right through the closed doors. At first the disciples were frightened, thinking that He was a ghost. But the Lord said, "Why are you troubled? Behold My hands and My feet, that I am He!" Then they realized that it was indeed their risen Lord!

Thomas, however, one of the disciples, had not been with the group that night. When the others told him that they had seen the Lord, he would not believe. He wanted more proof than just the words of the disciples. "Unless I see in His hands the mark of the nails," he said, "and put my finger into the mark of the nails, and put my hand into His side, I will not at all believe."

The next Sunday night, when the disciples were again gathered together, the Lord came to them a second time through closed doors. This time Thomas, too, was there. Tenderly rebuking His disciple, Jesus told him to put his finger into the nail prints and his hand into His side so that he would believe. Thomas had been stubborn and proud before, but now he confessed with his whole heart, "My Lord and my God!" The Lord answered, "Have you believed because you have seen Me, Thomas? Happy are they who have not seen, and have believed."

It is the Lord   *Thou knowest that I Love thee*

    Some time after this, by the sea of Galilee, Peter said to the six others who were with him, "I am going fishing." The others answered, "We will go with you, too." All night long they fished, but caught nothing. As it was beginning to get light, they saw a Stranger on the shore. He asked them if they had caught anything. "No," they replied. Then He said, "Throw the net to the right side of the ship." They did so, and soon the net was so full that they could hardly pull it up. John knew at once that only Jesus could have caused such a miracle. "It is the Lord!" he said excitedly. Eager Peter, always the first to act, jumped into the water and made his way to the shore, while the rest followed in the boat, dragging the net.

    Jesus had a fire going, and bread and fish ready for them to eat. After they had eaten breakfast, He turned to Peter and asked, "Simon, do you love Me more than these (other disciples do)?" Before Peter had denied his Lord, he had been so sure that he loved Jesus more than the others did. But now remembering how weak he had been, he humbly answered, "Yea, Lord, Thou knowest that I love Thee." Three times Peter had denied Jesus. So now the Lord asked him the same question three times. Each time Peter confessed that he loved Him. Then Jesus told him that he could again take his place alongside the other disciples for the work of caring for the flock of believers. (John 20-21 also Luke 24)

He showed Himself alive to them   *As they were watching. He was taken up*

JESUS GOES BACK TO HEAVEN

After that happy Easter morning when Jesus rose again from the dead, He did not stay with His disciples all the time, as He had done before. For forty days He showed Himself at different times to different people. He appeared on Easter morning to Mary Magdalene. Later that day He walked along with the two men who were going to Emmaus. Twice He came into the locked room where His disciples were gathered. And He even appeared to five hundred of his followers at once. Where He was in between these times the disciples did not know. But they did know that He was alive again.

After all that He had told them during the three years of His ministry, there was still so much that they did not understand. So during these forty days after His resurrection He explained to them why He had to suffer and die, why He rose again, and why He would soon have to leave them. He showed them from the books of Moses, the prophets, and the Psalms that God had told His people long ago that these things would happen.

However, the disciples still did not know what they were to do now that their Master would no longer be with them. Jesus commanded them first of all not to leave Jerusalem until they were baptized with the Holy Spirit. The Holy Spirit would be poured out upon them and would give them the power to do their work. Then Jesus told them what that work would be. "You shall be my witnesses,"

Why do you stand looking up?

Then they returned to Jerusalem

He said, both in Jerusalem, and in all Judea and Samaria, and unto the uttermost part of the earth" (Acts 1:8). Jesus wanted them to preach everywhere that He was the Son of God and that sins could be forgiven only by faith in Him. They were to start in Jerusalem, then go throughout the rest of Palestine, and from there unto all the world. But first they had to wait for the Holy Spirit.

The last time that Jesus was with His disciples was on the Mount of Olives, not far from Jerusalem. When He finished speaking to them, He lifted His hands to bless them. Then a very strange and wonderful thing happened. As they were looking at Him, He was carried right up into Heaven. They watched until a cloud hid Him and they could see Him no more. Then suddenly two angels dressed in white stood beside them. They told the disciples about something even more wonderful than what they had just seen. "This Jesus," they said, will come again some day on the clouds, just as you have seen Him go.

But for now Jesus was gone away from them. Yet the disciples were not sad, as they had been after He was crucified, for they knew that He was no longer in the tomb. He had gone to Heaven to be with His Father. And He had promised that the Spirit would come upon them. So they went back to Jerusalem joyfully to wait for the Holy Spirit. (Acts 1:1-14: Luke 24:44-53)

And forked tongues, like fire appeared

They were all together in one place

THE HOLY SPIRIT IS POURED OUT

The disciples did not have to wait long for the Holy Spirit to come upon them. Just ten days after Jesus ascended into Heaven, His disciples came together to celebrate the Jewish feast of Pentecost. Suddenly the whole house was filled with a noise like that of a strong wind blowing. Then, what looked like tongues of fire appeared on the heads of them all. At that very moment the disciples were filled with the Holy Spirit. No one can see the Spirit. But on the day of Pentecost, God used the signs of wind and fire to show the disciples that He was pouring out the Holy Spirit upon them.

At once they started talking in different languages. These men were simple Galileans and had probably never known any of these languages before. But now the Lord was working this miracle in them by means of His Holy Spirit. And as with all of His miracles, He was doing it for a special reason.

Jews from many different countries were in Jerusalem at that time to celebrate the feast of Pentecost. When they heard what was going on, a great crowd of them gathered around the disciples. Imagine how surprised they were to hear these Galileans talking in different languages. Each of these Jews heard in his own language about the wonderful works of God. They could not understand how such a thing could happen. But instead of praising God, some of them

But others made fun of them   *But Peter lifted up his voice and spoke*

made fun of the disciples and said they were drunk.

Jesus had told His disciples that they were to start telling others about Him in Jerusalem (Acts 1:8). Just ten days later they were given this wonderful chance to do that very thing. Peter stood up with the eleven and started to preach. What a change the Holy Spirit had made in Peter! Just two months before, when Jesus was taken prisoner, he had been afraid to tell a servant girl at the high priest's palace that he knew Jesus. And now he was preaching boldly to a great multitude.

First he explained to his listeners that the disciples were not drunk. The prophet Joel had foretold many years before that this would happen when God would pour out His Spirit. Peter then went on to tell them about Jesus. He explained how David had sung in the Psalms that God's Son who was Jesus of Nazareth could not stay in the tomb. He would ascend into Heaven and sit at God's right hand. Wicked men, Peter went on, had tried to get rid of Jesus, but God had other plans. He "made Him both Lord and Christ, this Jesus whom you crucified."

As those Jews listened to Peter, the Holy Spirit was working in their hearts. When he finished preaching, they said, "Brethren. what shall we do?" Peter told them that if they would truly repent of their sins and be baptized in the name of Jesus Christ, they would be forgiven. That day about three thousand people believed. (Acts 2:1-41)

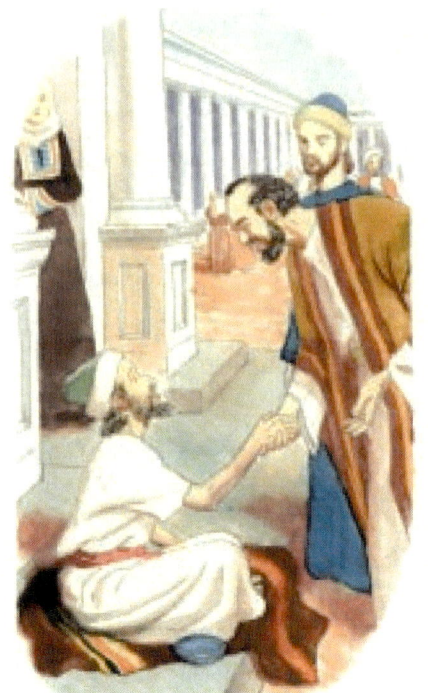
Rise up and walk!

Walking and leaping and praising God

THE LAME BEGGAR HEALED

It was three o'clock in the afternoon, the time of day when many of the Jews went up to the Temple to pray. As Peter and John were going into the Temple, they saw a beggar sitting at the gate called Beautiful. This man had been lame ever since he was born. He had never been able to run and play when he was a child. Now that he was older, he could not work because he could not walk. Every day he was carried to this same gate where he now sat begging.

As Peter and John drew near, he asked them for money. They stopped, looked down at him, and said, "Look at us." The man, of course, looked up at them, expecting to be given a coin. But Peter said, "Silver and gold have I none, but what I have I will give you. In the name of Jesus Christ of Nazareth, rise up and walk." Saying this, he took hold of his hand and raised him up. As the beggar leaped up, his feet and ankle-bones, which had always been weak and useless, now felt strong. First he stood a moment to see if it was really true. Then he tried walking. Entering the temple with Peter and John, he was so happy at the miracle that he started to leap about and praise God. Everyone turned around to see this man who was acting so strangely. When they recognized him as the beggar who had always sat at the Beautiful Gate, they could hardly believe the change that had taken place in him.

Why do you wonder at this?

They laid hands on them

    The beggar was so thankful to Peter and John for healing him that he would not let them go. As he held onto them, many people started to crowd around them. When Peter saw so many people there, he began to preach to them about Jesus. He told them that it was not he, nor John, who had healed this beggar in such a miraculous way.

    He said: "Men! Israelites! Why do you marvel at this, or why do you look at us, as if by our own power or holiness we had made him walk? It was faith in the name of Jesus Christ that made this man strong."

    "You Jews are the chosen people of God, the sons of the prophets," he went on. "Moses and the prophets had foretold that the Christ would be born from among you to bring you salvation first. Jesus of Nazareth was this Christ. But even after Pilate had decided to free Him, you would not have Him. You asked for a murderer to be set free instead, and you crucified the Lord Jesus. God, however, raised Him from the dead. I know that you and your rulers did not understand what you were doing. But if you will now repent of this great sin, you will be forgiven."

    Many who heard Peter believed. But the priests and Sadducees, troubled by this preaching, came up to Peter and John and arrested them. The next day they let them go after commanding them not to preach about Jesus any more. (Acts 3)

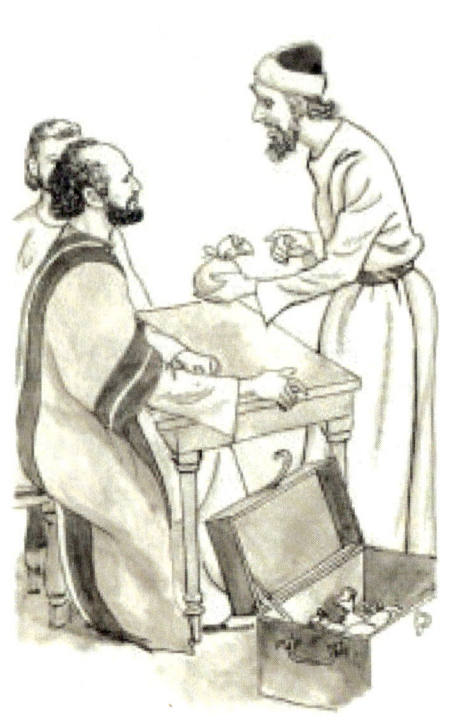 

Why did Satan fill your heart? *He fell down and died*

ANANIAS AND SAPPHIRA

In the early days of the New Testament church, the believers were so filled with the Holy Spirit that they lived as one big family of God. They loved the Lord and each other so much that many of the rich people gladly sold their houses and lands and gave the money to the apostles. The apostles then took that money and gave it to anyone who needed it. There was no one who was hungry or who did not have enough clothes to wear. Barnabas, who later went with Paul on his first missionary journey, was one of those who sold some land and brought the money to the apostles.

Another man was Ananias. But he and his wife, Sapphira, decided to keep some of the money for themselves and give only part of it to the apostles. That would have been perfectly all right, for they did not have to sell the land. Nor did they have to give any of that money away after they did sell it. But when Ananias took the money to Peter, he pretended that he was giving him the whole amount. He wanted people to think that he was better than he really was, that he was as good as Barnabas.

God told Peter what Ananias had done. So Peter said to him, "Why has Satan filled your heart to lie to the Holy Spirit? You have not lied unto men, but unto God." What Peter meant was that whenever we sin, we sin first of all against God, who has given us the commandments. David knew that, too. When

Later his wife came in   *And she fell down and died*

he treated Bathsheba and her husband Uriah very wickedly, he did not even say that he had sinned against them. Instead, he confessed to God: "Against Thee, Thee only, have I sinned, and done that which was evil in Thy sight" (Psalm 51:4). So Peter was actually saying to Ananias: "You think that you are just lying to me. But you are doing more than that. You are also lying to God."

As soon as Peter finished talking, Ananias fell down before him dead. God punished him right there suddenly and quickly. God does not always punish sin that fast. Sometimes He waits a long time. Sometimes He even waits until we die. But in this case, He punished Ananias immediately.

Some young men carried Ananias out to bury him. Three hours later his wife, Sapphira, came in, not knowing what had happened. Peter asked her if the amount of money which Ananias had brought was all that they had gotten from selling the land. He was giving her a chance to tell the truth. But since she had agreed with her husband beforehand to pretend to give the apostles all the money, she lied to Peter, too. Peter then told her that the men who had buried her husband were just coming back and they would bury her, too. At that very moment she fell down dead at Peter's feet. Then the young men carried her out to bury her next to her husband.

As you can imagine, great fear came upon the whole church and upon all who heard these things. (Acts 5)

Brothers and fathers, Listen! *And they threw him out of the city*

THE FIRST CHRISTIAN MARTYR

The Lord Jesus suffered a dreadful death on the cross to save His people. Since that time many Christians have been burned alive, thrown to the lions, stoned to death, or killed in some other horrible way because they loved Jesus. Such people are called martyrs. Jesus had told his disciples, "A servant is not greater than his lord. If they persecuted me, they will also persecute you" (John 15:20).

The first Christian martyr we know about was Stephen. The Bible says that he was "full of faith and of the Holy Spirit." Even though he was not one of the apostles, he was able to perform many miracles among the people.

But there were those who hated Stephen because he was a follower of Jesus. They tried to argue with him in the synagogue, but Stephen always knew how to answer them. Since they could not argue against him honestly, they did as they had done with Jesus. They gave men money to tell lies about what Stephen had taught. Then they stirred up the people against him. They seized him and dragged him before the Jewish council. There they told more lies about him. "This man never stops speaking against the Temple and the Law of Moses," they said. As Stephen listened to them argue, he did not get angry. His face was calm and beautiful. It looked almost like the face of an angel.

And they stoned Stephen   *And Saul was agreeing to his death*

   Then the high priest asked Stephen, "Are these things so?" Stephen did not answer that question directly. Instead, he started telling them stories about Abraham, Joseph, Moses, and David. He was not telling stories just to please the council, but to show them how disobedient the Jews had always been to God. "You stiff necked people!" he said, "Instead of listening to the prophets who had told that Christ would come, your fathers killed them. And you are no better. In fact, you are even worse, because you have killed the very One the prophets told about, Jesus Himself."

   When the Jews heard these words of Stephen, they were furious. They were not sorry for their sin like those who had listened to Peter on Pentecost. But Stephen stood there calmly, looking upward. He said, "Behold! I see the heavens opened and the Son of Man standing at the right hand of God." At that, the Jews stopped up their ears. They did not want to hear anymore. They all rushed upon Stephen and dragged him outside the city. There they began to stone him to death. Even as the stones were striking his body, Stephen was at peace. Knowing that he would soon be in Heaven, he said, "Lord Jesus, receive my spirit."

   Standing there watching was a young man named Saul, who was taking care of the coats of those who were stoning Stephen. From that day, Saul and many others began to drag men and women out of their homes and put them in prison. (Acts 6:8-8:3)

Phillip preached Christ to them *The Spirit said to Philip, Go near*

PHILIP THE EVANGELIST

These were dangerous days for the Christians. Most of them left Jerusalem for fear of being killed or put in prison. Only the apostles stayed there. But God had His plan in allowing men like Saul to persecute the Christians. Before ascending into Heaven, Jesus had told His disciples that they were to be His witnesses in Jerusalem, and in all Judea and Samaria (Acts 1:8). Now, as the believers fled to escape persecution, they carried with them the good news about Jesus. Thus, God's purposes were being fulfilled.

If Jesus had not told His disciples to witness for Him in Samaria, they probably would never have gone there. For although the Samaritans did not live far from Jerusalem, the Jews would have nothing to do with them. Do you remember how surprised the Samaritan woman had been when Jesus asked her for a drink?

But there was one disciple, named Philip, who began to preach in the city of Samaria. The Lord blessed Philip's work there. Great crowds of people listened to him and believed his words. He also healed many of their sick.

You might think that God would have wanted Philip to keep on preaching like that in other cities of Samaria. But no. God told Philip to leave those crowds and to go to the lonely, desert road that went from Jerusalem to Gaza. Philip did not ask why. He obeyed at once. But if Philip had wondered in his heart why God

Do you then know what you read?   *They went down to the water*

had sent him there where there were no houses or villages he soon found out. Along came a royal chariot with a very rich, important-looking man riding in it. This man probably a negro had charge of all the gold and silver of the queen of Ethiopia. Although he was not a Jew, he had made the long, tiring trip to Jerusalem to worship the God of the Jews. And now he was riding back home, reading out loud a part of the Old Testament.

    Philip ran up to the moving chariot and asked the man, "Do you understand what you are reading?" The Ethiopian answered, "How can I, unless someone should help me? Come, sit beside me, and explain it to me." The Ethiopian prince had been reading about the Servant of the Lord in Isaiah 53. He asked Philip, "Is the prophet talking about himself, or about someone else?" Philip said that the prophet, who lived many years before Jesus was even born, was telling what would happen to Jesus. He would be led as a sheep to be killed and would not open his mouth. Then, beginning with this passage of Scripture, Philip preached Jesus to him.

    Philip also said that those who believed in Jesus should be baptized. When they came to some water, the Ethiopian asked, "Here is water. Why can't I be baptized?" So the two men got out of the chariot and went down into the water. After he was baptized, the Ethiopian went on his way rejoicing. And Philip was caught away by the Spirit to preach in other cities. (Acts 8)

He fell down on the ground *He saw no one*

THE SALVATION OF SAUL

When Stephen was being stoned to death, a man named Saul stood by, taking care of the coats of those throwing the stones. From that day, he began putting many of Jesus' disciples in prison and even had some of them killed. Saul was a Pharisee and, like the other Pharisees who had crucified the Lord, he did not believe that Jesus was the Son of God. Saul thought that Jesus was an enemy of God, and he felt that he was doing the right thing by punishing His followers.

Most of the believers had fled from Jerusalem. Saul wanted to punish them, too. So one day he went to the high priest and asked if he could go to Damascus, a city about 150 miles north of Jerusalem. There he hoped to find more Christians and bring them back to Jerusalem to prison. The high priest gave him the letters he needed, and off he started.

It was about noon one day when Saul and his companions were nearing Damascus. Suddenly, a blinding light brighter than the sun shone around them. They all fell to the ground. Then Saul heard a voice saying to him, "Saul, Saul, why are you persecuting me?" Saul answered, "Who art Thou, Lord?" And the voice said, "I am Jesus whom you are persecuting. But get up and go into Damascus and there you will be told what to do."

He was three days without seeing   *And he instantly saw again*

Now Saul knew that he had been wrong! For in that heavenly light he saw and heard Jesus, who he thought was dead. Jesus must indeed be the Son of God, for no man could appear to him in such a way. Saul had thought that he had been persecuting only men. But now he realized that in doing so, he had also been persecuting the Lord Himself.

When Saul stood up again, he was blind. The men who were with him had to lead him by the hand. Saul had planned to enter the city with the power to punish Jesus' followers. But now, blind, helpless, and all mixed up, he had to be led like a little child. When he arrived at the house of a man called Judas, he did not eat or drink anything for three days. He was thinking of his past life, of the way he had persecuted the followers of Jesus, and of what had happened to him on the Damascus road.

Meanwhile, Jesus appeared in a vision to a man named Ananias. He told him to go to Saul and lay his hands upon him so that he could see again. At first Ananias was afraid to go, for he had heard of the dreadful things that Saul had been doing to the Christians. But Jesus said, "Go! I have chosen Saul to carry My name to many people and to suffer much for My sake." So Ananias obeyed, and as soon as he laid his hands on him, Saul could see again.

Then Saul went into the synagogues. But to everyone's surprise, instead of taking the Christians prisoner, he began preaching powerfully that Jesus was the Son of God! (Acts 9:1-22; also Acts 22)

He saw an angel in a vision   *It was let down on the earth*

A GENTILE BELIEVES

There was stationed at Cesarea a centurion called Cornelius. Although he was a Roman, he worshipped the God of Israel, prayed often, and gave much money to the poor.

One afternoon, an angel appeared to Cornelius in a vision and said: "Cornelius, your prayers and your gifts have been noticed by God. Send men to Joppa to bring back one Simon Peter, who is staying at the home of Simon the tanner. He will tell you how you may be saved" (Acts 11:14). Cornelius immediately obeyed. He sent three of his faithful servants to find Peter and bring him back.

But would Peter go with them to Cornelius' house? According to the Law of Moses, Jews were taught that Gentiles were unclean. And a Jew who ate with a Gentile, or even went into his house, became unclean. Before Peter would be willing to go, he had to be taught that the Gentiles were just as important to God as the Jews. In the church of Jesus Christ there could be neither Jew nor Greek, slave nor free, male nor female, for all are one in Christ.

As Cornelius' servants were nearing Joppa, Peter went up on the flat roof of Simon's house to pray. It was about noon and he was getting hungry. As he was praying$_5$ he saw in a vision a great sheet being let down from heaven by its four corners. In it there were all kinds of animals, birds, and creeping things. Then a voice said, "Rise, Peter; kill and eat." According to Moses' Law, there

340

Three men are looking for you   *Peter said, Jesus Christ is Lord of all*

were many kinds of unclean animals that the Jews were not allowed to eat. So Peter answered, "Not so, Lord; for I have never eaten anything that is common and unclean." Then the voice said, "What God has made clean you must not call unclean." This happened three times and then the sheet was lifted back up into heaven.

Just as Peter was wondering what this vision meant, Cornelius' servants stood at the door asking for him. The Holy Spirit told Peter that he should not be afraid to go with them. When Peter learned from the men that they had been sent by a Roman centurion a Gentile he understood the meaning of the vision. Not only were all animals now clean, but more important, the Gentiles were clean, too. It would be all right for him to go.

The next day Peter started out for Caesarea with some fellow-Christians. When they arrived, they found that Cornelius had gathered many of his family and friends in his home. After telling Peter about his vision, Cornelius said, "Now, therefore, we are all here present in the sight of God, to hear all things that have been commanded you by the Lord." What a wonderful group for Peter to preach to! Gentiles, yes, but now he knew that they were just as precious in God's sight as the Jews.

Peter preached Jesus to them and said that everyone Jew or Gentile who believes in Him shall be saved. Cornelius and his friends all believed Peter's words and were baptized that very day. (Acts 10).

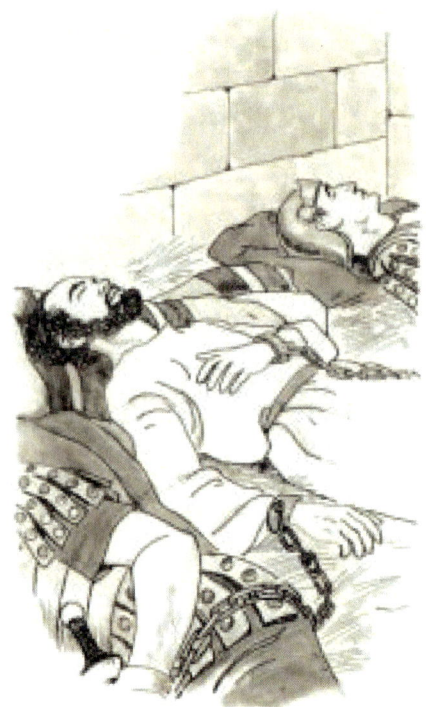
Peter was sleeping

An angel said, Get up quickly!

PETER DELIVERED FROM PRISON

After Stephen had been stoned to death, many Christians left Jerusalem. But the apostles stayed there (Acts 8:1) and for a time were not bothered. Finally, however, even they were to be perscuted. First, King Herod had James killed. He was the first of the twelve apostles to die for his Lord.

The Jews were very happy that James was dead. They hated to see the church of Christ growing so fast. They thought that if some of the leaders were killed, perhaps the church would die, too. When Herod saw how this pleased the Jews, he also seized Peter and put him in prison. He planned to have him killed right after the feast of the Passover. Meanwhile, he kept Peter in prison, under close guard. The Christians were very troubled by the way things were going. But what could such a small group do against Herod? They did the only thing they could do: they prayed earnestly to God. And God, who is more powerful than armies or kings, answered their prayers.

The night before Peter was to be killed, God sent an angel into his prison cell. The angel woke Peter, saying, "Get up quickly. Get dressed and follow me." As Peter stood up, the chains fell right off his hands. The two soldiers who were sleeping next to him did not wake up, nor did the other two who were guarding the door. Peter followed the angel through the prison as if in a dream. When they

The iron gate opened to them   *She didn't open the gate for pure joy*

came to the great outer gate, it swung open by itself and Peter was a free man! As he started walking along the street, the angel disappeared, and Peter began to realize that he was not dreaming.

He did not waste any time, for he knew he would not be safe for long. Quickly he hurried through the dark streets to the home of Mary, Mark's mother. Even though it was the middle of the night, many Christians were still there praying for him. Peter knocked. A girl named Rhoda came to the door and called, "Who is there?" "It is I, Peter," he said. In her happiness at hearing Peter's voice, she forgot to open the door for him, but ran back to the others, saying, "Peter is here!" "You're crazy!" they answered.

They had been praying hard that God would set Peter free. But when he stood before the gate in answer to their prayers, they would not even believe that it was he. God had given them what they asked for even though their faith in His power and goodness was so very weak. When Peter kept on knocking, they finally opened the door. Then they were so excited that he had to tell them to be quiet so that he could explain how the angel had set him free. But knowing that he would not be safe there, either, Peter went away again that very night.

In the morning, there was great excitement among the soldiers when they discovered that the prisoner was gone! Cruel Herod was so angry that Peter had escaped that he had all of the guards killed. (Acts 12:1-19)

They let them go   *Stand up on your feet!*

PAUL'S FIRST MISSIONARY JOURNEY

The Gospel had been preached in Jerusalem, Judea, and Samaria. Now it was to be carried beyond the land of Israel, "unto the furthest part of the earth" (Acts 1:8). The Holy Spirit said to the believers at Antioch in Syria: "I want Barnabas and Saul to leave this church to do the work to which I have called them." After fasting and praying, the Christians laid their hands on these two men and sent them off on their first missionary journey.

Barnabas and Saul first sailed to the island of Cyprus (see map), where Saul's name was changed to Paul. From there they sailed north to Asia Minor. In every city, they first went to the synagogues to preach to the Jews.

In Antioch of Pisidia (see map) they explained how God had promised long ago to raise up a Saviour from the family of David. But when this Saviour, Jesus, came to the Jews, they crucified Him. God the Father, however, raised Him from the dead, and He was seen alive by many of His disciples. Paul and Barnabas then told the Jews that if they trusted in Jesus, their sins would be forgiven. At first, many of the Jews believed. But the next Sabbath, when almost the whole city came together to hear Paul preach, they became very jealous and began arguing against Paul and Barnabas. The two missionaries, therefore, left the Jews and preached instead to the Gentiles. When the Jews saw that great numbers of Gentiles were believing the Word of the Lord, they became even more jealous.

The priest wanted to sacrifice   *They stoned Paul*

They stirred up the people against Paul and Barnabas and drove them out of the city. Leaving Antioch, the two missionaries went on to preach in Iconium and then in Lystra.

One day at Lystra, Paul stopped his preaching to heal a man who had never walked. Amazed at this miracle, the people cried out in their own language, "The gods have come down to us in the form of men." They thought that Barnabas was Zeus, the king of their false gods, and Paul they called Hermes, his messenger (because he did most of the talking). One of the priests was even about to offer up oxen as a sacrifice to them. When Paul and Barnabas realized what was happening, they cried out: "Sirs, what are you doing? We are not gods, but men, just as you are! We are bringing you the good news that you should turn from your idols unto the living God who made heaven and earth."

Some of the jealous Jews came to Lystra from Antioch and Iconium. Again they turned the crowds against the disciples. Those who just a short time before had wanted to worship them now stoned Paul and dragged him out of the city, thinking he was dead. But Paul miraculously got up and went on to preach in Derbe. After that, he revisited Lystra, Iconium, and Antioch to strengthen the believers there and to choose elders in every church. Then Paul and Barnabas returned home to Syrian Antioch to report how God had caused so many Gentiles to believe in the Lord Jesus. (Acts 13-14)

They laid on them many stripes   *Praying and singing hymns unto God*

THE PHILIPPIAN JAILOR

Some time after Paul had returned from his first missionary journey, he decided to go back to those cities where he had already preached to see how the Christians were getting along. This time he took with him another preacher named Silas. At Lystra, a young believer named Timothy also joined him.

After revisiting certain cities of Asia Minor, Paul came to the seaport of Troas. This city was across the Aegean Sea from the part of Greece called Macedonia (see map). One night, in a vision, Paul saw a man calling to him, "Come over into Macedonia and help us." From this, Paul understood that God was calling him to preach the Gospel to the people of Macedonia. So he and his company immediately set sail for that part of Greece.

The first of the many important Greek cities that Paul and his friends visited was Philippi. There, some evil men dragged Paul and Silas before the rulers of the city and told lies about them. The rulers believed the lies and had Paul and Silas beaten with wooden rods until their backs were torn and bleeding. Then they threw them into prison, saying to the jailor, "Don't let these men escape!" The jailor chained them in the inner prison and locked their feet in wooden stocks. Paul and Silas must have been very uncomfortable. But instead of feeling sorry for themselves, they prayed and sang hymns praising God.

Suddenly there was a great earthquake *What shall I do to be saved?*

Suddenly, about midnight, God caused an earthquake. The ground shook, the prison doors were opened, and the chains fell off all the prisoners. The jailor, waking from his sleep, saw the doors open. "The prisoners have escaped," he thought, "and I shall be killed because of it." So he drew his own sword to kill himself. But Paul cried out, "Do no harm to yourself, for we are all here!"

Calling for lights, the jailor rushed into the inner prison and fell down trembling before Paul and Silas. The earthquake had frightened him greatly. He could not understand why the prisoners, though unchained, had not escaped. Seeing that Paul and Silas were not like most prisoners, he brought them out and asked them, "Sirs, what shall I do to be saved?" Paul and Silas told him the good news, Believe on the Lord Jesus, and you shall be saved, and your household." Then they told the jailor and his household about the Lord Jesus, and every one of them believed Pauls and Silas' words. That very hour of the night, the jailor washed their wounded backs and he and his household were baptized. Then he took them into his own house and gave them something to eat.

The next day the rulers of the city ordered the jailor to set Paul and Silas free. But Paul sent back word, "We, who are Roman citizens, were beaten when we had done no wrong. Let them come themselves and bring us out!" Frightened to hear that Paul and Silas were Romans, the rulers themselves went to the prison to set them free. Then they begged them to leave the city. (Acts 15:36-16:40)

Paul saw the city was full of idols *I found also an altar*

PAUL ON MARS HILL

After leaving Luke at Philippi, Paul went on to Thessalonica with Silas and Timothy (see map). As usual, he went first to the synagogue to preach. Some of the Jews and many of the Greeks believed that Jesus was the Christ. But as at Antioch, Lystra, and Iconium, the Jews who were jealous of Paul stirred up crowds of people against him, so that he and his friends were forced to leave the city.

But the Jews were still not satisfied. They followed Paul to Berea, for they had heard that many people there believed his preaching. In Berea they caused more trouble, and once again Paul had to flee.

This time Paul went south to Athens, the most glorious city of all Greece. He had to leave Berea without Silas and Timothy, so he waited at Athens for them. Athens had once been the most beautiful city in the world. Many beautiful white marble temples and statues could still be seen there. But Paul was not interested in the beauty he saw. He was troubled that these people were worshipping idols instead of the true God.

Paul could not keep quiet about the way he felt. He talked in the synagogue. He even went into the marketplace and talked with any who would listen. There were many learned men who sat around in the marketplace, doing nothing else than "either to tell or to hear some new thing." They were so curious

They brought him to Mars Hill   *Some indeed made fun of it*

to hear what Paul had to say about Jesus and the resurrection that they brought him to Mars Hill. They said, "You bring strange things to our ears. We would like to know, therefore, what these things mean.

Paul was glad to explain to them about Jesus. This time he did not talk about what the Old Testament said, for these people had never read it. So he began: "Men of Athens, I can see from all the temples and idols in this city that you are very religious. Yet with all these gods you still have not found what you're looking for. As I was walking through your city I saw an altar that said, 'TO AN UNKNOWN GOD.' Since you do not know whom you worship, I make Him known to you. The God who made the heavens and the earth does not live in temples, for He is Lord over all. Nor does He need anything that we men can give to Him, for it is He who gives us life and breath and all things. All men should seek after Him. But they have not. In the past, God has overlooked their sins. But now He commands everyone everywhere to repent. For one day He will judge the world by Jesus Christ, whom He has raised from the dead."

When he spoke of the resurrection of the dead, some of them laughed. Others wanted to hear Paul at another time. And there were also a few who did believe. But Paul never preached to them again. He left Athens, and went to Corinth. (Acts 17)

They were tent makers by trade *We have our riches from this work*

PAUL AT EPHESUS

When Paul stopped off at Ephesus on the way home from his second missionary journey, he told the Jews, "I will return unto you if it is God's will." Paul kept his promise. On his third journey after revisiting the churches in Galatia and Phrygia, he returned to Ephesus. For the first three months, Paul preached in the synagogue. But as usual, the unbelieving Jews turned many people against him. So he left the synagogue, taking his disciples with him. Then for over two years, Paul taught both Jews and Greeks in Tyrannus' school. He also spent many hours working as a tent maker in order to earn enough money to live on.

Because of Paul's faithful preaching, great numbers of people believed the word of the Lord, not only in Ephesus but in all parts of Asia Minor. Many of those who became Christians had formerly worshipped the goddess Diana, whose beautiful temple stood in Ephesus. The silversmiths had made much money selling little silver statues and temples of Diana to the worshippers. But as more and more people believed in Jesus, they stopped buying the silver statues of Diana.

Greatly upset, Demetrius, one of the silversmiths, called the craftsmen together and said: This Paul is persuading people not to worship our great goddess Diana any more. Soon no one will want to buy our silver trinkets. And we will become poor men." The silversmiths became so angry when they

The people rushed into the theater *There was much crying by all*

heard this that they stirred up the whole city. The people rushed into the great amphitheater, yelling and shouting. Paul wanted to go in, too, to talk to them, but his friends would not let him. They knew it would be too dangerous. When Alexander, a Jew, tried to quiet the mob, they all started chanting, "Great is Diana of the Ephesians." This they kept up for two hours. Finally the townclerk, warning the people that they would get into trouble with the Romans for such an uproar, sent them home.

When the city had calmed down, Paul left Ephesus to preach some more in Macedonia and Greece. On his way back from there, he was in such a hurry to get to Jerusalem that he did not want to take the time to stop at Ephesus again. Instead, he landed at Miletus (see map) and sent for the Ephesian elders to come to him. He reminded them of how he had taught them the whole counsel of God day and night; with tears, for three years. He added:

"The Holy Spirit has made you shepherds over this church which the Lord bought with His own blood. You must feed them with the word of God and watch over them so that they will not be led away from the Lord. And now I give you up unto God and to the word of His grace, for you will never see my face again."

Saying this, he kneeled down and prayed with them. The elder kissed Paul good-bye and wept, especially because he had said that they would never see him again. (Acts 19)

This is the man *They were trying to kill him*

PAUL AT JERUSALEM

Paul had told the Ephesian elders at Miletus: "I do not know what is going to happen to me in Jerusalem, except that in every city the Holy Spirit has told me that bonds and troubles await me." Yet Paul still wanted to get back to Jerusalem in time for Pentecost.

At both Tyre and Cesarea (see map), his friends also warned him that the Jews at Jerusalem would bind him and hand him over to the Gentiles. But Paul answered his friends in faith, "not only am ready to be bound, but also to die at Jerusalem for the name of the Lord Jesus." When they saw that they could not change Paul's mind, they said, "The Lord's will be done."

Paul did go on to Jerusalem. The elders there were glad to see him again and praised God that through Paul's preaching so many Gentiles had become Christians.

A week later, when Paul was in the Temple, certain Jews from Asia rushed up to him. They cried out: "This is the man who teaches all men everywhere against the Law and the Temple. And furthermore, he also has brought Greeks into the Temple, and has defiled this holy place." Paul had indeed walked about the city with a Greek, but he had not brought him into the Temple.

At once, a great, excited crowd gathered around. They did not wait to find out if the charge was true, but dragged Paul out of the Temple and were about

The captain ran down upon them

He spoke to them in Hebrew

to kill him. But Roman soldiers came running up to put a stop to the uproar. When they had taken Paul and bound him, the chief captain asked the crowd who Paul was and what he had done. But he learned nothing from all the shouting. So he commanded the soldiers to carry Paul into the nearby fortress. At the top of the stairs, Paul asked the chief captain if he could speak to the angry crowd.

    Paul did not want to try to save himself. But he loved his people and wanted one more chance to preach to them about Jesus. Standing on the steps of the fortress, he waved his hand for them to be quiet. Then he spoke to them in Hebrew: "Brethren and fathers, I am a Jew who was brought up in the Jewish law and customs, just as you were. And once I, too, thought I was serving God by persecuting the Christians. But one day on the way to Damascus, the Lord Jesus appeared to me in a blinding light. He told me that I was fighting against God and Himself. After that, I wanted to tell all the Jews about Jesus. But He said, "Go, for I will send you far away to the Gentiles."

    "To the Gentiles?" The Jews would not listen any more! They thought Israel was the chosen people of God and His salvation was for them only and not for the Gentiles! "Away with this fellow!" they shouted.

    Paul was now bound and in the hands of the Gentiles, just as the Holy Spirit and his friends had warned would happen. (Acts 21:17-40)

He stretched him out with straps *He set Paul among them*

THE PLOT AGAINST PAUL

Claudius Lysias, the chief captain, still did not know why the Jews were so angry with Paul. He commanded his soldiers to take him into the fortress and find out by whipping him. The soldiers obeyed. They tied Paul up with straps and were about to lash him when he said, "Is it lawful for you to whip a Roman before it has been shown that he has done something wrong?" When the chief captain heard of this, he said, "Tell me, are you a Roman?': Paul said, "Yes." The captain said, "I bought my citizenship with a great sum of money." Paul answered, "But I was born a Roman!" The captain was afraid when he heard this, for according to Roman law, a Roman citizen could not be whipped or even bound until proved guilty.

The next day the captain called together the Jewish council and set Paul before them. He still wanted to find out what wrong Paul had done. But when Paul spoke of the resurrection of the dead, the Pharisees and Sadducees got into such an argument about the resurrection that the chief captain was afraid that Paul would be torn to pieces by them. He ordered his soldiers to take Paul back to the fortress.

The next night, as Paul lay in prison, the Lord Jesus stood by him to comfort him. "Be of good courage, Paul," He said. "For as you have told about Me at Jerusalem, so you must also bear witness at Rome." The Lord was still

The captain asked, What is it? *The soldiers brought him by night*

with him! And He had promised Paul that he would yet get to Rome. Because Rome was the most important city of that day, Paul had wanted for a long time to go there to preach.

When it was morning, forty Jews got together and swore that they would neither eat nor drink until they had killed Paul. They asked the council to have the chief captain bring Paul down again to be questioned. They planned to hide along the way and to rush out and kill him before he reached the council.

A son of Paul's sister heard of this plan. He ran to the fortress and told his uncle Paul. Paul sent his nephew at once to the chief captain. The officer took him aside and asked, "What is it you want to tell me?" The captain was very worried when he heard of the plot to kill Paul. He sent the young man away saying, "Don't tell anyone that you have told me this."

That same night he commanded two hundred soldiers, seventy horsemen, and two hundred spearmen to start out for Cesarea with Paul. Again, God was using the power of the Roman empire to take care of His servant. After travelling all night with Paul, the foot soldiers returned to Jerusalem, while the seventy horsemen went on with him to Gesarea. There the soldiers turned Paul over to Felix, the governor, with a letter from the chief captain, telling about Paul's case. Felix then commanded Paul to be kept in Herod's palace until the Jews came from Jerusalem to accuse him (Acts 23:12-33).

I will hear you fully when they come

Tertullus began to accuse

PAUL ON TRIAL

Paul was safe in Herod's palace. The plotting Jews could not reach him there. After five days Ananias, the high priest, and certain elders arrived in Gesarea from Jerusalem. With them came Tertullus, a clever public speaker. The Jews had chosen him to present their case against Paul. When they were all gathered before Felix, Tertullus began.

"Most excellent Felix," he said, "this man is a disturbing fellow. He has been stirring up trouble among all the Jews throughout the world. He is one of the leaders of the sect of the Nazarenes. Furthermore, he tried to dishonor the Temple." The other Jews that were there all agreed that these things were so.

Then Felix motioned to Paul to speak. One by one, Paul showed that the charges they made against him were false.

" I am no troublemaker," he answered. went to Jerusalem to worship only twelve days ago. I argued with no man. Nor did I stir up a crowd in the Temple, in the synagogues, or in the city. As for the second charge, it is true that I follow the Way (which they call the sect of the Nazarenes). But I, too, believe all the things written in the Law and the prophets. I believe, as they do, that there will be a resurrection of both the good and the evil. As for dishonoring the Temple, that is not true either. I came to Jerusalem to bring gifts to the Jews from the Gentile churches. When certain Jews from Asia took hold of me, I was

He commanded him to be kept

Felix came with Drusilla

worshipping in the Temple."

Felix could see that Paul had not done the things the Jews had said he did. But Felix was not a good and honest governor. He wanted the Jews to like him. So he did not set Paul free. Instead, he said, "When Lysias, the chief captain, comes down, I will know more fully the things about you."

We do not know if Lysias ever came to Cesarea. But for two whole years Paul was kept a prisoner. He was treated kindly, however, and his friends were allowed to visit him. Felix sent for him often, hoping that Paul would give him money to be set free. Paul, of course, did not do so. But he did speak to him and his wife, Drusilla, about faith in Christ Jesus. He said that a person who believes in Jesus must not do evil things. He warned them that God will judge everyone at the Last Day the Day of Judgment. Felix was frightened by this. But he always put off changing his ways.

At the end of two years Porcius Festus became governor in Felix's place. But to please the Jews, Felix did not set Paul free before he left. Two years had passed since Jesus had told Paul that he must witness for Him at Rome'. Yet during all this time Paul firmly believed that the Lord would keep His promise. (Acts 24)

They begged him, asking a favor   *King Agrippa and Bernice came*

PAUL BEFORE FESTUS AND AGRIPPA

Three days after Festus became the new governor, he went up to Jerusalem. There, the chief priests and leaders of the Jews told him all about Paul and asked to have him brought back to Jerusalem. Again, they secretly planned to kill him on the way. However, Festus answered: "Paul is being kept at Cesarea. If you wish to accuse him before me, you must go there."

So when Festus returned to Cesarea, the Jews went, too. They made many serious charges against Paul, hut they could prove none of them. However, like Felix before him, Festus wanted to please the leaders of the Jews. He asked Paul, "Are you willing to go up to Jerusalem to be judged before me?"

Paul was not afraid to die for the Lord Jesus. But he did not want to throw his life away foolishly. So he answered: "If I have done anything worthy of death, I do not refuse to die. But if none of those things is true about which these men accuse me, no man can turn me over to their will. I appeal to Caesar." (By appealing to Caesar, Paul asked to be judged by the emperor himself at Rome.) Festus answered, "You have appealed to Caesar: to Caesar you shall go."

A few days later, King Agrippa and his sister, Bernice, came to visit the new governor. Festus told the king about Paul. This man had not been accused of the usual evil things, he explained, but only about some questions of the of the Jewish religion. King Agrippa was very interested in Paul's case and asked

On the next day Paul was brought

This man might have been set free

to hear him.

The next day Paul was brought before Festus, King Agrippa, Bernice, and many important men. Festus explained: "It seems unreasonable to me to send a prisoner to Caesar without saying what wrong he has done. I hope that you, King Agrippa, who know so much about the Jews, will be able to help me write the letter." Agrippa turned to Paul and said, "You may speak for yourself."

Paul began: was brought up a Pharisee and persecuted the Christians both in our country and in foreign cities. But one day, as I was going to Damascus, Jesus appeared to me in a blinding light. He told me that I was to be His witness among the Jews and also the Gentiles. I was not disobedient to this heavenly vision, but preached that everyone should repent and turn to God. What I taught about Jesus' suffering and resurrection was only what the prophets and Moses said would happen."

At this, Festus interrupted, "You are mad, Paul!" But Paul went on: "King Agrippa, do you believe the prophets? I know that you do believe." Agrippa knew that Paul was not mad. Perhaps he almost wanted to believe the things that Paul had been saying. Yet he did not. He said to Paul, "You almost persuade me to become a Christian."

After talking with Festus, then the king rose up, and said, "This man might have been set free if he had not appealed to Caesar." (Acts 26)

We set sail *We were violently tossed by the storm*

PAUL'S SHIPWRECK

At last Paul was on his way to Rome! When in Ephesus he had said, "must see Rome," he had probably not expected to be going there as a prisoner. But God had His own plans for him.

A Roman centurion put Paul and certain other prisoners aboard a small ship. Luke (who wrote about the trip) and Aristarchus (a Christian friend from Thessalonica) also went along. Setting sail from Cesarea, they followed along the coast of Asia Minor as far as Myra (see map). There the centurion changed his prisoners over to a larger ship carrying wheat from Egypt to Italy.

However, it was now fall, and travel by sea was becoming very dangerous. Soon it would stop completely for the winter. Only with great difficulty was this large ship able to cross the rough, open water between Cnidus and the island of Crete (see map). Paul then warned them: "Sirs, if you go on now, great harm will come to the cargo, the ship, and our lives." But the centurion and ship master decided to try to sail to a better port in which to spend the winter.

Hardly had they set sail when a fierce storm broke upon them. They were driven helplessly before the wind, for the sailors could no longer steer the ship. Then they tried to lighten the load by throwing overboard everything they did not need. For days the storm beat upon them. Since neither sun nor stars shone all that time, they did not even know where they were. All hope was gone that

Be of good cheer, Men!

They all escaped safe to the land

they would ever be saved.

Then Paul stood up and said: "Sirs, you should have listened to me and not set sail from Crete. But be of good cheer. The ship will be lost, but no one will drown. Last night an angel of the God I serve appeared to me and said: 'Fear not, Paul, you must stand before Caesar. And God will save the lives of all who are with you, for your sake.' But first we shall be wrecked upon a certain island."

On the fourteenth night of the storm, the sailors discovered that they were getting close to land. They began to lower the small boat to escape in it. Seeing them, Paul said to the centurion, "Unless these men stay on the ship, you cannot be saved." So the soldiers cut the ropes, letting the boat fall into the water.

As it began to get light, Paul said: "This is the fourteenth day since you have eaten. I beg you to take some food to strengthen yourselves." And taking bread, he gave thanks to God and began to eat. Cheered by his words, the rest also took food.

When it was day, the sailors tried to run the ship up on the beach of the island. However, it struck ground and began to break up as the waves beat upon it. The centurion commanded everyone to try to get to land, either by swimming or by holding on to boards. Thus everyone — soldiers, sailors, and prisoners — arrived safe on land, as the angel had said. (Acts 27)

They had kindled a fire   *A viper fastened upon his hand*

PAUL ARRIVES AT ROME

The shipwrecked travelers must have been happy to reach land once again. But as they came out of the water, they shivered in their wet clothing, for it was a cold, rainy day. Some of the natives of the island (called Melita) saw the wreck and hurried to the shore to help. They built a big fire so that the travelers could get warm and dry. Paul, too, helped gather wood. As he was throwing a bundle of sticks on the fire, a poisonous snake came out of the wood because of the heat, and clung to Paul's hand. The natives said to each other: "This man must be a murderer. He has escaped from the sea, but the gods will not let him live." When Paul just shook the snake off into the fire, the people watched closely to see if he would become swollen or fall down dead. But when he did not, they thought he must be a god.

Since no ships could put out to sea during the winter, Paul and the others with him had to spend three months on the island, They were treated with much kindness by the natives. Paul and his friends healed all who were sick, and we can be sure that he also preached to them about Jesus.

When spring finally came, the travelers were once more on their way. Another ship from Egypt took them to a city about 150 miles south of Rome. From there they had to go the rest of the way on foot.

The brothers came out to meet us

Persuading them from morning to evening

News of Paul's coming reached Rome ahead of him. Some of the believers traveled many miles south to meet him on the way. When Paul saw them, he thanked God and took courage.

At Rome, Paul was treated very well for a prisoner. He was always chained to a soldier, and he could not walk freely about the streets. But he was allowed to live in a house which he rented, rather than in a prison.

Shortly after he arrived in Rome, Paul invited the Jews to come to his house on a certain day since he was not able to go to the synagogue himself. Many came, and Paul reasoned with them from morning until evening. He tried to show from the Law of Moses and the prophets that Jesus was the Messiah they had been waiting for. Some believed that day. But as in Antioch, Lystra, Jerusalem, and so many other cities, most of them did not. Before they left his house, Paul rebuked them for not receiving the message of salvation which they had heard from him. "Be it known unto you, therefore," he said to them, "that the salvation of God is sent to the Gentiles, and they will hear."

For two whole years Paul lived in the house which he rented. Although he was still a prisoner, he could have visitors whenever he wished. All that time he preached and taught freely about the kingdom of God and the Lord Jesus Christ. What happened to him after those two years we do not know, for the Bible does not tell us. (Acts 28)

Peter was kept in prison　　　　*Behold! We turn to the Gentiles*

THE OLIVE TREE

The Israelites or Jews were the chosen people of God. He gave to them His special promises, the Ten Commandments, and also instructions for their worship of Him. He led them out of Egypt and brought them into the promised land of Canaan. But the greatest blessing of all was that the Saviour, Jesus Christ, was one of them and came to bring salvation first of all to them.

However, most of the Jews, although not all of them, rejected Jesus. Not only did they crucify Him, but they did all they could to stop the spread of the Gospel. Stephen was stoned to death. James, the brother of John, was beheaded. Peter was thrown into prison. Saul before he became Paul arrested many men and women. And when Paul went on his missionary journeys, the unbelieving Jews in Antioch, Lystra, Thessalonica, and many other places turned the Gentiles against him.

Because the Jews rejected Jesus, the Gospel was brought to the Gentiles. Paul told the Jews at Antioch: "It was right that the word of God should be spoken to you first, but because you thrust it away, and you do not judge yourselves worthy of everlasting life, 'Behold'. We turn to the Gentiles" (Acts 13:46). Paul hoped that through his preaching many Gentiles would be saved. But he also hoped that when his own people the Jews saw God's blessings coming to the Gentiles, they would again want to have a place in God's favor.

Some of the branches were broken off   *Your were grafted in among them*

To the Christians in Rome, Paul once explained this relationship between Jews and Gentiles. The chosen people of God, he said, are like an olive tree. But because some of them did not believe that Jesus was the Messiah, God broke them off the tree, like branches. In their place, He grafted branches of the wild olive tree — Romans and other Gentiles — who believed that Jesus was the Saviour. Thus, believing Romans took the place of unbelieving Jews.

But, wrote Paul, the Romans should never be proud because they replaced the Jews. Since the Jews were broken off because of their unbelief and the Romans were grafted in because of their faith, they must be careful to remain faithful. Otherwise, God will break them off, too. For if He did not spare the natural branches (the Jews), but broke them off because of their unbelief, how much more quickly will He break off the wild branches (the Romans) if they are unbelieving. Therefore, warned Paul, "Be not high minded, but fear."

Finally, Paul wrote that if the Jews should turn from their unbelief and accept Jesus as he is certain many will. God is also able to graft them back into the tree. For if He can graft wild branches into the olive tree, how much more can He graft the natural branches back into the tree from which they were first broken off. (Romans 11:11-24)

There is no authority except from God   *It does not wear the sword in vain*

OBEDIENCE TO RULERS

Because the early Christians in Rome did not feel that they should obey the heathen rulers over them, Paul wrote to urge them to obey their government. For, he said, all rulers whether they are emperors, kings, presidents, or governors receive from God their right to rule. When Pilate said to Jesus, "Do you not know that I have the authority to crucify you, and I have the authority to let you go?" Jesus answered him, "You would have no authority against Me if it were not given to you from above" (John 19:10).

Therefore, said Paul, since the authority of rulers comes to them from God, anyone who disobeys the rulers also disobeys God. And he will be punished for his disobedience not only by the rulers, but also by God. God established the governments of the world in order to protect and help those who do good and to punish those who do evil. Those who do good do not need to fear the government, explained Paul, "for the rulers are not frightening to good works, but to evil." But those who disobey have cause to fear, for God has given the rulers the right to use the sword to punish evil doers.

A person may disobey the government, however, when the rulers ask him to do that which is against God's will. For example, Jesus had commanded His disciples to preach the Gospel to all nations (Matt. 28:19). So when Peter and John were ordered by the Jewish rulers not to preach about Jesus anymore, they

If it is right in the sight of God

Give to Caesar the things of Caesar

answered, "Whether it is right in the sight of God to listen to you rather than God, you judge" (Acts 4:19). Then they went right on preaching. In this case, the apostles had the right and even the duty to disobey the Jewish rulers.

However, when the rulers ask that which it is lawful for them to ask, all citizens must be obedient unto them, not only for fear of being punished, but also because God has commanded it. Nor should they obey unwillingly. But rather, they should give "fear to whom fear is due, and honor to whom honor is due."

Paul also wrote that the rulers must be given, through taxes, the money which they need to carry out their work. The Jews, trying to trick Jesus, once asked Him if it was right to pay tribute (or taxes) to the Roman emperor. Asking for a Roman coin, He pointed to it and said, "Whose image and writing is this?" When they replied that it was Caesar's, He said, "Give therefore to Caesar the things of Caesar, and unto God the things of God."

Christian citizens owe one more thing to the rulers besides obedience, respect, honor, and taxes. Paul, in writing to Timothy, said that they must pray "for kings and all that are in high places; that we may lead a peaceable and quiet life, in all godliness and honor" (I Tim. 2:2). Even though the rulers themselves do not love and honor God, Christians must pray that they will keep good order for the welfare of men. (Romans 13:1-7)

He stayed with them and worked

And persuaded both Jews and Greeks

GOD'S FIELD AND GOD'S TEMPLE

After Paul had preached on Mars Hill in Athens (Acts 17), he travelled about forty miles west to Corinth.

At first, Paul went into the Jewish synagogue every Sabbath to preach that Jesus was the Christ. But when most of the Jews refused to believe, Paul left the synagogue and began preaching in a house next door to it. For a year and a half Paul worked faithfully in that city. As a result, a great number of the Corinthians believed in the Lord.

Paul then left Corinth, and another Jew named Apollos came there and took up the work. Apollos knew the Scriptures thoroughly and could preach in a powerful way. He was of great help to the church and caused the believers to grow in their faith.

After a while, however, Paul received word that the church was being split into groups. Some of the members were saying that they were followers of Paul others, Apollos. Others claimed Peter as their head; and still others said they were Christ's.

Paul at once wrote to the church to rebuke them for these divisions. As believers in Christ, they all should be one in Him, and not followers of the different preachers. "Has Christ been divided?" he asked them. "Was Paul crucified for you? Or were you baptized into the name of Paul?" "Who then is

I planted, Apollos watered   *I have laid the foundations*

Paul?" he questioned. "And who is Apollos? They are but ministers through whom you believed."

Like a farmer, Paul said, he had planted the seed of the Word in the field (the Corinthian church). Apollos then watered the seed by his preaching. But through His Holy Spirit, God was the One who had caused the seed of the Word to grow in the hearts of the Corinthians. So, no glory could come to Paul, who planted, or to Apollos, who watered, but only to God who caused the growth. Neither Paul nor Apollos could be leaders of different groups, for they were but fellow-workers for the same Lord and Saviour.

After speaking of the divisions in the Corinthian church, Paul then began to talk of the church as the temple of God and the ministers as builders. Paul had begun the work in Corinth by laying the foundation of the temple. That foundation was Jesus Christ, "for other foundation can no man lay." Other ministers came after Paul and built upon the foundation. But each one, wrote Paul, should be careful how he builds on it. For in the Day of Judgment, each minister's work will be tested by fire. The work of those who built with gold, silver, and precious stones that is, with the wisdom of God will stand the test. But the work of those who built with wood, hay, and stubble that is, with their own wisdom will be burned up. "Each one shall receive his own reward according to his own labor." (I Corinthians 1:10-17)

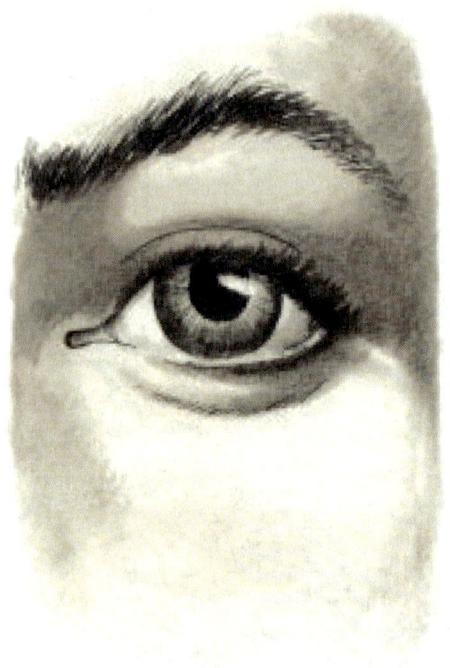
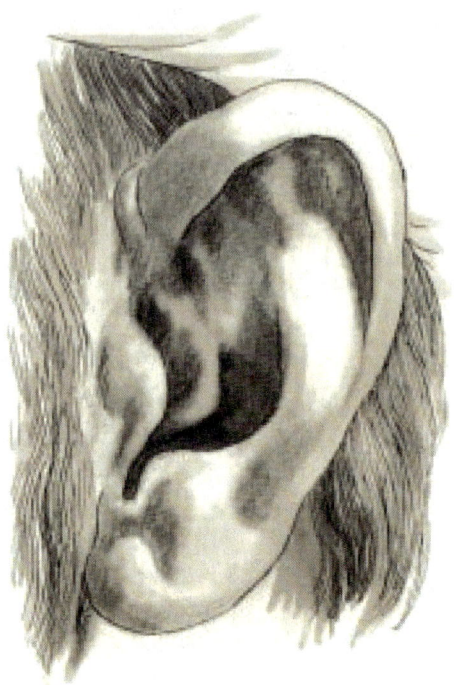

The body is not one member   *Is it therefore not of the body?*

THE BODY OF CHRIST

Paul once wrote to the Corinthian church that they were all members of the body of Christ. That sounds strange, does it not? But Paul was using picture language to explain something very important to those Corinthians.

Man's body, he wrote, is one whole made up of many different members, or parts. For example, there are legs and feet, arms and hands, eyes and ears, a head, a nose, and a mouth. God made them all different. But each one is important because He gave each one its own special work to do. And so it would be wrong for the hand, for example, to think that it was more useful or more important than the foot, or for the ear to think that it was not as good as the eye. Paul asked, "If the whole body were an eye, where were the hearing? And if the whole were hearing, where were the smelling?" Even though the ear cannot see, it can hear. And even though a hand cannot walk, it can hold things. Each part is useful for the body as a whole. "And the eye is not able to say to the hand, I have no need for you. Nor again can the head say to the feet, I have no need of you."

The same thing is true of the church. The church is called the body of Christ, and every true member is just one part of that body. Each member has his own special work to do and is very important. These members form a complete body, the church.

The eye cannot say, I have no need of you   *Nor can the head say it to the feet*

Paul tells us that in the days of the young church, some people were apostles, some were prophet and others were teachers. Some could heal the sick; others could talk in strange languages. Not everyone did the same kind of work. Yet each one was important and each was necessary for the life of the church.

Today, people cannot be prophets or perform miracles. But there is other work which they can do. Some can be ministers. Some can teach; others can visit the sick and lonely. The church, like the body, is made up of all different members, each with his own special work. It would not be good if everyone were a minister, for that would be like having a body that was all eye or all hand!

Not only is the church the body of Christ; but Christ is its Head (Eph. 4:15). The head is the most important part of our body and controls everything that each arm or leg or eye does. When Herodias wanted to have John the Baptist killed, she had her daughter ask King Herod for John's head. She knew that without his head, John could not live.

In the same way, the Lord Jesus is the most important part of the church and controls all the members of it. Through His Holy Spirit, He gives to each one the strength and ability to do what He wants them to do. Without Christ as the Head, the church is dead. (I Corinthians 12)

You do not sow the body *And another flesh of beasts*

THE RESURRECTION HOPE

The simple Gospel which Paul had preached to the Corinthians was that Christ died for their sins, was buried, and was raised on the third day. This Gospel they had believed when Paul had been with them. But now some in the Corinthian church were saying that there was no resurrection of the dead. Paul, therefore, wrote them to correct their wrong ideas.

How is it possible, he asked them, to believe that Christ rose from the dead and yet not to believe that there is a resurrection of the dead? To say that there is no resurrection of the dead is to say that Christ was not raised. And if Christ was not raised, then the whole Gospel is destroyed, and all preaching is meaningless. Moreover, wrote Paul, he and his fellow-preachers would be liars since they said that God raised up Christ. Furthermore, the faith of the Corinthians would be useless; their sins would still not be forgiven. And those who had already died in the faith would be lost. "If we have hoped in Christ in this life only," he said, "we are of all men most miserable." Then there was no sense in Paul's suffering so many dangers and hardships for the Gospel. If the dead are not raised, he said, "Let us eat and drink, tomorrow we die."

"But," rejoiced Paul, "now Christ has been raised from among the dead. He became the first-fruit of those who have fallen asleep." Just as the first ripened grain is a promise of more grain later on in the harvest, so the resurrection of

And another flesh of fishes

Another glory of the moon and stars

Christ is a promise of the resurrection of all the dead.

But some might wonder what the body will be like when it is resurrected. Paul explained to them that the resurrection body will not be the same as the one we have now. When a farmer sows wheat, he does not sow the plant, but only a tiny seed. Yet after the seed is buried in the ground, a wheat plant which does not look anything like the seed springs up from it. Likewise, after our body dies and is buried, an entirely different body a heavenly one will be raised from it.

We should not be puzzled about two such different bodies, wrote Paul. For even in this life there are many different kinds of living creatures: some are men, others are animals, still others are birds and fish. Furthermore, the earth is very different from the sun, moon, and stars. Even the stars differ one from another. If God has created so many different kinds of bodies in this life, then we must not doubt that He can remake our earthly bodies into ones that are fitted for Heaven.

This will not happen right away when we die. At death the soul of the believer goes to Heaven. But the body waits in the grave until Christ returns. At that time, said Paul, God will change that earthly body into a heavenly one in the twinkling of an eye. With such a hope, the Christian can say, "death, where is your sting? O grave, where is your victory?" (I Corinthians 15)

They let him down in a basket *I received forty stripes minus one*

THE SUFFERINGS OF PAUL

In the year and a half that Paul had preached and worked in the Greek city of Corinth during his second journey, he had established a large church there. But some time after he left, false teachers began to turn the believers away from Christ by claiming that they were the true apostles and that Paul was not. Therefore, they said, the Corinthians should believe their teachings rather than Paul's.

When the chief of apostles heard about this, he knew that unless he could show the Corinthians that these men were telling lies about him, the work which he had done among them would soon be destroyed. Paul did not like to boast. He even called it "foolishness." But he decided that he would have to do so in order to prove that he was indeed a real apostle of Christ and therefore that his Gospel was true.

Paul explained to the Corinthians that he had worked harder and suffered much more for the Gospel of Christ than had any of those false teachers. Right at the very start of his ministry when he began preaching at Damascus his troubles began. The Jews in that city became so furious when they heard this former Pharisee preaching Christ that they plotted to kill him. Day and night they watched the city gates, making it impossible for Paul to escape that way. So one night, some Christian friends helped him. They fastened a heavy rope to a

I passed a day in the deep

In danger of robbers

large basket. Then, through a window of one of the houses built on the city wall, they carefully let down the basket with Paul in it until it touched the ground. Paul then climbed out and slipped away into the night.

That was just the beginning of his troubles, of which Luke (in the Book of Acts) tells us only a few. Five times, wrote Paul, the Jews gave him thirty-nine lashes with the whip. Three times one of them in Philippi the Gentiles beat him with wooden rods. Another time, in Lystra, the people stoned him until they thought he was dead. He was shipwrecked three times (not counting the last great shipwreck on the way to Rome). During one of these storms, he had to stay in the water for a day and a night.

Besides, as Paul travelled from city to city to preach the Gospel, he was continually in danger. There were deep rivers and hot deserts to cross. There were robbers hiding along the way waiting to attack travellers. The unbelieving Jews, the Gentiles, and even false Christians made trouble for him everywhere. His work was hard and long. He often suffered from hunger, thirst, the cold, and lack of sleep. Besides all this, Paul was continually concerned with the problems and care of all the churches which he had founded.

Truly, there was no one who could claim to have been a more faithful apostle than Paul! Therefore, he urged the Corinthians to hold to the Gospel which he had preached, and not to the false gospel of those ministers of Satan. (2 Corinthians 11)

You received me as an angel of God

I went away into Arabia

PAUL, THE TRUE APOSTLE

When, on one of his missionary journeys, Paul began preaching in the region of Galatia, the people welcomed him as if he had been "an angel of God." And they believed his message that salvation comes only by trusting in Jesus Christ.

After Paul left, however, some Jewish Christians began to trouble these churches. They claimed that Paul did not even have the right to he called an apostle and said that his teachings were false. They began to persuade the Galatians that a person cannot be saved by only believing in Jesus, but that he must also keep the Law of Moses.

When Paul heard that the Galatians were so quickly turning away from the simple Gospel which he had taught them, he was both amazed and displeased. He wrote to warn them that these men were not just adding a little to the Gospel of Christ but were, in fact, turning it right around. And "if we," he told them, "or an angel from Heaven, should preach any other gospel unto you than that which we have preached unto you, let him be accursed" (Galatians 1:8).

Paul assured them that his Gospel was true, for he had not been taught it by men, but had received it directly from the Lord Jesus. When Jesus appeared to him on the way to Damascus (Acts 9), He had made it clear to Paul that the very Gospel against which he had been fighting so bitterly was the truth of God.

I went up to see Peter   *Not for an hour did we give in*

Not only did Christ reveal the Gospel directly to him, Paul went on, but He also commanded him to preach it to the Gentiles. He was not one of the original twelve apostles. But since he had been appointed for his work by the Lord Himself, he was equal to them in every way. Thus, after his experience on the Damascus road, he did not find it necessary to go to Jerusalem to get the approval of the other apostles. Instead, he went away into the desert of Arabia. There, alone with God, he could better prepare himself for his great work. Paul told how he did go to Jerusalem three years later, but only to get acquainted with Peter and James. He was not seeking their approval of him as an apostle.

Fourteen years later, after having preached among many Gentiles, he again went to Jerusalem, taking with him Barnabas and Titus. Titus was a Greek Christian, and, as such, had not been circumcised. As a result, a great argument arose between Paul and Barnabas and some Jewish Christians. The Jewish Christians claimed that unless Titus was circumcised according to the custom of Moses, he could not be saved. Paul and Barnabas, however, stood firm and would not give in an inch to them, no "not even for an hour" (Galatians 2:5). For to hold that circumcision was necessary for salvation was to say that the death of Christ was not enough.

The leaders of the church at Jerusalem agreed with Paul. Certainly, then, the Galatian Christians should not now doubt the truth of his preaching. (Galatians 1-2:5)

Gave us the right hands of fellowship   *He was eating with the Gentiles*

BY FAITH ALONE

The leaders of the church at Jerusalem — James, Peter, and John — did not correct or add to the Gospel which Paul had been preaching among the Gentiles. They agreed with him that Christians did not need to keep the Law of Moses in order to be saved. And learning of the great numbers who had believed his preaching, they realized that God had sent him to the Gentiles even as He had sent Peter to the Jews. Therefore, these three leaders gave to Paul and Barnabas the right hands of fellowship, showing that they recognized their work as being of God.

Peter believed that the works of the Law were not necessary for salvation. But one time Paul had to rebuke him for not upholding this truth as he should have. While visiting Paul in Syrian Antioch, Peter at first ate freely with the Gentile Christians. However, when some Jewish Christians came to Antioch from Jerusalem, he stopped doing so. He was afraid of what they might think if they saw him eating with Gentiles. For these men still held that Christians had to keep the old Jewish laws such as not eating with Gentiles if they wished to be saved.

Paul saw that by giving in to the false idea of these Jewish Christians, Peter was doing harm to the Gospel. So he rebuked him in front of everyone. Paul insisted not only to Peter but also to the Galatian Christians that man is not justified (declared to be righteous by God) by the works of the Law, but "through

I withstood him to his face   *Throw out the slave woman*

faith in Jesus Christ for by the works of the Law shall no flesh be justified" (Galatians 2:16).

The Galatians had at first believed this Gospel of salvation by faith rather than by works. But now that they were turning away from it, Paul asked them, "foolish Galatians, who has bewitched you, that you should not obey the truth?" (Galatians 3:1) He reminded them that even Abraham was not counted righteous because of his works, but rather because of his faith in God's promises. And all who are of faith are the sons of believing Abraham.

Those who are counted righteous because of their faith, however, are not sons like Ishmael, but like Isaac. Abraham, explained Paul, had two sons Ishmael, who was born of Hagar, a slave woman, in a natural way; and Isaac, who was born of Sarah, a free woman, in a miraculous way. Although Ishmael was the first-born, he was not the one who inherited the blessings of God. For as the son of a slave woman, he could not share in the promises made to Isaac, the son of the free woman. What is more, when he mocked Isaac, both he and his mother, Hagar, were driven away.

All those who receive God's promises in faith, Paul continued, are like Isaac. But all who try to earn Heaven by their own works by being slaves to the Law are like Ishmael. They, like him, shall be cast out and shall have no part in the inheritance. (Galatians 2:6-4:31)

In the school of Tyrannus *Children, obey your parents*

CHOSEN FOR HOLINESS

While Paul was a prisoner in Rome, he had much time to talk about Jesus to his many visitors, and even to his Roman guards. He also used this time to write letters to the young churches.

On Paul's third missionary journey, he had spent almost three years in the city of Ephesus (see map), first preaching in the synagogue, and later in the school of Tyrannus (Acts 19). His work there was so successful that not only was a strong church established in Ephesus itself, but the Word of God spread to all the area around it. It was to these Gentile Christians that Paul wrote from Rome the beautiful "Letter to the Ephesians."

The great apostle reminded them that before God even created the world, He had chosen them to be His own adopted children. He had not elected them instead of others because they were so much better than the rest. No, He chose them "according to the good pleasure of His will" (Ephesians 1:5), not because they were holy, but in order that they might become "holy and blameless before Him in love" (Ephesians 1:4). Like everyone else, they had been spiritually dead in sins. But by the same great power with which God raised Jesus from the dead, He also made them alive spiritually so that they might enter the kingdom of Heaven. They had done nothing to earn God's love. Rather, wrote Paul, "by grace are you saved, through faith and this not of yourselves, for it is the gift of God not of works, lest any man should boast" (Ephesians 2:8, 9).

Obey your masters

Put on the whole armor of God

Therefore, since God had called them out of death into life, out of darkness into light, Paul urged them to behave themselves as true children of God. All around them were the heathen, who were lying, stealing, hating, fighting, committing adultery, and worshipping idols. They themselves had formerly done all these things, too. "You were once darkness," wrote Paul, "but now you are light in the Lord, walk as children of light" (5:8).

Also in the homes, said Paul, they should live as Christians. The wife must obey the husband who is the head of the family even as the church obeys Christ who is its Head. The husband, in turn, must love his wife, even as Christ loved the church and gave Himself up for it. The children must obey their parents. But the parents must also take good care of their children. Servants must be obedient to their masters. And the masters must be kind to their servants. Love should be the rule in the home.

Paul knew that trying to live as God's children would be a continual battle against Satan. Therefore, urged Paul, "Put on the whole armor of God:" the girdle of truth, the breastplate of righteousness, the shoes of the Gospel, the shield of faith, the helmet of salvation, and the sword of the Word of God. In their own strength they would be overcome by Satan, but with the armor of God and much prayer they would be able to stand firm against the attacks of the Devil. (Ephesians)

We spoke unto the women   *They dragged them*

REJOICE IN THE LORD!

Philippi, in northern Greece (see map), was the first city in Europe to hear the Gospel of Jesus Christ. On Paul's second missionary journey, he went there with Silas, Timothy, and Luke because of a vision he had one night (Acts 16). Since there was no Jewish synagogue in Philippi, they went outside the city gate to a place by a river where some women usually gathered for prayer. Paul spoke to them about Jesus, and Lydia, a rich woman who sold purple dyes, came to believe and was baptized. She also invited Paul and his friends to stay at her home.

    Some time later, Paul and Silas were dragged into the market-place before the rulers of the city. They had done no wrong but were beaten with wooden rods and thrown into prison.

    Soon after Paul was set free, he left Philippi. Although he had not been there very long, he had been able to start a church. It was a small but faithful group and very dear to Paul's heart. Several times the Philippians sent money to help him out in his journeys. And when they heard that he was a prisoner in Rome, they sent Epaphroditus, one of their members, to him with another gift.

    While in Rome working with Paul, Epaphroditus became very sick and almost died. But, to Paul's joy, God spared his life. Now that he was well again, Paul decided to send him back home with a letter for the Philippians.

Your messenger to my need

I have learned to be content

In this letter, Paul thanked them for their gift. He also told that he was still a prisoner for the sake of the Gospel. His trial before the emperor had begun, but he did not yet know whether he would be set free or put to death. Yet in all of this, he could write: "Do not be anxious about anything. But in everything, by prayer and by petition, let your desires be made known unto God. And the peace of God which passes all understanding shall keep your hearts and minds through Christ Jesus" (Philippians 4:6, 7).

In all of his troubles, Paul not only had peace in his heart, but also joy. His joy did not depend on whether he was free or in chains; whether he was allowed to live or was killed. His joy came, rather, from loving and serving his Lord. "For to me to live is Christ," he wrote, "and to die is gain" (Philippians 1:21). If he should live, he could be of further help to the churches. But if he should have to die, then he could be with Christ in Heaven, which was far better.

Meanwhile, Paul wrote, even his imprisonment had worked out for the good. As different guards, in turn, were chained to him, he had an opportunity to tell them about the Lord. After a time, the whole palace guard had heard the Gospel. Furthermore, many of the Christians in Rome, seeing Paul's boldness, gained courage to preach the Word without fear. Paul's joy was sure, for he knew that "all things work together for good to those who love God." (Philippians)

He declared to us your love   *I sent him to you*

CHRIST, OUR ALL IN ALL

During the three years that Paul was in Ephesus (see map), the Word of the Lord spread throughout the whole area called Asia (Acts 19:10). Probably during that time, Epaphras, a fellow-worker of Pauls, travelled the one hundred miles eastward to the three cities of Colosse, Laodicea, and Hierapolis to preach the Word.

Then, while Paul was a prisoner in Rome, Epaphras came to visit him. He brought news of the believers in Colosse, whom Paul had never known personally. The imprisoned apostle rejoiced to hear of their faith in Jesus Christ and of their love toward each other. But Epaphras also told him of certain false teachings which were creeping into the church. Whenever Paul heard of errors in a church, he was very sorrowful. So he wrote to warn the Colossians against these teachings. Paul sent this letter with Tychichus, a fellow-minister, and Onesimus. It was Tychichus also who delivered the letter from Paul to the church at Ephesus.

Paul instructed the Colossians to have his letter read not only in their own church, but also in the nearby church in Laodicea. Apparently, both the Laodiceans and the Colossians were being troubled by the same errors. Someone in the Colossian church was teaching what he thought was a higher wisdom than could be found in the simple Gospel. So in his letter, Paul warned the Colossians against any so-called "wisdom" which did not agree with the Gospel which

When this letter is read among you *You may not handle, taste, touch*

Epaphras had preached to them. Wisdom which was of men, he said, and not of God, was false and useless. For there could be no higher wisdom than Christ, "in whom are all the treasures of wisdom and knowledge hidden" (Colossians 2:3).

The Colossians were also being taught that they had to keep the old Jewish laws concerning circumcision, feast days, new moons, and clean and unclean foods. Paul answered that those had been useful before Christ came because they pointed forward to Him. But now that He had come, they were no longer of any value.

Thirdly, the Colossians were being told that in order to become more holy, they had to refuse their bodies many things. The body was evil, they were taught, and only by holding down the desires of the body could the soul rise to greater heights. Paul replied that none of these rules "you may not handle, you may not taste, you may not touch" (Colossians 2:21) could help them to become more holy. Only by setting their hearts and minds on Christ could they overcome sin.

They were wrong, he argued, to seek wisdom and holiness outside of Christ, for there is no one higher than He. He is, after all, the Lord of creation and the Lord of the church. He is the image, or picture, of God the Father, whom no man has even seen. Therefore, Paul urged, they ought not to be carried away by false wisdom and rules. They should, rather, "be filled with the knowledge of His will in all wisdom and understanding." (Colossians 1:9)

And set the city in an uproar   *They dragged Jason before the judges*

CHRIST'S RETURN

After their shameful beating and imprisonment in Philippi, Paul and Silas, started out for Thessalonica (see map). After they arrived, Paul taught in the Jewish synagogue for three Sabbaths. Some of the Jews, but especially the Greeks accepted his preaching, not as the word of men but, as it truly was, the Word of God.

But other Jews became jealous of Paul. Gathering together a mob of rough fellows, they attacked the house of a man named Jason, where the missionaries had been staying. Not finding them there, they dragged Jason and some other Christians before the rulers of the city and accused them of taking in men who "turned the world upside down." When the rulers made sure that the Christians would not allow such an uproar to happen again, they set them free.

These believers felt that Paul and his friends should leave Thessalonica at once. So when night came, they secretly sent them off to Berea (see map). Paul was sorry to be forced to leave such a young church so soon and so suddenly. He still wanted to explain much more to them. So when he reached Athens, he sent Timothy and Silas back to strengthen and comfort them.

Paul had already gone on to Corinth and started his work there when Timothy and Silas joined him (Acts 18:5). He rejoiced to hear them tell that the Thessalonians were not only standing firm in their faith, but were also

They sent away Paul and Silas   *Work with your own hands*

carrying the Gospel to the region around them. However, certain false ideas were also troubling them.

For example, while Paul was in Thessalonica, he had taught that one day Jesus would return to take the believers up to Heaven with Him. After he had left, some of the Christians had died, and their families feared that these dead could not take part in Christ's return. So Paul now wrote to explain that when Jesus comes down from Heaven with His angels and with the trumpet of God, those believers who have already died will be raised first. Then they who are still alive will also be carried up into Heaven to be with the Lord forever. Paul reminded the Thessalonians that no one knows when this great Day will be. For those who are not looking for it, it will come as a thief in the night. But those who are ready and watching will not be taken by surprise.

Some, however, were so sure that the Lord would return at any moment that they did not bother to work any more. But Paul wrote that the Lord would not come back that quickly. First there would be a period of great unbelief. And the Lawless One, the man of sin who would, himself, pretend to be God would appear. Then Jesus would come down from Heaven in great power and glory to destroy the man of sin and to punish all who have not obeyed the Gospel. Therefore, urged Paul, until that day they should work with their own hands. (1 & 2 Thessalonians; Acts 17

From a babe you have known the Scriptures   *Men, why do you do these things?*

TIMOTHY IS CHOSEN

Two of the books in the New Testament are letters, or epistles, which Paul wrote to Timothy. From what Paul says in these epistles, as well as from what Luke tells us in the Book of Acts, we know many things about this young man.

Timothy lived in Lystra, a city of Asia Minor (see map) His father was a Greek, but both his mother, Eunice, and his grandmother, Lois, were faithful Jewish women. They knew and loved the Old Testament, and as soon as Timothy was old enough to understand, they began to teach it to him. In one of the letters to Timothy, Paul once said, "From a babe you have known the Holy Scriptures which are able to make you wise unto salvation through faith which is in Christ Jesus" (II Tim. 3:15). Since the New Testament had not been written at that time, the "scnptures" which Paul spoke about were the books of the Old Testament. From them Timothy had learned at his mother's knees of the Lord's dealings with the Israelites and of the Messiah whom He had promised to send to His people. Like every faithful Jew. Timothy looked forward eagerly to the coming of the Messiah.

Then one day, when Timothy was a very young man, two strangers came to his home town. These men, Paul and Barnabas, began to preach about this Messiah, a certain Jesus, whom God had sent to be the Saviour of men. In the crowd which was listening to these two preachers there sat a man who had been

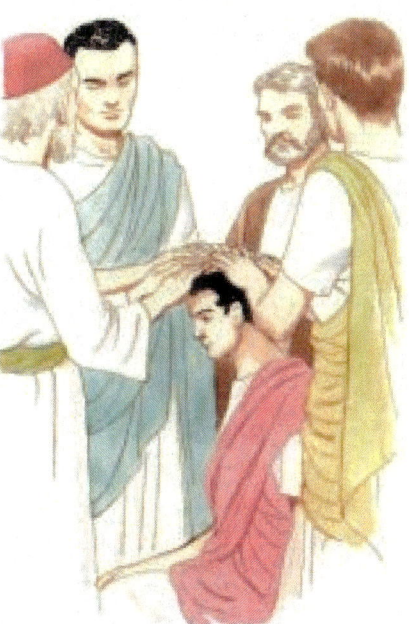

A disciple was there, named Timothy   *The laying on of hands of the elders*

lame from birth. Seeing that he had faith to be healed, Paul commanded him, "Stand up on your feet." For the first time in his life, the lame man stood up and walked and jumped!

Timothy must have either seen or heard about all the excitement which this miracle caused. If he was in the crowd, he would certainly have seen the priests about to sacrifice oxen to Paul and Barnabas, thinking that they were gods. He would also have heard the missionaries cry out, "Sirs, why do you do these things?" Then they explained that they were not gods, but that they had come to tell about the only true God.

At any rate, before Paul and Barnabas were forced to leave Lystra, Timothy heard Paul preach the Gospel and he believed.

About four years later, on his second missionary journey — Paul came back to Lystra to see how the Christians there were getting along. This time he met Timothy again and found that he had grown a great deal in the Christian faith and was well spoken of by the believers at Lystra and Iconium. Paul liked the young disciple so much that he asked him to leave his family and friends and go with him as a missionary to other cities and countries.

When Timothy agreed, Paul and the Lystran elders laid their hands upon him and prayed that the Holy Spirit might fit him for the great work to which he was being called. Then Paul continued his journey, taking Timothy with him. (Acts 14-16)

Preach the word   *But call upon him as a father*

ADVICE TO TIMOTHY

Paul was never sorry that he had chosen Timothy to be his helper. Even though Timothy was much younger than Paul, and not as bold and fearless, he served well and faithfully with him, right up until Paul's death. The great apostle thought so much of his young friend that he once wrote to the Philippians concerning him: "I have no man likeminded, who will care truly for your state. For they all seek their own, not the things of Jesus Christ. But you know the proof of him, that, as a child serves a father, so he served with me in furtherance of the Gospel" (Phil. 2:20-22).

Timothy usually went with Paul as he travelled from city to city to spread the Gospel. But once, when Paul left Ephesus to go to Macedonia, and another time, when Paul was in prison in Rome, Timothy stayed in Ephesus to take care of the church there. It was a difficult task for such a young man, yet Paul knew his young friend well enough to entrust the work to him. However, he did write him two letters to give him some advice for the problems which he would have to face.

In these letters, Paul tenderly calls Timothy his "true child in the faith." For through his preaching Timothy had come to know the Lord Jesus. Now Paul wrote him to take care that his own faith remained strong and pure. "Hold the pattern of sound words which you have heard from me," he told Timothy (II Timothy 1:13). "Be an example to them that believe, in word, in manner of life,

Do the work of an evangelist   *Try to come to me quickly*

in love, in faith, in purity" (I Tim. 4:12).

Then he urged him to spread the Word to others by preaching and teaching. And finally, he urged him to stand firm against false teachings. For there were many men in the church at Ephesus who were trying to lead the believers away from the true faith with their fables and endless questionings. Timothy must never stop fighting against the teachings of these men.

"Preach the word," Paul wrote him. "Be urgent in season, out of season; reprove, rebuke, exhort, with all longsuffering and teaching ... Be sober in all things, suffer hardship, do the work of an evangelist, fulfill your ministry" (II Tim. 4:2-5).

Then Paul told Timothy what kind of men should be chosen as elders to help in the important work of watching over the flock of the church — of the Lord Jesus. He also gave other advice so that Timothy might "know how men ought to behave themselves in the house of God, which is the church of the living God, the pillar and ground of the truth" (I Tim. 3:15).

Finally, at the end of his second letter, Paul begged Timothy to come to him before winter and bring his cloak and books that he had left at Troas. Except for Luke, all Paul's friends had left him. And as he sat in his prison cell in Rome, he longed to see his "beloved child" once more before he was to be killed for his faith. (I and II Timothy)

And to the church in your house   *I beseech you for my child*

A RUNAWAY SLAVE

In the city of Colosse in Asia Minor (see map) there lived a rich man named Philemon. Although Paul had never visited this city, Philemon had met the apostle somewhere. Through hearing Paul preach, Philemon had become a Christian. Since that time, he had used his riches for the work of the Lord: he had helped many fellow-Christians who were in need, and he had opened up his home as a place of worship for the believers in Colosse.

It was to this Christian that Paul wrote "The Letter to Philemon." Usually Paul's letters either were addressed to a whole church or at least dealt with church matters. But this short letter was written to one man only, and for a very personal reason.

One of Philemon's slaves, called Onesimus, had run away from his master, perhaps even stealing some of his money before he left (verse 18). After traveling far, Onesimus had arrived in Rome. The apostle Paul happened to be in Rome at that. time, too. He was a prisoner, but was allowed to live in a rented house and to receive all who wished to visit him. When, for some reason or other, Onesimus came to see him, Paul spoke to him as he did to everyone about the Lord Jesus.

As a result, Onesimus came to believe in the Lord and his whole life was changed. No longer was he a dishonest, runaway slave but a "faithful and beloved brother." Paul liked Onesimus and wanted very much to have him

Whom I now have sent back to you

Receive him as myself

stay in Rome to serve him while he was a prisoner. But Onesimus still belonged to Philemon, and Paul did not want to keep him there without his master's consent. He must first go back to Philemon.

Because Onesimus was afraid that he might be severely punished for having run away, Paul wrote a letter to Philemon for him to take along. In it he said: "beseech you for my child, whom I have begotten in my bonds, Onesimus, who once was not profitable to you, but now is profitable to you and to me: whom I have sent back to you" (verse 10). He went on to suggest that God could use even the former faithlessness of Onesimus to a good purpose:

"Perhaps," wrote Paul, "because of this he was separated from you for a time, so that you might possess him for ever no longer as a bondslave, but above a bondslave, a beloved brother" (verses 15, 16). Even though Onesimus would return as a slave, there would now be a difference. Master and slave would be brothers in Christ. For, as Paul wrote elsewhere, "there can be neither bond nor free for you all are one in Christ Jesus" (Gal. 3:28). Paul, then, begged Philemon to pardon his slave and to receive him again in love.

As he sent Onesimus off, Paul had no fears concerning the way, the slave would be treated. He was sure that Philemon would show even greater love and forgiveness than he was asking. (Philemon)

Make all things according to the pattern

Every high priest is to offer sacrifices

THE GREAT HIGH PRIEST

The example of Old Testament saints did not prove to be enough to stir up again a living and warm faith in these backsliding Jewish Christians. So this letter to the Hebrews was written to encourage them to greater faith by showing them how great a salvation Jesus had won for them. In Old Testament times God told the Israelites exactly how they were to worship Him. He gave to Moses on Mt. Sinai careful instructions about the building of the tabernacle, the dress and work of the priests, and the animals to be sacrificed.

According to these instructions, the place of worship, or tabernacle, was to be a large tent made up of two rooms: the Holy Place, with its candlestick, altar of incense, and table of show- bread; and the Holy of Holies, in which stood only the ark. These two rooms were separated by a heavy curtain, or veil, as it was called. Every day, after offering the same sacrifices before the tabernacle, the priests came into the Holy Place to pray to God. But no one was allowed to go past the veil into the Holy of Holies, that is, into Gods presence except the High Priest. And he could go there only once a year, on the great Day of Atonement. With the blood of bulls and goats which he had sacrificed outside, he would then make atonement first for his own sins and then for the sins of the people.

All of this service, because it was commanded by God, was good and holy.

And he sprinkled with blood

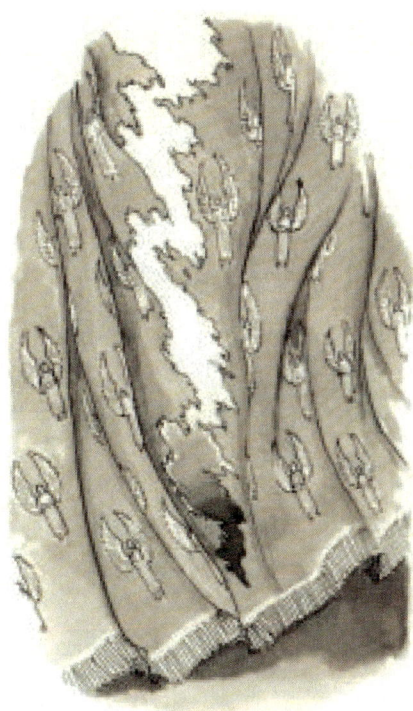
A new and living way through the veil

But it was only a copy, or shadow, of better things to come. Worth nothing in itself, it only pointed to the great High Priest, Jesus Christ, and to His perfect sacrifice on the cross.

Jesus' sacrifice was far better than that of the other high priests. Unlike the Old Testament high priests, Jesus did not have to make a sacrifice for His own sins first, before making one for the sins of His people, because He was without sin. Moreover, the blood which He offered was not the blood of bulls and goats, which can never take away sins. He offered His own precious blood on the cross of Calvary. Nor did He have to offer the same sacrifice year after year, as did the high priests. "But He, when He had offered one sacrifice for sins for ever, sat down on the right hand of God" (Hebrews 10:12). The moment His sacrifice was finished, that is, when He breathed His last breath on the cross, the veil in the Temple was torn from top to bottom. By this miracle, God showed that the way into His presence was now open not just to the high priest once a year, but at all times to anyone who came to Him through Christ. With such a High Priest, who is "able to save to the uttermost them that come unto God through Him" (Hebrews 7:25), the readers should take courage. "Let us," urged the writer, "hold fast to what we say and draw near with boldness unto the throne of grace, so that we may receive mercy, and may find grace to help us in time of need" (Hebrews 8-10).

By faith Noah prepared an ark   *By faith Abraham offered up Isaac*

FAITH UNTO THE END

"The letter to the Hebrews" was written to Jews who had been Christians for quite some time. At first, they had been strong and faithful believers. Even when they had to suffer persecution and had to lose many of their possessions because of their faith, they did so cheerfully (Hebrews 11:32-34)

But after a while, they began to slip backwards. Whereas they should have grown enough spiritually to be able to teach others, they themselves had to be taught the simplest things all over again. They were no longer faithful in prayer or in worship services. They had also become tired of doing good to others.

It was, then, to encourage these Jewish believers in their Christian faith and life that the author wrote this letter. Warning them that only those who remain faithful to the end will enjoy the blessings which Christ has promised, he wrote, "Be careful, my brothers, lest there be in any of you an evil heart of unbelief, in falling away from the living God" (Hebrews 3:12). He reminded them of what happened to the children of Israel whom God had brought out of Egypt. They had started out so well. But because they lost faith later on and doubted God's promises, they had to die in the wilderness without entering the land of Canaan.

There were, however, many others in the Old Testament who had never doubted God's promises, but had continued in faith.

They passed through the Red Sea

The walls of Jericho fall down

By faith Noah, for example, built an ark far from any water, because he believed that God would send the flood as He had promised. When the flood did come, he and his family were saved in the ark, while those who had laughed at him were drowned.

By faith Abraham was willing to offer up his only son, Isaac, when God tested him. Abraham could not understand why God wanted him to sacrifice the very one through whom He had promised the blessings. Yet he trusted God and obeyed. As he was about to kill Isaac on the altar, God stopped him and told him to offer in his place a ram caught in a nearby bush.

By faith Moses led the children of Israel through the Red Sea, trusting that God would hold the waters back until they had crossed over. Whereas the Egyptians who tried to do the same thing without faith were swallowed up by the sea.

What those Jewish Christians needed most of all was patience in their faith. They knew the truth and had believed it. Yet their sins and troubles were causing them to become careless and down hearted. Therefore the writer urged them to follow the examples of Noah, Abraham, Moses and other "heroes of faith": "Let us also," he said, "lay aside every weight and the sin which does so easily beset us, and let us run with patience the race that is set before us, looking unto Jesus, the Author and Finisher of our faith" (Hebrews 11)

These all continued in prayer   *Paul went in with us unto James*

JAMES WRITES TO THE TWELVE TRIBES

As time went on, James became more and more important in the church at Jerusalem. Paul speaks of him as one of the men on which the church depended, along with Peter and John (Gal. 2:9). James ministered to the Jewish Christians, rather than to the Gentiles. Even when many of them fled from Jerusalem because of persecutions, he still kept in touch with them. So when he heard that their Christian life was not what it should be, he wrote this letter to them.

Knowing that these scattered groups were having many trials and temptations, James first calls their attention to God s purpose in all these things. "Count it all joy when you fall into different kinds of temptations," he said (James 1:2). You will prove you have faith, and you will find your patience will grow because of these things. If you do not have the heavenly wisdom to know what to do, or how to stand for your Lord, then ask God, he tells them. Finally, he gives them the rich assurance that if they endure temptation, then God will certainly give them the crown of life which He had promised to those who love Him.

It is good to have faith in God, he went on, but that is not enough. "The demons also believe and shudder" (James 2:19). Even the demons who cannot be saved have a kind of faith. A faith, however, which is real and living and which saves, will produce good works. Good works never cause a man to get to

Sit here in a good place   *He prayed, and the sky gave rain*

Heaven, but they do show that his faith is a live faith. For "faith," said James, it "does not have works, is dead" (James 2:17)

He also warned his readers not to show greater honor to the rich than to the poor. If a rich man comes into their synagogue, wearing a gold ring and fine clothing, it is wrong to give him a seat of honor, while telling a poor, ragged man to remain standing or to sit in a lowly place. They should not honor men according to the way they are dressed, but should show the same kindness to all.

James had also heard that these Christians were praying, but that they did not seem to get answers to their prayers. One reason was that they did not really believe that God could or would answer them. They had to ask in faith, James told them, "for he that doubts is like the surge of the sea driven by the wind and tossed. For let not that man think that he shall receive anything of the Lord" (James 1:6, 7). Another reason was that their prayers were selfish. They were asking God only for things they wanted and not for things God wanted. If they learned to pray correctly, they could find that prayer could do great things. Elijah, for example, prayed earnestly that it would not rain. And for three and a half years not a drop of rain fell in Israel. Then when he prayed for rain, God again heard his prayer and sent it.

With these and many other words, James showed his readers what it meant to live a Christian life. (James 1-5)

Patiently endure it, doing good   *Where is the promise of His coming?*

TRIALS AND TEMPTATIONS

As a result of Paul's three missionary journeys, many people in Asia Minor came to believe in the Lord. Some of these new Christians were Jews. But most of them had worshipped idols and had led lives of drunkenness, adultery, stealing, and the like.

After they became Christians, life was not always easy for them. Sometimes servants were mistreated by their heathen masters. Wives were sometimes mistreated by their unbelieving husbands.

The believers were becoming downhearted. They could not understand why they should have to suffer so much for doing good. They wondered if it was really worth being a Christian after all, and they were greatly tempted to slip back into their old way of life. It was to comfort and strengthen these discouraged Christians that the apostle Peter sent two letters.

They should not think it strange, he wrote, that they had to suffer as Christians, for God's people have always been persecuted. Nor should they return evil for evil, but should follow the example of Christ in His suffering. For He "did not speak evil in return when evil was being spoken to Him. He did not threaten when He was suffering" (I Pet. 2:23). He left it to God the Father to judge His persecutors.

It would be easier for them to bear persecutions patiently, Peter continued,

Bringing the flood upon the world   *He turned the cities into ashes*

if they would remember the great reward they would receive at Christ's return, an inheritance that could not rot or fade away was being kept in Heaven for them.

Besides the persecutions from the unbelievers outside the church, these Christians were also being troubled by false teachers within. Mockers were questioning whether Jesus really was going to return to judge the world. After all, things were not any different from what they always had been. And if there was no judgment to fear, they taught, then why not sin?

Peter pointed out that things have not always been the same, but that God once did wipe out the ungodly world with the flood. Furthermore, although it may seem like a long time to men before Christ returns, it is not long for God. For "one day is with the Lord as a thousand years, and a thousand years as one day" (II Pet. 3:8). The Lord is not slow in fulfilling His promise of judgment. On the contrary, because He is merciful, He is allowing much time for people to turn to Him. The day will surely come in which the heavens shall pass away with a great noise "and the earth and the works in it shall be burned up" (II Pet. 3:10). And then there will be new heavens and a new earth.

As for the mockers, Peter warned, let them tremble. For if God did not spare the angels who sinned, but threw them out of Heaven; if He destroyed with the flood all the sinful world except Noah and his family; surely He will also destroy these false prophets. (Peter 1-2)

See if they are of God

Do not receive him into your house

THE APOSTLE OF LOVE

John, "the disciple whom Jesus loved," wrote the Gospel of John, three epistles (or letters), and the book of Revelation. They were all written when he was an old man, perhaps sixty years after Jesus died.

John wrote his first epistle to a group of believers to warn them against false teachers. There were many people, he said, who once had been members of the church without being true believers. Then they had left the church and were trying to lead others astray. These men claimed to be speaking for God, but John wrote that anyone who was of God would obey His commandment. "And this is His commandment, that we should believe on the name of His Son, Jesus Christ, and that we should love one another." These false teachers denied that Jesus was the Christ, the Son of God. John wrote that such people were liars and antichrists. They could not be called true prophets of God, for only he who "believes that Jesus is the Christ has been born of God."

Furthermore, they could not be true prophets because they said that it was not necessary to love one another. John answered: "If anyone should say, 'I love God,' and should hate his brother, he is a liar" (I John 4:20). God, who is perfect love, has shown what it means to love. For He proved His love when He sent His only Son to be the Saviour of men. Thus, out of His great love, He made it possible for sinful men, through faith in that Saviour, to be called children of God

We ought then to receive such

He throws them out of the church

and to have eternal life. "If God so loved us," said John, then "we ought also to love one another" (I John 4:11). "He that does not love never knew God, because God is love" (I John 4:8) Therefore, John warned his readers, "Do not believe every spirit (every teaching), but test the spirits to see if they are of God" (I John 4:1).

In his second letter, the aged apostle also warned a lady to beware of false prophets, for there were many of them travelling about. Such liars should not be welcomed, nor even greeted.

His third epistle John sent to a rich man named Gaius. He praised him for his kindness to travelling preachers. These preachers depended on fellow-Christians for housing and food, for they would not accept any help from the heathen. By taking them into his home and helping them on their way again, Gaius was sharing in the work of the Gospel. But John spoke sharply against a man named Diotrephes, who wanted to be the most important person in the church. This man said unkind things about the apostle himself. He refused to have travelling preachers as his guests and even threw out of the church those who wanted to be kind to them. John said that he would deal with him when he came. But he warned Gaius not to follow after such a man. For "he that does good is of God, but he that does evil has not seen God" (John 1-2-3)

I heard a loud voice behind me

You allow that woman Jezebel to teach

THE VISION OF JOHN

One day God sent a vision to the apostle John by an angel. He heard behind him a great voice a voice like a trumpet or like the thundering of waves on a beach, saying: "What you see write in a book and send it to the churches which are in Asia to Ephesus, and to Smyrna, and to Pergamos, and to Thyatira, and to Sardis, and to Philadelphia, and to Laodicea" (see map).

Turning around, John saw seven golden lamp stands with Christ walking among them. His face was as bright as the sun, His eyes like flaming fire, and He held seven stars in His right hand. Overcome by such a glorious sight, the apostle fell down at Jesus' feet as if he were dead. But the Lord laid His right hand on His trembling servant and said "Do not fear. I am the First and the Last, and the Living One. And I became dead, and behold! I am alive for ever and ever. Write, therefore, the mystery of the seven golden lamp stands which are the seven churches and of the seven stars which are the angels of the seven churches."

These seven churches were real churches in the western part of Asia Minor. But they were also examples of churches everywhere in all ages. Therefore, the messages which Jesus gave John to write to them are also messages for every church.

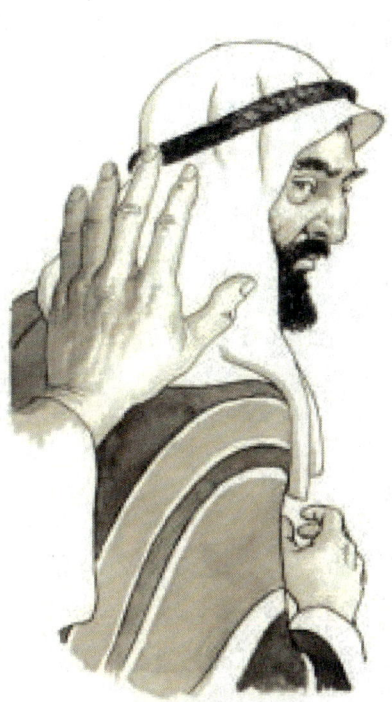

I know that you cannot bear evil men　　　　*You are neither hot nor cold*

    The believers in these churches were being greatly persecuted and tempted. The Jews dragged many of them before the Roman rulers, accusing them of doing wrong. As a result, many Christians were cast into prison, burned to death, thrown to wild animals, or sent far away. The heathen were tempting them to take part in their wicked feasts and celebrations.

    The Lord praised the church at Smyrna for remaining true to Him through all their persecutions. He rebuked the church at Thyatira for allowing Jezebel to teach. And He praised the believers at Ephesus for driving the false teachers out. He found fault with those in Sardis for their dead faith; only a few were leading holy lives. The Laodiceans were rich in worldly goods, but He rebuked them for not knowing how lukewarm and blind and poor and naked in spirit they were. And He praised the Philadelphians for their faithful witnessing to Him.

    The task of the churches was to be like lamps shining in the dark and sinful world. Therefore, according to how they were fulfilling this task, the Lord rebuked, comforted, praised, and warned them. And to those who would overcome evil and remain true to Him, He promised them a new Heaven and a new earth, the New Jerusalem, where they should live and rule with Him forever. And He encourages their hope when, as the Lamb of God who finally conquers all, He says, " come quickly." Even so, come, Lord Jesus! (Revelation)

Aaron

Abraham

Adam

Daniel

David

Elijah

Elisha

Ezekiel

Isaac

Jacob

Jeremiah

Jonah

Joseph

Joshua

Moses

Noah

Samson

Solomon

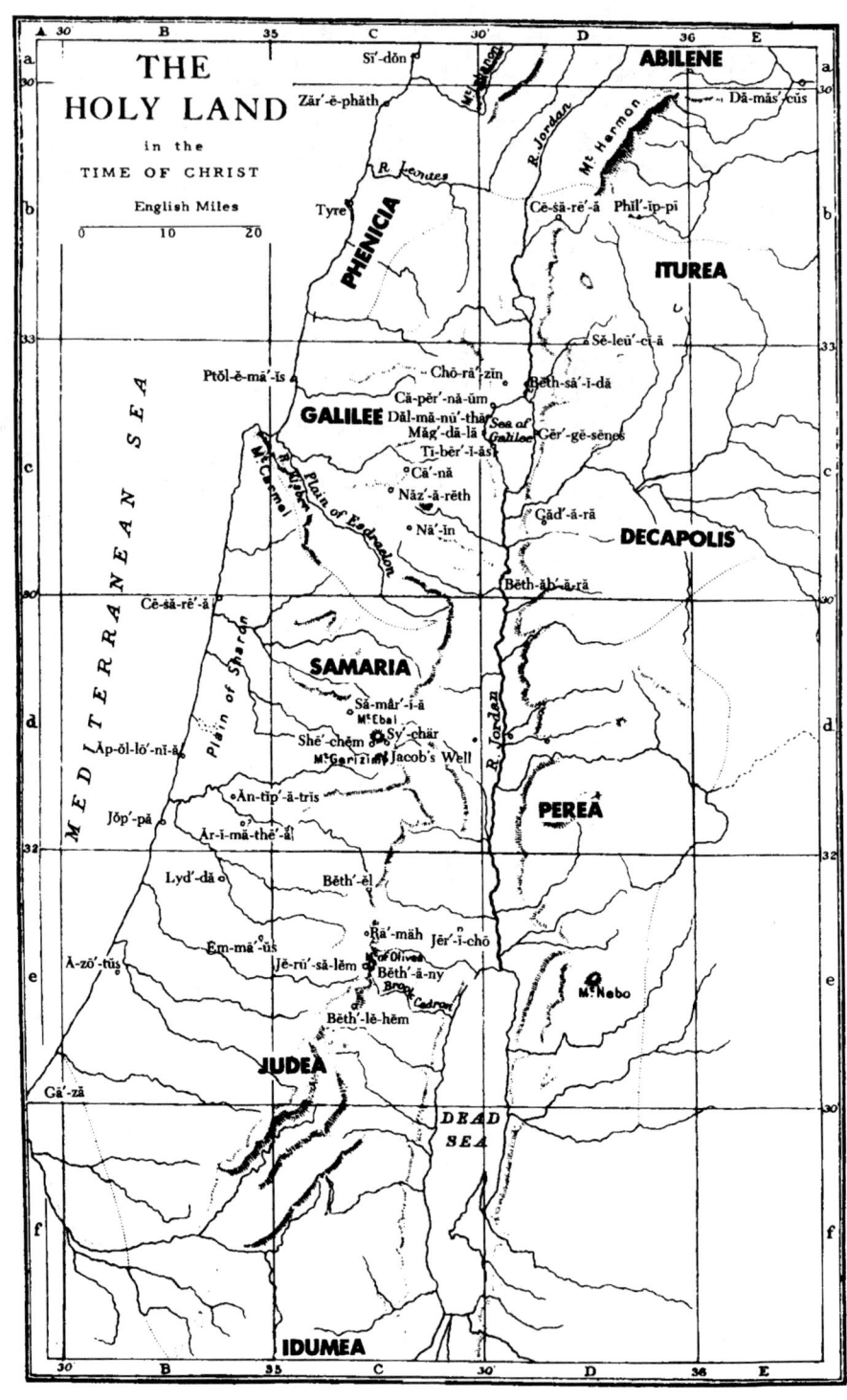

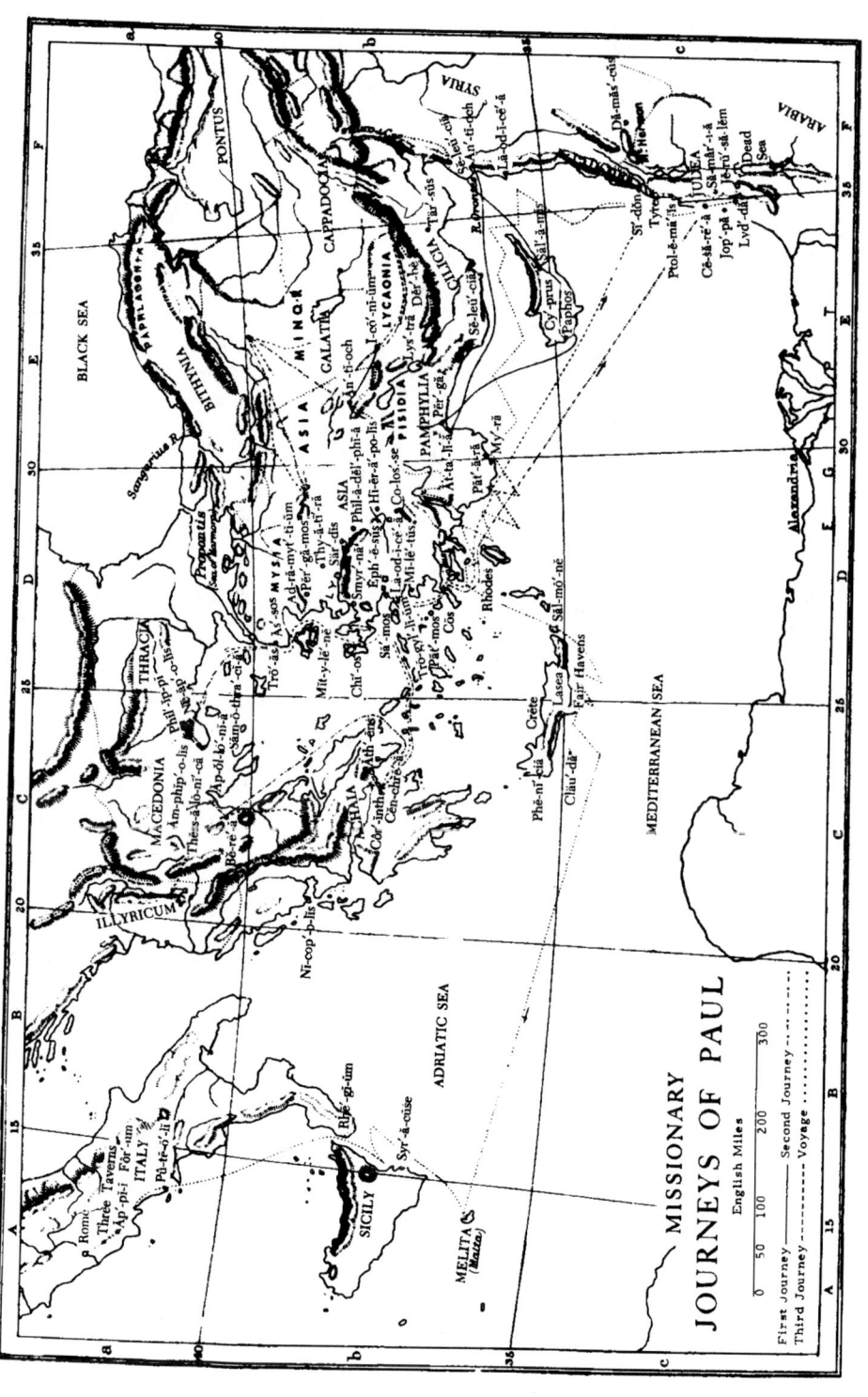

Printed in the United States of America